Poverty:

VIEWS FROM THE LEFT

D1507940

Poverty:

VIEWS FROM
THE LEFT

EDITED BY

Jeremy Larner & Irving Howe

WILLIAM MORROW & COMPANY, INC.

New York

Second Printing, February 1969

Published simultaneously in Canada by
George J. McLeod Limited, Toronto.

Printed in the United States of America.

Table of Contents

Introduction

This is not—we hope—just another book on poverty. We expect it will prove useful in the classroom, but it is meant as more than a mere academic survey. We hope it will indicate the problems and possibilities awaiting everyone committed not only to understanding poverty in America but to joining in common action to eradicate that scourge.

The war on poverty in America has barely begun, and the resources assigned to that war are grotesquely insufficient. But it is a good sign that so many Americans are now aroused by the problem of poverty and debating the complex issues which surround it. Ever since our colleague Michael Harrington published his now famous book *The Other America* in 1962, the issue has been in the forefront of American political life. And there it must remain till adequate action is taken. Since, however, it now becomes clear that the eradication of poverty is not a simple matter, to be effected through one piece of legislation or a single action or slogan, it is necessary for radicals and reformers to tackle the details and nuances of a great many contingent social and economic areas. This book, consequently, is incomplete; it has to be. Certain problems concerning poverty are here closely examined; others barely touched upon. In part this is due to the usual limitations of space, resources and intelligence. In part it is due to the fact that the more closely we study the phenomenon of poverty, the more new problems define themselves and multiply.

Most of these essays first appeared in *Dissent* magazine, or were jointly commissioned for *Dissent* and this book. They represent, roughly speaking, the views of the democratic left in the United States in regard to American poverty. But, as must always occur among people who believe in democratic politics, there are significant differences of opinion among the contributors. Between Michael Harrington and Stephan Thernstrom, for example, there is an important divergence as to the nature of the "new poor," or even as to whether this category has much significance. And while the article we print here by Laura Carper on the Moynihan Report is sharply critical, it seems fair to add that there are contributors to *Dissent* who feel much more sympathetic to the Moynihan analysis. The reader will note other differences and divergences in attitudes toward the importance of integration, the need for local autonomy, the efficacy of various welfare methods, etc. Since our writers share only political and moral values—not an infallible doctrine— we believe that differences of opinion and emphasis are perfectly natural and desirable.

All the contributors to this book are united, however, in a passionate sense of urgency: a conviction that in a nation as rich as the United States it is an utter moral scandal that even the slightest remnant of poverty should remain—let alone the vast areas that continue to blight our social landscape. We offer this volume to everyone involved in the fight against poverty— in the local communities, in government agencies, in the trade unions, in the colleges, in the Civil Rights movement—with the hope that it will contribute to new forms of popular activity that will end American poverty once and for all.

The Editors

There are eight degrees or steps in the duty of giving. . . . The Eighth, and most meritorious of all, is to anticipate charity by preventing poverty; namely to assist the reduced fellow man, either by a considerable gift, or a sum of money, or by teaching him a trade, or by putting him in the way of business, so that he may earn an honest livelihood, and not be forced to the dreadful alternative of holding out his hand for charity. . . .

Maimonides

"You can't tire me," said Mrs. Pardiggle [a visiting social worker]. "I enjoy hard work, and the harder you make mine, the better I like it."

"Then make it easy for her!" growled the man upon the floor. "I wants it done, and over. I wants a end of these liberties took with my place. I wants an end of being drawed like a badger. Now you're a-going to poll-pry and question according to custom—I know what you're a-going to be up to. Well! You haven't got no occasion to be up to it. I'll save you the trouble. Is my daughter a-washin? Yes, she *is* a-washin. Look at the water. Smell it! That's wot we drinks. How do you like it, and what do you think of gin instead! An't my place dirty? Yes, it is dirty—it's nat'rally dirty, and it's nat'-rally onwholesome; and we've had five dirty and on-wholesome children, as is all dead infants, and so much the better for them, and for us besides. Have I read the little book wot you left? No, I an't read the little book wot you left. There an't nobody here as knows how to read it; and if there wos, it wouldn't be suitable to me. It's a book fit for a babby, and I'm not a babby. If you was to leave me a doll, I shouldn't nuss it. How have I been conducting of myself? Why, I've been drunk for three days; and I'da been drunk four if I'da had the money. Don't I never mean for to go to church? No, I don't never mean for to go to church. I shouldn't be expected there, if I did; the beadle's too gen-teel for me. And how did my wife get that black eye? Why, I give it her; and if she says I didn't, she's a lie!"

—Charles Dickens, *Bleak House*

STRUGGLE

Though my sanity has lapsed
My will has not collapsed.
My arch-enemy is despair,
For I know I must continue to care.

I struggle to keep heart,
For I know when it and I part,
There will be just an empty shell of a man,
And you could see I lost, the minute I began.

I struggle to try
To become something worthwhile,
As not to have my mind,
Sectioned in the "out" file.

—M.J.B.,
age 15, an inmate of Youth House,
a prison school in the Bronx.

The Politics
of Poverty

MICHAEL HARRINGTON

Can poverty in the United States be abolished within the limits of the welfare state? Or does the present commitment to end the scandal of economic misery in the richest nation history has known require measures which will go beyond the present theories and practices of American society?

The answer is, I think, clear enough. The Johnson administration's War on Poverty is basically inadequate, a fact which can be demonstrated by the government's own figures. The liberal-labor proposals for social investments which would both generate jobs and destroy the very physical environment of poverty represent a considerable advance over the present program and deserve vigorous support. But even these measures have implications which are considerably more radical than liberal reform. Understanding that the poor need a planned allocation of resources in their favor is but a first step toward the knowledge that a revolutionary technology is subverting some of the most cherished myths and principles of the entire society and demands fundamental changes in our economic and social structure.

13

In short, the goal announced in the Economic Opportunity Act is much more profound than its framers suspected. "It is, therefore, the policy of the United States," that law proclaims, "to eliminate the paradox of poverty in the midst of plenty in the Nation by opening to everyone the opportunity to live in decency and dignity." This sounds reassuring. It is the American rhetoric and the wisdom of the New Deal: the state intervenes to guarantee the citizen a fair chance in the private economy.

In fact, however, living up to these familiar goals is going to take unfamiliar action. For specific and historical reasons, the accumulated American knowledge about how to abolish poverty applies less and less each day. Unless there are profound changes in the American economy and society—new ways of allocating resources and distributing wealth—the economic underworld of the poor will not only persist but probably grow.

In saying these things, I do not want simply to dismiss the Johnson administration's War on Poverty (or John F. Kennedy's tremendously important first steps in this direction). If it is necessary to point out considerable, and even basic, inadequacies in the government's current programs, the very possibility of serious discussion of poverty in this country is a gain which one owes in part to that program. But now that a start has been made, there is no point in fostering the illusion that a sort of Federal Community Chest is going to get together the men of good will, the Henry Fords and Walter Reuthers, Russell Longs and Martin Luther Kings, and by a little more generous welfare-ism do away with a national shame. The task is much more difficult than that; the remedies are much more radical.

In developing this analysis, one need not enter into any argument over the exact, statistical nature of poverty in the United States. A small library of books written in recent years has demonstrated the brutal fact that tens of millions of

Americans are poor. For convenience, the definitions and figures used here will be those published by the government in the Economic Reports of 1964 and 1965. We discuss, then, a misery which, in a most cautious and prudent statement, embraces thirty-five million Americans and particularly afflicts the aging, the young, the non-white, and certain categories of workers and farmers. (It should be noted that a recent study of the Social Security Administration is even grimmer than the Economic Reports. It finds "about fifty million Americans, one quarter of the population," who "live within the bleak circle of poverty or at least hover around its edge.")

How can these thirty-five million—or perhaps even fifty million—be given "the opportunity to live in decency and dignity"?

To begin with, one must understand the obsolescence of much of the traditional American wisdom about abolishing poverty. The "old," pre-World War II poor, whose experiences dominate so much of our present thinking, were different kinds of people than the poor of the 1960s and they faced different problems.

The old poor lived at a time when economic opportunity was a trend of the economy itself. They suffered terribly, to be sure, and by statistical indices of living standard and life expectancy many were worse off than the impoverished of 1965. But they also participated in that incredible growth of American capitalism, a development which, in Colin Clark's figures, saw a 4500 per cent increase in the net income from manufacturing between 1860 and 1953. The farmers came to the city in good times to better their luck. They were not driven into the metropolis as bewildered, despairing exiles, which is so often the case today. And the insatiable manpower needs of mass production meant that there were jobs for grade school dropouts and for Eastern European immigrants who could hardly speak English.

There was objective, realistic reason for hope—and the old

poor of the cities were hopeful. The immigrants, for instance, often brought a language or a culture with them. The resultant solidarity provided the basis for self-help institutions within the culture of poverty: for political machines, churches, social clubs, and the like. In a good many instances aspiration and hunger for learning became a way of life.[1]

These internal resources of the old poor were used in the creation of the big-city political machines, one of the first welfare systems in the United States. But they also provided the basis for something more than "self-help" and group benevolence. In the 1930s they played a role in a climactic moment of American social history. Millions of the old poor participated in the organization of unions, particularly the CIO, and in the political struggle for the New Deal. They— and their ethnic drives and community hopes—became an important constituent of a new political coalition which translated into law many of the reforms advocated by liberals and socialists of an earlier generation—the Wagner Act, Social Security, minimum wage, etc.

Naturally, the resultant welfare-ism was permeated by the experience and some of the assumptions of the old poor.

In Arthur Schlesinger, Jr.'s analysis of the Roosevelt years there is a distinction between the "first" and "second" New Deals which is quite relevant at this point. The first New Deal was supported by very significant sectors of American business. It was dominated by the NRA, which gave legal recognition to an old corporate dream of the anti-anti-trusters: that something like the European cartel could be given American citizenship. This was a period in which the Chamber of Commerce was talking about a planned economy—planned by business.

[1] The various national groups had different patterns of response and varying degrees of success. Some of these contrasting patterns are analyzed in *Beyond the Melting Pot* (Massachusetts Institute of Technology, 1964) by Glazer and Moynihan and in *The Ghetto Game* (Sheed, 1962) by Dennis Clark.

By the end of Roosevelt's first term this initial New Deal was breaking up. Parts of the labor movement were restive, millions were listening to demagogues like Huey Long, business was souring on FDR. The Supreme Court ended the NRA and Roosevelt turned toward his left. Paradoxically he did so by moving away from the concept of planning and toward the "free market." The result was the second New Deal, which was *the* New Deal of the liberal nostalgia and, more importantly, the source of welfare theory and antipoverty wisdom to this moment.

The heart of the second New Deal was Keynesian. To be sure, some of the old pledges were redeemed: "floors" were provided for some of the aging and the workers in Social Security and minimum wage legislation; collective bargaining was recognized as a national policy (though it took several years of militant union activity to make the promise real). *Still, the American percentage of the gross national product devoted to direct social benefits has yet to achieve even half the level of the typical European contribution.* And the basic assumption of the second New Deal was that government intervention should not plan but stimulate the economy and that the private sector and initiative would continue to be the mainspring of progress. Public works were thus a temporary expedient and, as the second New Deal went on, they shifted from planned social investments toward projects designed primarily to get money into the economy.

The second New Deal did not succeed in its avowed aim of ending the Depression. That did not happen until the massive armaments spending of the war period. Nevertheless, Roosevelt did define the fundamentals of the American welfare state: modest contributions in direct welfare spending, a legal framework for the conflict between labor and management, and a government commitment to stimulate, or brake, the private economy in the interest of orderly growth without depression.

After World War II there was only one amendment in principle to the wisdom of the thirties. It centered around programs for training and retraining.

In 1956, for the first time in history, there were more white-collar than blue-collar workers in the United States. At the same time unemployment, while well below Depression levels, was chronic and persistent even in the good years. The diagnosis of this situation made by the Kennedy administration, and followed by President Johnson, had two main elements. Growth rates were lagging and the government must therefore stimulate the economy by deficits even at a time of business prosperity; and certain individuals required special help if they were to survive in the labor market.

The training-retraining component was built into a series of laws: Area Redevelopment, Manpower Development and Training, Economic Opportunity, and even the Federal Aid to Education Act of 1965. Some workers, it was acknowledged, were not participating in the general economic advance or were even being expelled from it by automation. They, and a growing number of high school dropouts, were denied economic opportunity because they lacked the right skills. The government was to give them the training, or the retraining, which would change this situation. At the same time neo-Keynesian tax cuts were to spur the nation and create the employment for the training-retraining graduates.

This general perspective is reflected in many pieces of current legislation. It is the foundation of the War on Poverty and summarizes bitter experience and arduously acquired knowledge. It will certainly help some people and probably not hurt many and is, on balance, to the good. Still, this approach misses the fundamental problem of the poor today. To understand why, it is necessary to turn to the new poor.

The basic reason why the poor of today differ from those of a generation ago, and therefore require radical measures if their poverty is to be abolished, is that the economy has changed much in a generation. In absolute terms and objective indices, the impoverished today are better off than their predecessors in misery; but relatively speaking, in terms of hope and economic opportunity, their plight is much worse. Moreover, this economic fact has all kinds of social and psychological consequences for the poor and it therefore cannot be described in simple, statistical terms.

For instance, because of their peculiarly underprivileged place in history and the economy, the new poor have fewer internal resources with which to combat their degradation and to seize chances when they appear.

Perhaps the most terrible example of how contemporary poverty affects group psychology is found among American Negroes. Negroes, who make up a large portion of the new poor, were systematically stripped of their African heritage under slavery. Every human institution—religion, the family, the tribe, or the community—was abolished as far as that was possible. After the Civil War this terrible violation by white America of the very spirit of the Negro continued through indirect economic pressures rather than the overt coercion of slavery. The Negro male was often emasculated socially, i.e., denied the chance to earn a living, to be the real head of a family, to function as a father. The result was a matriarchal tendency in Negro life.

Sociologists like Franklin Frazier have documented this terrible history in detail. One aspect of their analysis is particularly important here. The high percentage of broken families within Negro life, particularly in the Northern ghettos, makes the black masses of the 1960s much more difficult to organize than the predominantly white masses who formed the CIO. On the other hand, there is a paradoxical sense in which the very virulence of American racism has given Negroes a certain minimal solidarity, based on color, which is denied to many of the white poor.

So it is that the other principal groups of the new poor also

have tremendous problems built into the very structure of
their life. The farm worker who comes to the city today is
not drawn by economic opportunity but driven by the fact
that he has been made obsolete by agricultural modernization.
(In 1929, 25.1 per cent of the population was engaged in
farming; in 1964, 6.7 per cent. And the latter figure under-
estimates the actual trend. If one spoke of those Americans
engaged in *market* farming, i.e., the well-off rural people who
are subsidized by the government, they would number well under 5 per cent of the population.) The result is exile colonies of
the rural poor in cities like Cincinnati, St. Louis, and Chicago.

In the depressed areas the typical pattern is that those with
viable skills, or youth and hope, leave. Those who stay behind tend to lack militancy and aggressiveness. Where the old
spirit does remain, as among the miners of Hazard, Kentucky,
the poor face the fact that much federal depressed-areas legislation—the Appalachia Act, for instance—is constructed on a
trickle-down theory. The government, in keeping with the
conventional, neo-Keynesian wisdom, makes public investments in the infrastructure by building roads and dams. And
the first recipients of aid are the local business people. Their
prosperity is supposed eventually to provide jobs for the poor
people in the area. But of course it is precisely against this
middle class that the proudest and most aggressive of the
miners have battled. So the law which is supposed to help
them may well be used to discipline them.

Some white, urban workers are also caught in this downward spiral of pessimism. About half of the families of the
poor are headed by an employed worker. These people work
long, hard hours in jobs which are not covered by the minimum wage law (17.6 million workers in private industry are
not) and in which the minimum wage set by law is lower than
the accepted poverty line. They are in the occupations—laun-
dry work, lowly service functions in restaurants, hotels, and
hospitals, etc.—which in general are not organized by unions.

The new poor are thus in a different, and much more difficult, position than the old poor. In saying this, I do not want to romanticize the misery and exploitation of the past, or to imply that the poverty-stricken of today somehow just don't possess the spirit of their predecessors and never will. There is no point in repeating the error of the artisans of the AFL who, in the 1930s, looked down upon the industrial workers and predicted that they would never organize into an effective union. But there are two reasons why the new poor do not have a *present* potential for militant action equal to that of auto and steel workers in the thirties. For one thing, they are not assembled together daily in huge and organizable units like the mass-production factory. They live in chaotic slums and work at jobs which the union has never reached. But much more important, the new poor do not even have the economic hope which existed in 1936 and 1937, when the CIO emerged. Then, with a brief recessionary interlude, the economy was reviving, and the worker could believe that his job would be there tomorrow even if he joined and fought for the union. *But the new poor are the automation poor.* In fact, as will be made clear shortly, they have no reason to expect that present government plans will provide them with something to do which will be both useful and decently paid. To the extent that they are demoralized, their attitude derives from an accurate perception of the future as well as from the terrible heritage of the past.

Several ideas follow from this initial analysis of the new poor. In the face of the massive, and in many ways unprecedented, indignities which the poor suffer, superficial liberals should stop telling them to pull themselves up by the bootstraps "as we did." And superficial radicals should stop thinking that the new poor will instinctively be more disciplined, cohesive, and revolutionary than the workers of the CIO. But above all—and this point should emerge more plainly as I go on—this definition of the new poverty adds a crucial dimension to the demand that the federal government generate the jobs which will provide these people with economic hope. Such a program will not simply provide work for large numbers of individuals. It is hoped that it will provide a social setting in which entire groups of the poor will militantly organize themselves.

Having made this first definition of the new poverty, I must emphasize that it is, to an extraordinary degree, a youthful phenomenon. The problem of the poor is not automatically dying out with the older generation but is being most tenaciously posed by the youth.

In the 1964 Report of the Council of Economic Advisers, poverty was defined as an income of $3000 or less for a family. That was a bold way of putting the term and it gave a fair, if modest, estimate of the quantitative dimensions of our national scandal. But by omitting reference to family size and geographical location, the Administration was imprecise as to the exact qualitative composition of the problem. During 1964 the Social Security Administration refined the criteria and the new data became the basis for the 1965 Economic Report. The approximate number of the poor was not changed by these revisions. But, "most important, the estimated number of children in poverty rises by more than one third, from eleven million to fifteen million. That means that one fourth of the nation's children live in families that are poor."

In short, young people in America are "more" poor than the population as a whole. A fifth of the country, but a fourth of the youth, live in the other America. Of the thirty-five million defined as poor by the Council of Economic Advisers, over 40 per cent are young people. And one of the terrible things we have learned about present-day poverty—it was brilliantly documented in a Department of Labor Study of Selective Service Rejectees in 1964—is that it tends to be hereditary. Almost all of the old poor were children of people with little education, but they lived in communities which often made education an important community value. They worked in an economy which, in the long run, provided a market for uneducated muscle. Both of these advantages have been profoundly modified in the new poverty and in a good many places they don't exist at all. A quarter of the young men who take the draft exam fail because they are not educated enough to train as army privates (they are typically in their early twenties when they take the test). And they are, to a depressing degree, the children of the poor.

If all other things remain constant, one could then expect these 25 per cent of the youth who are poor to become heads of families—or, more precisely, heads of large families, for that is one of the patterns of poverty. And this would mean that impoverishment has a great future in this country. However, it is now the express purpose of the Administration not to let all things remain constant. These young people have been made the crux of the Economic Opportunity Act and of federal aid to education. So the question remains: faced by a poverty which is peculiarly corrosive in its impact on individual psychology and the internal resources of various subgroups of the poor, can present government programs provide "economic opportunity" for millions of impoverished youth in a period of automation and cybernation?

The answer to this question involves a manpower revolution and the fact that, even with the various Administration measures, the poor youth are so unequipped to meet this change that there is no present prospect that the majority of them will enjoy economic opportunity.

First of all, there is the manpower revolution itself (the phrase is taken from the 1964 Majority Report of the Senate Subcommittee on Employment and Manpower, chaired by Senator Joseph Clark). Between 1957 and 1963, the Senate Subcommittee found, there were substantial increases in output and even new industries in the non-agricultural, goods-producing sector of the economy—and yet employment in this sector decreased by 300,000 jobs. Indeed, the report continued, state and local governments provided approximately one third of the increase in wage and salary employment. So that when one looked for those areas in which jobs were being generated, it turned out that the private, profit-making, non-farm economy had given rise to only 300,000 new jobs in the six-year period, virtually all in the non-goods-producing sector.

These developments were, of course, part of a long-range pattern. In 1956, 39.4 per cent of the workers in the United States were white-collar, 38.8 per cent blue-collar. By 1964 the proportion had reached 44.2 per cent white-collar, 36.3 per cent blue-collar. The assembly line, through automation and cybernation, was becoming more and more productive, capable of increasing output while decreasing employment or keeping it stable. The state and local governmental sector was growing because of the increasing complexity of urban life and an enormous increase in education brought about by the postwar baby boom. And the private service sector—private schools, hospitals, restaurants, hostelries, etc.—was also burgeoning as a result of the general affluence.

Between 1957 and 1963, the result of these trends was that chronic high rates of unemployment (above 5 per cent on the official figures; nearer 10 per cent when one computed in the workers "expelled" from the labor market, the part-time unemployed, and so on) often co-existed with prosperity. Furthermore, these new jobs tended in contrary directions: occupations for the highly skilled with good pay; menial, janitorial employments at poverty or near-poverty pay.

In 1965 it seemed to some publicists that the 1957–63 figures described an aberration rather than a trend. From 1957 to 1962, they said, there had indeed been an average annual decline in blue-collar work of 120,000. But from 1962 to 1964 there had been a gain of 550,000 in this category. The crisis, they said, was over, and the manpower patterns of the late fifties constituted, not a revolution, but a temporary response to low growth rates. So the tax cut had done its proper work, and with some judicious training and retraining there would be work for the employable poor.

The President of the United States and the Department of Labor were not so optimistic. The 1965 Manpower Report noted that, even with the extraordinary stimulus of the tax cut, goods-producing industries barely held their own as a percentage of total employment. And President Johnson said, "In the long run, the need for semiskilled production workers and for many types of unskilled workers will continue to shrink in relation to demand in other occupational fields. . . . Most of the employment rise and the greatest rates of increase in 1964 were not in goods-production industries but in trades, services, and state and local government activities."

In short, the blue-collar unskilled and semiskilled jobs which had provided for so many of the old poor their occupational exit from poverty are declining. Where there is an increasing demand for simple muscle power, in the public and private service industries, it is more often than not in low-paid janitorial or dishwashing occupations. Thus one of the most fundamental propositions of the old antipoverty wisdom—that in the long run the private economy will generate new and better-paying work—applies less and less every day. It is now possible to have prosperity and decreasing opportunity for the poor.

Even this analysis understates the problem. For the American economy labors under the pressure of increasing population. It is not simply that the poor are tragically youthful but that the entire society is getting younger. And this could intensify some of these problematic manpower trends.

According to the Department of Labor, the United States will require over 101 million jobs by 1980. Between 1964 and 1970 the labor force will grow at a rate of 1.5 million a year. Just to accommodate this increase—and *without* reducing unemployment—would require job generation on a scale not even achieved during the Korean War. And if one adds the absolutely reasonable goal (it should be axiomatic with the neo-Keynesians) of reducing unemployment, as officially defined, to 3 per cent by 1969, that would take, according to AFL-CIO Research Director Nathaniel Goldfinger, 1.9 million new jobs a year.

The government is extremely pessimistic about its ability to measure up to these extraordinary job quotas. In order to meet the 1964–70 manpower requirements, Washington reports that an annual 4 per cent increase in gross national product will be needed during the entire period. And it then says, "But at no time in our recent peacetime history have we been able to sustain a rate of increase in the gross national product of 4 per cent for more than a brief period." That is to say, the welfare state and economic measures of the past are, by Administration admission, probably not equal to the labor force requirements of the future.

As in all things, this grim proposition will be truer for some people than for others: the poor, and the fifteen million poor youth among them in particular, will bear the brunt of the trend.

About a third of American youth today drop out of education before they leave high school. They have an unemployment rate of 15 per cent (and it is almost double that for Negro dropouts); of the 1963 dropouts who did find employment, 45 per cent wound up as laborers or as menials; and these people typically, the government tells us, do not upgrade their skills. This one third of the youth includes a majority of the young poor. In a time of automation they provide a reserve army for poverty.

But, someone might reply, this is precisely the reason for the considerable investments which the government is now making in various education programs, from preschool training under Community Action to postschool training under the

Job Corps and retraining for middle-aged workers under Manpower Development and Training. This notion begs the question. For all of the training and retraining in the world cannot change the fact that the government itself, in the 1965 Manpower Report, has no confidence that the requisite number of jobs will be generated.

The Department of Labor projections on the educational attainment of the work force in 1975 are even more revealing. In 1964 the Senate Subcommittee estimated that a young worker needed fourteen years of schooling—two years beyond high school—in order to have a really good chance for economic opportunity. But in 1975, when the skill requirements for the available decent jobs will presumably be much higher, more than one fourth (26.6 per cent) of the workers twenty-five to thirty-four years of age will be without a high school diploma. This society apparently plans for them to be either unemployed or janitors, i.e., poor.

Thus the newness of poverty, and the consequent obsolescence of so much of President Johnson's current program, can be defined in the following way. The decisive factor, the terrible novelty, of impoverishment today is that it takes place in a time of automation. Under such circumstances the systematically undereducated and undertrained (which is another way of saying "the poor") are justifiably pessimistic. Thus far the government has offered them the possibility of further education and training but, at the same time, essentially says that it really doesn't expect to have enough decent jobs for its own graduates. All this reinforces the cynicism and resistance to organization which characterizes poor communities.

The situation is particularly acute for the fifteen million young people who are poor and the even larger number (one in three) who are high-school dropouts in the age of post-high-school technology. This is the "growth potential" of American poverty. There are liberal critics ("critical supporters" might be a better term) of the Administration's program who have recognized many of these problems. They have consequently proposed what I would call a third New Deal: that the nation politically allocate resources to the public sector (consciously directing, rather than simply stimulating, at least a part of the economy) in order to create positive, useful jobs which would raise the quality of life of the entire society. These proposals are excellent as far as they go—but they do not go far enough. As a next, and giant, step in American life, they are certainly worthy of support, but they raise issues and pose problems which have radical implications for the very structure of the society.

In brilliant testimony before the Joint Committee on the Economic Report in February 1965, John Kenneth Galbraith spoke of "reactionary Keynesianism." This is the thesis that one promotes economic growth by expanding private, individual consumption through policies like the tax cut, but not by making planned investments in social consumption. "I am not quite sure what the advantage is," Galbraith said, "in having a few more dollars to spend if the air is too dirty to breathe, the water too polluted to drink, the commuters are losing out in the struggle to get in and out of the city, the streets are filthy and the schools so bad that the young perhaps wisely stay away, and hoodlums roll citizens for some of the dollars they saved in the tax cut."

Galbraith's point is particularly relevant to the new poverty. When one cuts taxes and uses other methods to increase individual consumption, that allows individuals to choose how the public subsidy will be spent. Moreover, as Leon Keyserling demonstrated at length in regard to the 1964 cut, the rich will get the lion's share of this decision-making power. The corporations will presumably spend their rebates on becoming more efficient, i.e., requiring fewer workers; and wealthy individuals will scarcely invest theirs in slum clearance or public schools.

As Galbraith testified with considerable wit, this approach

is, in the long run, disastrous even from the viewpoint of the well off. For a "prosperity" that leaves slums and ghettos standing and creates a desperate generation of uneducated youth will be threatened, not by revolution, but by constant outbreaks of individual, nihilistic violence. In addition to discomfiting the good citizenry, such a situation costs them money. The announced initial cost of Mayor Wagner's "war on crime" in New York City was greater than the first investment in his "war on poverty."

But beyond this middle-class cost accountancy, the poor themselves are deeply involved in this matter. The Community Action Programs under Title II of the Economic Opportunity Act propose to ameliorate the educational, familial, and psychological ravages of slum life. But no one has yet proposed the most crucial and obvious thing: to do away with the slums altogether. The poor are, by income definition, not in the "free" housing market (I use the quotation marks because private residential construction—for the middle class and the rich—is subsidized by an extraordinary array of governmental programs). There are not enough low-rent public housing units and those which do exist, while an advance over a crowded, rat-infested tenement, tend to be segregated by class and race and to have other disadvantages.

Thus there is no reason to expect that the slums will disappear by the "natural" workings of the economy. Yet so long as the slums do exist, Community Action will have a first aid rather than a surgical quality. And obviously, doing away with the slums will take a whole range of public responses: creating new towns, breaking the class and race barriers which block off the suburbs, rehabilitating structurally sound housing (but this project, which is sometimes put forward as a panacea, requires moving—and housing—three quarters of the people who live in the present charming but miserable unit), and so on.

As the poor themselves have understood in several "urban

renewal" battles, such an undertaking requires that the new, low-cost housing be supplied first and that demolition occur only after the residents have been rehoused. In any case, all of these new departures are theoretically possible. The only (and enormous) obstacle in their way is political. Another argument can be advanced in their favor: if the Community Action Program is to work, a new environment for community has to be created. And that is a positive, job-generating way of investing resources in social consumption as contrasted to priming the pump with tax cuts.

This one instance of housing points how far the United States must go beyond the notion that poverty can be abolished by tax cuts and various new forms of vocational training. There must be a conscious governmental creation of a labor market in which the poor can find economic opportunity, and this can be done only by social investments which will also attack the environmental structure of poverty. There must be, in short, a planned expansion of the public sector of the economy, particularly with regard to housing, education, and transportation.

Such a program can be found on the democratic left wing of American liberalism. It is, in one form or another, professed by the AFL-CIO, Leon Keyserling's Conference on Economic Progress, the ADA, and many other groups, and it was the subject of Myrdal's *Challenge to Affluence*. It is, therefore, politically possible, a giant step forward in American life— and still this side of radicalism.

Essentially, this social investment approach would involve the adoption of some kind of indicative national economic planning. As far back as the Full Employment Bill of 1945, the Democrats argued that the gross national product was too important a determinant of economic and social life to be left to the fates or the so-called free market. But their proposals were reduced to the statements of intent in the Employment Act of 1946. Now there are once more serious proposals to catch up with what we almost knew as a nation twenty years ago. The Clark Subcommittee of 1964 thus favored giving the President and the Council of Economic Advisers the responsibility for developing a national budget for all sectors of the economy, public and private, of estimating the GNP and unemployment which would result from this projection, and, if the figures pointed to a jobless level of 3 per cent or more, coming in with programs to create a GNP big enough to fit the employment needs of the society. The subcommittee further put forward an immediate proposal to reduce unemployment to below 3 per cent by 1968 through annual increments of $5 billion in social spending.

This tack was not taken by the Johnson administration. With a strange fatalism, Washington in 1965 clearly implied that it had no confidence that its economic policies would reduce unemployment even to the 4 per cent "interim" acceptable level; and, as noted earlier, the White House and the Department of Labor do not think that our current capacities and development will meet the needs of the manpower revolution during the next five years. With ingenuity and brilliance we have predicted chronic high unemployment. Leaving that prophecy to come true, we propose to abolish poverty at the same time.

The nation need not passively accept such a contradictory perspective. Instead, we could move toward a more radical liberalism by means of programs and policies which are now advocated by the labor and liberal movements. In so doing, the United States would undertake its third New Deal.

The centerpiece of the first New Deal was the business-dominated planning of the NRA and that of the second New Deal, Keynesian intervention to stimulate the private economy. "Now," John Kenneth Galbraith has written, "Keynesian policies are the new orthodoxy. Economists are everywhere to be seen enjoying their new and pleasantly uncontroversial role. Like their predecessors who averted their eyes from un-

employment, many are now able to ignore . . . the new problem, which is an atrocious allocation of resources between
private wants and public needs, especially those of our cities.
(In a sense, *the Keynesian success has brought back an older
problem of economics, that of resource allocation, in a new
form.*)" (Italics mine.) I would add only one comment to
Galbraith's analysis. So long as the present situation persists,
the poor will be the most helpless victims of America's atrocious
allocation of resources; and the moment something is done,
they will be the first beneficiaries, in terms both of finding
decent employment and of building a new environment for
themselves.

In short, the essence of the third New Deal is social investment, a conscious and political allocation of resources to meet
public needs. Such a program can obviously be carried out
within the general limits of the welfare state, i.e., it does not
propose any basic change in the ownership of American industry. Yet it is also clear that the business wing of the Johnson
coalition would be extremely hostile to a third New Deal. Even
more important than Henry Ford's reaction is the fact that
a third New Deal would pose radical questions about the nation's economy and social structure, which could signify both
a culmination of liberalism and a most important point of
departure for radicalism. I want to labor this point a bit, because it has implications for the political strategy of a real
war on poverty, pointing up the necessity for the mobilization
of a new and militant coalition which will include, but not be
confined to, the poor.

The social investment approach assumes that the gross national product is not an economic fate played out on the free
market but a subject for political debate and determination.
In the Clark Subcommittee proposals, for instance, if a projected GNP does not fit the nation's social aims, then the
government creates a new, more appropriate GNP. A major
instrument of such a policy is the expansion of the public

sector. There are two arguments for such a tack: the private, goods-producing sector will not create jobs for the poor, so there must be a conscious generation of work in the public sector; in the course of providing the needed quantity of jobs through the public sector, we will be able to transform the quality of American life.

Now all this is compatible with the corporate ownership of American industry. And yet the social investment approach takes liberalism to a junction with radicalism. It goes beyond Lyndon Johnson, of course; but more than that, it points toward the other side of the welfare state.

To begin with, this approach proposes a modest allocation of economic resources on the basis of social usefulness rather than private profit. As the Clark Subcommittee and others have put it, this would still leave the great mass of the economy in private hands. Yet it is a most important opening wedge for establishing a principle which could be extended until there is democratic control of major economic decisions. As one socialist French planner said of the situation in his own country, it opens up the possibility that the legislature could become the stockholders' meeting of the entire national economy.

But there is another possibility, and here France's present rather than its possible future is the model. If the big corporations were to be shrewd about all this and join wholeheartedly in indicative planning, they could shape it to *their* collective ends rather than to those of the society. Thus, under Gaullist planning in France, there has been a redistribution of income in favor of the rich. The entire French economy has become more efficient and, in the absence of effective counteraction by the democratic left, the chief beneficiaries have been the largest shareholders. If there is a "reactionary Keynesianism," there is also "reactionary planning." If this is to be avoided, it can only be through the power of an organized popular movement against the political power and interest of the corporations. And this I regard as a radical undertaking.

It is in this context that one must place the importance of the self-organization of the poor and their participation in a larger coalition. The point of community organization today is not, as too many seem to think, "self-help," neighborhood uplift. In Harlem, Kenneth Clark points out in his *Dark Ghetto*, people on a block organized to clean up the street. That, Clark says, was a wrong thing to do, for it implied acceptance of the theory that the street was litter-strewn because its Negro inhabitants were at fault. In point of fact the real culprit was the city administration which, in this instance, as in practically every other, provides inferior public services for Negro areas. And the real demand, Clark concludes, should have been political organization to force the city to give the street its due.

At the 1965 Conference of Mayors various metropolitan chief executives understood these political implications of community organization, even if they were a bit hysterical in the doing. The right of the poor to participate in the War on Poverty was, some of them said, "Marxism," the class struggle. This was an incredible overstatement of the present state of affairs but it at least had the virtue of understanding what might happen if the poor were no longer welfare dependent but militant activists.

Such militant activism among the poor cannot be wished into existence. If the argument of this essay is correct, one of the consequences of a liberal program for the generation of new jobs would be that it might well create the economic setting for a radical movement of self-organization among the poor. Such a mobilization could take place in two main areas: around the indignities of daily life in the slum in the form of community unions, tenants' councils, and the like; and through the penetration of the labor movement into the American economic underworld in the form of unionizing and transforming poverty jobs. In any case, such new institutions of the poor would have an important place in the national (liberal-labor-religious-radical) coalition which would be required to make planning an instrument of the popular will rather than of the corporation.

Finally, there are in these liberal proposals for social investments radical implications for the quality of American life. The issue is not simply providing a given quantity of work, important as that is to the new poor. It is also one of providing the right kind of socially useful work. And this will require that new occupational categories be consciously created. The middle class has defined some new pursuits for its children already: the occupation of graduate student as a first career; the foundation industry with its fellowships and consultantships; Peace Corps and VISTA volunteer; and so on. And now, under the impetus of the War on Poverty, there are tentative new definitions of work for the poor themselves.

The "indigenous" neighborhood worker—the slum dweller recruited for paid social work because of his existential training in poverty—is already appearing in various Community Action Programs. Other possibilities are being explored: teacher's aide, community organizer, research assistant. Significantly, these new occupations tend to appear in the public and "human care" sector of the economy. This trend owes at least as much to technological necessity as to the popular conscience. For it is the private and goods-producing part of the economy which automates; and it is in the service, and particularly the public service, sector that new needs and opportunities appear.

But here again the political dimension is extremely important. Governmental support of the indigenous neighborhood worker could turn into an excellent way of recruiting the best leaders of the poor into an apparatus controlled by City Hall. This would not be the case if a coalition were activated between the poor and other movements for social change. One of the important functions of such a coalition would be to provide a financial base so that indigenous community organizers could be completely independent of government, responsive only to their own constituents.

In short, a program of social investments in the public sector is a liberal, politically possible proposal with radical implications. At the outset it leaves the corporate domination of the economy intact, but it also introduces the counterprinciple of social usefulness into our economic affairs. Whether or not this principle will develop into the basis of fundamental economic decision is a political question. It depends, above all, on the emergence of a new coalition which will see to it not only that planning and social investment are extended but that they are extended in a democratic way. And these implications of the liberal proposals are clearly radical.

In considering the problem of poverty, then, I suggest that we raise the issue of the future of society itself.

The poor were, as noted before, the first part of the American population to cross the frontier of automation. Tragically, for them it meant entry into the new poverty. But these problems will not stop at a $3000 income line or be confined to thirty-five or even fifty million Americans. For these trends point to the possibility that entire areas of work—union-organized work, clerical work, executive work, as well as poverty work—will be abolished. The Administration has been skeptical of such prophecies, but in the 1965 transmission of the Manpower Report, President Johnson implied that the real argument is not whether, but when, extraordinary transformations will take place. "New technology," the President said, "will not *soon* curtail need for human labor." (Italics mine.) In short, *someday* new technology could curtail need for human labor.

If this is the case, then the program outlined in this paper points deeper than reform and well beyond poverty. The problem is not simply the massive one of liberating thirty-five to fifty million people from their misery and providing useful occupations for fifteen million youngsters. This undertaking is but the first installment in the redefinition of work for the society as a whole. And the economy of the future will thus have to allocate resources and plan for an unprecedented situation in which work, as traditionally defined, will no longer be the main fact about human life.

There are glimpses of this futurism in current, and sober, proposals. There are now bills providing benefits which would allow workers to exit earlier from the economy into retirement (this is necessary because the new technology cannot read the Social Security fine print about aging starting for a man at sixty-five) and to permit young workers to enter it later (by providing everyone with at least fourteen years of free public education). These are not simply fragments of change; they could be steps toward redefining the working lifetime of society.

Thus the immediate and politically possible need in the war against poverty is for a third New Deal, a radical liberalism. This would involve the assignment of planning responsibilities to the Council of Economic Advisers, massive social investments, the creation of a new human care sector of the economy which would employ college graduates and high school dropouts. To one degree or another, the considerable political forces of the labor, civil rights, and liberal movements are committed to taking this path. Radicals should join with them.

At the same time it is the vocation of the radical to point out that even a third New Deal is not enough. The thoroughgoing reforms which the new poor need today if they are even to begin to catch up with automation merely anticipate the basic transformations which the entire society will require tomorrow if it is to make its revolutionary technology humane. For more and more resources will have to be allocated to education, to leisure, to the "non-productive" and socially useful sector.

The plight of the new poor is radical. To help these tens of millions out of their present misery demands at least a third

New Deal. And in achieving that the society will be forced to think about, and to embark upon, a far more fundamental restructuring. Such a development will not occur automatically. There are now reactionary Keynesians, and there will be reactionary third New Dealers who will want to use the new social techniques to maintain the old social subordinations. If they are to be defeated, the war against poverty will not be based simply on economic models and blueprints for change. Its driving force will be a new political coalition—the poor, the unions, the best of the religious movements, the liberals, the radicals—everyone whose aim will be the democratization of economic and social power.

1966

America's Schizophrenic View of the Poor

PAUL JACOBS

I

How old-fashioned, almost quaint, the word "pauper" appears today. One thinks of Oliver Twist asking the beadle for a bit more porridge or of an aged couple trudging over the hill to the poorhouse. Yet at least 8,000,000 of the estimated 35,000,000 people living in poverty today are actual paupers, dependent solely on public or private charity. But we prefer to speak of these paupers as "the disadvantaged," the "hard-to-reach," the "senior-citizens," or as the "long-term unemployed" with "culturally deprived children" who are born, unfortunately, into a "cycle of poverty" which gives them no chance to get out of the "poverty pocket" or "poverty belt." Are these less offensive terms merely euphemisms, or do they suggest that basic changes have taken place in the American attitude towards the poor?

An ideological schizophrenia with a complex history characterizes the American view of poverty. On the one hand, we believe achievement is related primarily to self-reliance and

From the book, *The State of the Nation*, edited by David Boroff. © 1965 by The Nation Centennial, Inc. Published by Prentice-Hall, Inc., Englewood Cliffs, New Jersey.

self-help; on the other, we have been forced to concede that failure cannot always be laid at the door of the individual. Both these views are embodied in the constellation of ideas on which President Johnson's War Against Poverty is based. As a result, that program is schizophrenic, too. It assumes that poverty will be eliminated if only society can alter the circumstances which have barred the poor from access to work, the "American way of life." But it does not question whether such a way of life is possible for all in the new technological order, nor does it seek to alter, in any profound sense, the economic and political system. Instead, the existence of poverty is viewed as an impersonal—and soluble—"paradox." The program's cheerful optimism reflects an almost mystical belief in the infinite potentials of American society. Poverty, like polio, will be defeated when the right vaccine is found.

The first American colonists brought with them from Puritan England the comparatively new doctrine which combined the view that man had a religious duty to achieve material success with the concept that giving direct financial aid to the poor destroyed their character.

Typically Puritan was John Locke's proposal in 1697 "that all men, sound of limb and mind, begging in maritime counties out of their own parish shall be seized by an officer of the parish or by an inhabitant and brought before the next J.P. and be sent . . . to the next seaport town, there to be kept at hard labor till some of H.M. Ships coming in, give an opportunity of putting them on board, where they will serve 3 years under strict discipline at soldiers' pay." So, too, Locke suggested that paupers' children between the ages of three and fourteen be taken away from their parents and put in working schools where "what is necessary for their relief will more effectually have that use if distributed to them in bread at school. . . . And to this may be added, without any trouble in cold weather, if it be thought needful, a little warm water gruel, for the same fire that warms the room may be made to boil a pot of it."

In colonial America, such Puritan doctrines were buttressed by the belief that every man, except the Negro slave, could break through the class barriers that had held them down in aristocratic England and Europe. In this view, the poor were poor only because of some flaw in their character; therefore, not society, but only their families, bore any responsibility towards them. Only the Negro slaves, for whom poverty was considered the natural state, were exempt from this judgment, and their care was given to their masters. The only explanation for any others who were poor was the one characteristically offered by the Humane Society in 1809, when it said that "by a just and inflexible law of Providence, misery is ordained to be the companion and punishment of vice."

The most popular methods for dealing with the non-slave poor who had no families or friends to care for them were to auction off those incapable of working to the persons asking the smallest amount to care for them, to put them in "alms-houses," or to "bind out" the able-bodied as indentured servants. This was usually done by state or local governments; no one dreamed of any federal responsibility for the poor.

Such attitudes began to waver, however, in the first quarter of the nineteenth century, when the vision of an eternally expanding and ever-more-prosperous country became clouded over by recurring economic depressions. Grudgingly, it was conceded that "non-employment" resulting in poverty was not necessarily the fault of the workers. For those "whose cry was, not for bread and fuel of charity but for Work!" as Horace Greeley described them, destitution was often the ugly consequence of unemployment. The popular faith in the American ideals of self-sufficiency and self help was shaken by this kind of talk. Nevertheless, as late as 1854 President Franklin Pierce, vetoing a bill to grant public land for the use of states to help care for the indigent insane, argued that the government could not become "the great almoner of public charity throughout the United States."

The severe depression of 1857–1859 forced changes in methods of dealing with the poor. Private charity funds weren't adequate to tide over the unemployed, and public funds had to be appropriated by cities. Now, for the first time in the country's brief history, the unemployed organized in protest, demonstrating and marching to force local governments to take action. Shortly there followed the Civil War, which left the South as an entire region of poverty. In the wake of the war, private charity and philanthropy developed on a large scale, while there grew a reluctant acceptance of the fact that the federal government had to assume responsibility for some part of veterans' care and provide for the families of dead soldiers.

But no one, except nineteenth century radicals, questioned the basic assumption that the free enterprise system was created by God to bring about the Kingdom of Heaven, or something close to it, here on earth. Economic dislocations were believed to be only temporary disturbances from which the country could, and would, always quickly recover. The depression of 1873, like that of the late 1850's, brought about demonstrations of the unemployed which were crushed by the police. Private charity remained the main form of welfare during the latter half of the nineteenth century. Public work projects were adopted only reluctantly, because administration of welfare programs by corrupt officials often led to their abuse for political purposes. In the spring of 1894, thousands of unemployed marchers from all parts of the country gathered in Washington to petition Congress. This was "Coxey's Army." Coxey and a few other marchers were arrested and received short prison sentences for "walking on the grass" and carrying banners. The House Committee on Labor refused to hear Coxey's proposals, and before the end of the year, the first national movement of the poor and unemployed had collapsed.

Meanwhile, the reform and settlement house movements had started focusing attention on the social and economic conditions creating poverty. Even so, these social workers remained committed to the thesis that the dole destroyed the character of the recipients. In 1883, Josephine Shaw Lowell, the great welfare worker, wrote that using public funds to support the poor in their homes was evil because "the principle underlying [the practice] is not that the proceeds of all men's labor is to be fairly divided among all but that the idle, improvident and even vicious man has the right to live in idleness and vice upon the proceeds of the labor of his industrious and virtuous fellow citizen."

Characteristically, Jane Addams poignantly describes her mixed reactions to this policy in the case of a young man who came to Hull House to secure help for his family:

I told him one day of the opportunity for work on the drainage canal and intimated that if any employment were obtainable, he ought to exhaust that possibility before asking for help. The man replied that he had always worked indoors and that he could not endure outside work in the winter. . . . He did not come again for relief but worked for two days digging on the canal where he contracted pneumonia and died a week later. I have never lost trace of the two little children he left behind him although I cannot see them without a bitter consciousness that it was at their expense I learned that life cannot be administered by definite rules and regulations; that wisdom to deal with a man's difficulties comes only through some knowledge of his life and habits as a whole; and that to treat an isolated episode is almost sure to invite blundering.

The viewpoint of the business community towards the reformers' concern about the "deserving poor" was expressed bluntly by Elbert Hubbard in 1899:

We have been recently hearing much maudlin sympathy expressed for the "downtrodden denizen of the sweatshop". . . . Nothing is said about the employer who grows old before his time in a vain attempt to get frowsy ne'er-do-wells to do intelligent work; and his long, patient striving with the "help" that does nothing but loaf when his back is turned. In every store and factory there is a

constant weeding-out process going on. . . . It is the survival of the
fittest. Self-interest prompts every employer to keep the best—those
who can carry a message to Garcia.

Gradually, however, needy children, the aged, the blind, the
deaf, the mentally retarded and widows with children were
exempted from the strictures of social Darwinism. Pensions
for the blind were authorized by law in Ohio in 1898 and
gradually in other states. In 1911, Illinois passed a law
providing cash payments to widows with young children, and
over a period of years the boundaries of these laws were
extended to take in not only children with dead fathers but
those whose fathers had deserted them. But the application of
these laws was discretionary rather than mandatory, and since
the costs were almost always assumed by the local communities, rather than the states, the grants were very often not
made or were inadequate.

The first old-age assistance law was passed in 1915—not in
a state, but in the Territory of Alaska. In 1923 Montana and
Nevada became the first states to enact such legislation. Only
28 states had such laws in 1934, and even then the restrictions
on eligibility were very severe and the amount of aid very
limited. During the depression that followed the panic of 1907,
and during the depression of 1914–1915, the fate of the able-
bodied unemployed was left almost completely in the hands of
private charity.

The traditional commitment of the country to laissez-faire
capitalism was still very strong in the postwar depression of
1920–22. The federal government took the position that only
private industry could solve the problem of unemployment and
that the responsibility for relief of the unemployed rested with
the local communities.

In September, 1921, President Warren Harding told the Na-
tionwide Conference on Unemployment that "I would have
little enthusiasm for any proposed relief which seeks either

palliation or tonic from the public treasury. The excess of stimulation from that source is to be reckoned a cause of trouble rather than a source of cure. . . ." Curiously, organized labor sided with the President and the employer class in opposing public relief for the unemployed. The American Federation of Labor had always opposed such relief and continued its opposition to any form of federal unemployment insurance even after the Great Depression of 1929. At its 1930 convention, William Green spoke in ringing 18th-century terms: "The American workman, proud of his freedom and his liberty, is not yet willing to make himself a ward of the state and a ward of the government. . . . We cannot deal with such a tragedy in a visionary way."

Even in the following year, with at least 7,000,000 people expected to be unemployed during the winter, the AFL termed federal unemployment insurance as "unsuited to our economic and political requirements here and unsatisfactory to American working men and women." It was not until July, 1932, when 11,000,000 workers were unemployed, that the AFL executive council reluctantly instructed President Green to draft a plan of unemployment insurance.

Social workers, too, opposed the "federal dole." Influenced strongly by Freud, they had moved, during the twenties, from the muckraking role of urging environmental reform to a greater emphasis on the psychological problems of their clients. This new psychological orientation, with its emphasis on the individual solution of problems, blended very well with the older traditions of self-help and social Darwinism. From it evolved a belief that the best way to help unemployed able-bodied workers was not through a federally controlled "dole" program, administered by politicians, but through locally administered private programs over which the social workers could exercise some professional control.

But by the summer of 1931 this re-affirmation of local responsibility was beginning to face strong opposition among social workers appalled by the effects of the Great Depression, and by the spring of 1932, the profession as a whole was united behind the urgent need for federal intervention.

The character of that intervention was set by Franklin Delano Roosevelt while he was governor of New York, and can be found today in President Johnson's program. In August, 1931, Roosevelt had called an emergency session of the New York legislature, and one month later got a bill passed setting up the Temporary Emergency Relief Administration. TERA sponsored relief programs that were to be administered by local communities: the amounts allocated to each community were to be based both on the community's needs and their effectiveness in drawing upon their own resources. Thus, TERA was, in a sense, a compromise between the older tradition of self-help and the terrifying need for governmental action. It was headed by Harry Hopkins, a professional social worker, who gave the highest priority to work relief, for he was deeply concerned that the recipients of aid not lose the self-esteem which social workers believed would be destroyed by direct aid.

II

The argument over whether or not federal funds should be used to aid the needy had actually ended in the summer of 1932, when President Hoover had reluctantly approved federal loans to finance 80 per cent of all state and local aid to the unemployed (loans which obviously were not going to be repaid). The summer of 1932 was catastrophic for the Republicans: thousands of unemployed veterans had converged on Washington to exert pressure for the passage of a bonus bill, and were driven from the capital by force —an act which outraged the country. Roosevelt, as President, took immediate steps to meet the terrible crisis. In March, 1933, the Civilian Conservation Corps was established to provide work camps for youth; in May, the Federal Emergency Relief Administration was created; in June, public employment offices to be operated by the states were authorized; and in November, Roosevelt issued an executive order setting up the Civilian Works Agency to operate a federal work program. In January, 1935, Roosevelt proposed that Congress set up the Works Progress Administration. But his message to Congress reflected his commitment to the traditional attitude toward the dole: "The lessons of History," he said, "show conclusively that continued dependence upon relief induces a spiritual and moral disintegration fundamentally destructive to the national fiber. To dole out relief in this way is . . . a subtle destroyer of the human spirit."

Roosevelt also asked, at this time, that Congress act in the field of social security by establishing a federal-state partnership to finance old-age assistance, aid to the blind and aid to needy children. In August, the Social Security Act was passed, providing also for a federal tax on employer payrolls to finance unemployment insurance. The passage of this legislation, as well as the establishment of the Department of Health, Education and Welfare, formalized the federal government's acceptance of responsibility for social welfare. (The first government job that Lyndon B. Johnson ever held was as a WPA administrator, an experience he obviously has never forgotten, for clear echoes of that experience can be found in his antipoverty program.)

The New Deal welfare program changed an essential tenet of American life, but only in a limited way. Responsibility for the economic well-being of individuals was now vested in the government, but the responsibilities were carried out in ways that did no violence to traditional attitudes. Unemployment insurance and social security pensions were not given to all citizens as a matter of right; unemployment insurance was paid only to those who had been working for specified periods of time; payments to the aged were based on a system to which the workers contributed. The amounts paid out varied, too, in relation to the amounts paid in; nor did anyone question the right of the state to refuse unemployment insurance payments to the unemployed worker who refused to accept what was considered a suitable job. States' rights were also carefully preserved, and the emphasis of the program—accepted by the political leaders, the administrative staff and their social-worker allies—was on helping the depression victims adjust to their now somewhat better condition.

The fear shared by reformers and conservatives alike that unemployment relief and unemployment insurance would have the effect of pauperizing the recipient turned out to be ground-less. Bakke, in *The Unemployed Worker,* a study of the depression victims, came to the general conclusion that "Un-employment Insurance has not made paupers." Nevertheless, over and over again, the "no handout" theme was emphasized by the administrative liberals running the programs. Together with the social workers, they adopted a kind of progressive paternalism towards the poor in which Roosevelt represented the kindly father figure.

But the establishment of federal work and relief programs also brought about the development of organized groups of the unemployed who, demanding better treatment or increased relief budgets, frequently met with bitter opposition from the welfare administration and from the police. However, some welfare administrators understood that these groups played an important role in dramatizing the plight of the unemployed.

In 1939 and 1940, another and more rebellious voice was raised—that of the Back of the Yards movement in Chicago, which brought together a variety of community, religious, and labor organizations centered in the stockyards. The BYM was overtly a pressure group, committed to tying local actions into programs of larger social reconstruction. In words that have a clear resonance today, for they are echoed by important seg-ments of the civil rights movement, one of their spokesmen defined the organization's aims:

We are sick of the social-worker approach. The battle against slum conditions and slum areas is our prime objective, as it must be the prime objective of all organizations and individuals who seek to do significant work for social betterment.

Many liberals are disturbed by the Back of the Yards Neighborhood Council because they feel it is a pressure group which fights in a tough vicious way in which no holds are barred. It does fight viciously.

We in Back of the Yards are fighting for our bread and butter, our homes, our families, and for our very lives. . . . These liberals fail to realize that the achievement and constructive use of power can help people better themselves.

The force we rely upon is the power that can only be generated by democratic organizations. The liberals cannot believe this because they are remote from the people and have never seen or felt the vitality of democracy in action.

World War II brought an end to the depression, at least for the white majority, and with it also came a temporary easing of the ideological schizophrenia that the country had suffered during the thirties. The society concentrated its attention on the war efforts, which seemed, as a concomitant, to have brought prosperity to all. In fact, nothing of the sort had happened: the aged, the dependent, and the disabled were only a little better off than they had been during the depression, while the Negroes, the largest minority group, were only in a relatively better position.

At the end of World War II, memories of the depression resulted in the passage of the Full Employment Act of 1946, which again reflected the dual commitment so characteristic of American society. The Act affirmed federal responsibility for providing "conditions under which there will be afforded useful employment opportunities, including self-employment, for those willing, able and seeking to work and to promote maximum employment, production and purchasing power"; but, simultaneously, it insisted that this responsibility had to be carried out "in a manner calculated to foster and promote free competitive enterprise."

Fortunately, the law faced no real test in the first ten years of its enactment, for employment remained relatively high except for brief recessions in 1949 and 1954. To be sure, some industries revealed a high rate of unemployment, and some groups—particularly Negroes and older workers—were quite clearly at a disadvantage. But only the unions and a few economists raised the issue of unemployment in any forceful terms; the Republican Administration and the business community remained optimistic about a future upturn and insistent that the prewar values were still verities. The National Association of Manufacturers for example, bitterly opposed the United Auto Workers' demand for a supplementary unemployment insurance plan that would guarantee income for a longer time. Said the NAM: "Guaranteed wage demands are based on the theory that employment is man's natural state and that when unemployment occurs employers should be held responsible. Actually, people cannot be employed until someone takes positive action which results in the creation of jobs."

III

Beginning in 1956, the unemployment rate rose steadily, from 4.2 per cent to 5.6 per cent. Even worse, inside the overall rate was buried a differential rate for Negroes that was having a sharp effect in the Negro community: Negroes were actually slipping backwards and were relatively worse off than they had been in the immediate postwar period. But now a more aggressive mood prevailed among the Negroes and other minority groups, stimulated in part by the expansion of community and race relations agencies that were often supported by foundation funds.

These agencies were the post-World War II counterparts of the social welfare and reform groups of the late nineteenth and early twentieth centuries. But their focus had shifted to the improvement of inter-group and inter-religious relations, primarily through the establishment of community agencies with broad representation from all segments of the community. Generally, their operations were in the hands of professional staffs, backed by a board whose individual members either had personal or organizational prestige. And although the agencies recognized very quickly that the problems they confronted had to be dealt with in an integrated fashion, involving all aspects of community life, their actual operations involved very few members of the groups on whose behalf they spoke. In this approach they differed sharply from such organizations as the Back of the Yards movement, with its emphasis on participation in decision-making by as many members of the community as possible.

Inevitably, then, reform became professionalized, and the reformers learned to operate within the context of society, rather than attempting to make radical changes in it. Even more important, the new breed of reformers became the experts to whom society deferred for dealing with community problems—including the one of poverty, which was again being discovered.

The discovery wasn't a sudden one, nor was it complete. In 1958, John Galbraith's *The Affluent Society* divided the "new poverty" into two main components: case and insular poverty. Case poverty referred to those individuals who suffer from some personal disability that prevents them from joining in the national upward trend, while insular poverty referred to an entire area, such as the Appalachians, where everybody was adversely affected by the economic downgrading that had taken place.

But most people were more heartened by the title of Galbraith's book than dismayed by its contents. And the civil rights movement, which was not yet directly connected with, nor concerned about, poverty absorbed the attention of the government and the reformers. Robert Lampman's work on unequal income distribution failed to draw the notice it deserved, and when, in 1962, Michael Harrington's *The Other America* was published, it received equally little attention. But a year later, Dwight MacDonald wrote a long review-article about poverty in *The New Yorker* praising Harrington's book, and the rush was on. Poverty had been rediscovered.

The rediscovery came at a most opportune time for American liberals. Their earlier struggle on behalf of the Negroes had been replaced by the Negroes' struggle on their own behalf —one from which the white liberals were being pointedly excluded. In foreign policy, the cold war consensus had eliminated any real differentiation between the liberal voice and that of the conservatives. And the Kennedy administration had brought to Washington a group of people who combined a commitment to *Realpolitik* with a rosy vision of the liberal future. At the same time, the Administration grew increasingly concerned with the problem of poverty, especially as it related to the intensification of the Negro struggle; indeed, the Negro became the personification of the poverty problem.

The assassination of the President cut short the Administration's plans in this field, and thus Johnson was able to make the antipoverty program his own.

Johnson's interests in developing the program were manifold. It was one of the first with which his Administration could be identified as initiator, rather than merely as executor. Such a program, moreover, represented a fairly safe political means of dealing with the race relations crisis, for few could openly defend the poverty level in which so many Negroes still lived. To be antipoverty was certainly good politics in an election year. And finally, Johnson, unlike any other recent President, had spent his formative years in a poor part of the country and so had some direct personal experience with the traumas created by the depression of the thirties.

Johnson's choice of Sargent Shriver to head up the anti-poverty program was characteristic. Shriver, who was a symbol of the Kennedy style, had directed the Peace Corps operation remarkably well. He was an attractive figure against whom very little personal antagonism had developed anywhere in the country. If he knew nothing of poverty either personally or through academic study, he could be expected to learn very quickly, as indeed he did. And clearly, he was committed, sincerely, to the notion that some changes were in order. As a business leader in Chicago, Shriver had been actively engaged in community activities, and was familiar with the agency and foundation approach to civic problems.

The Peace Corps had attracted people to the Kennedy administration who might not otherwise have been willing to join the government: liberal professionals with genuine commitment to limited change, and sincere volunteers, especially young ones, who were becoming involved in social problems but who, for one reason or another, were outside the civil rights movement.

The "war on poverty" attracted the same kinds of people—in some cases, the very same people. And Shriver, who was familiar with these types, liked them, and has proved willing to take some risks on their behalf. Under him, the "war on poverty" did not so much professionalize reform as bring professional reformers into the governmental orbit.

But despite manifestly good intentions, the program was handicapped from the start by the schizophrenia that has always marked the American view of the poor. For political reasons, it had to be defined immediately, in Shriver's words, as "not a hand-out program—or an individual case-work program." Instead, the main emphasis has been put on projects which, again in Shriver's words, are "prudent, practical, focused and patriotic." The program is designed to give some of the poor opportunity to participate more fully in the American way of life, through better education and jobs. The basic assumptions were stated by the President's Council of Economic Advisers in their 1964 report: "Americans want to *earn* the American standard of living by their own efforts and contributions."

Thus, no attempt was then made to initiate new payments, or to increase the amounts of money now paid, to unemployables—the 4,174,728 recipients of Aid to Families with Dependent Children (whose average payment per family is $138 monthly); the 2,160,943 recipients of old-age assistance (average payment $78.88 per month); the 691,000 people who receive general assistance of $31.36 per month; the blind and the totally disabled. All these groups are still considered to be the "undeserving poor," no matter by what euphemism they are called.

So it is the "deserving" poor who are the main targets of the antipoverty effort. Its major emphases are on youth education and employment, on planned regional and community development, and on vocational training and retraining. But the programs are severely limited, almost all of them merely extensions of older programs. And the "war on poverty" was sold to the American public as a "cheap" war—one that would cost taxpayers very little.

As part of the effort to make the campaign seem a natural extension of society, some programs have been placed in the hands of business groups, especially those in the systems-development field. Computer techniques are applied to the operation of Job Corps camps and training programs; the latest methods of teaching by machine are used.

But all the programs are handicapped by the need its administrators feel to maintain good "public relations" and to avoid risking Congressional disapproval. Admission to the Job Corps is limited to young people without long histories of arrests for serious offenses; no volunteers from VISTA, the domestic counterpart of the Peace Corps, can be sent to a local community, except to mental hospitals, unless the community leaders request their presence. And the major portion of anti-poverty funds are focused on community-action programs submitted by broadly based community groups. But such great emphasis on local community support places even non-risk programs in jeopardy. In a good many cities and areas, conflicts among local political interests and among community groups have held back development of even limited programs.

Only one new dimension was added to the "war on poverty": the poor were to be involved, as much as possible, in making decisions about their own future. But paternalism dies hard, and so the involvement of the poor has been limited—at times hardly noticeable—at the political level. When an organization such as Mobilization for Youth in New York encourages a rent strike, powerful forces rush in on the landlord's behalf to attack the organization. And even if Mobilization for Youth, or a similar body, can survive such attacks, inevitably it becomes more cautious.

The poor are encouraged to find new careers, new work opportunities; but when jobs are created in fields hitherto dominated by professional trade or labor organizations, great resistance is encountered. Unions resist those parts of the poverty program which they believe menace their direct interest; business organizations act similarly; and community groups seek to exploit the program for their own selfish purposes. Too often, the latter regard the "war on poverty" as a kind of "fuller employment act" for their own professional staffs, rather than as an opportunity for the poor to make their own decisions, even bad ones.

The program has suffered, too, from conflicting political interests at local, state, and federal levels. The mayor wants to control the disposition of the funds in his area; the governor, given a veto authority over the program by the act, may seek to exercise it to further his political interests; the local Congressmen are convinced that they, too, have a stake in how the money is spent. Such political problems become especially acute when community groups are also involved, since these groups tend to support the political interests which provide them the best opportunity for carrying out their program. The poor seem lost, very often, in this tangled forest of politics and private and public agencies.

The basic idea of the "war on poverty" suggests that the enemy is impersonal, a matter of "unfortunate" circumstances like "ignorance" or "disease." But, in fact, there are people and institutions who have a vested interest in the continuation of poverty: employers who pay substandard and marginal wages; agricultural groups that refuse to pay living wages or to maintain decent housing for migrant farm workers; racists who understand the connection between maintaining the fiction of white supremacy and the reality of low wages. Yet, since such groups exercise a strong political influence in the society which is being called upon to support the "war," they go unmentioned in the propaganda.

Still another basic difficulty is that the program's success, especially for the youth, depends upon the creation of enough jobs to employ those who have gone through the training courses. If there aren't enough jobs, then the aspirations of the poor will have been raised without any opportunity for them to be satisfied.

But with all its limitations, this new effort to diminish the number of Americans living in poverty may help at least some people; and from it may flow consequences altogether unexpected by the Congress which approved it. Perhaps stimulated by the program, the poor will organize on their own behalf. If that happens, the country may yet be forced to adopt the kind of pre-Puritan ideas expressed about the poor by our Leveller ancestors in England, who in 1648 petitioned "that the too long continued shame of this nation, viz. permission of any to suffer such poverty as to beg their bread, may be effectu-

ally remedied: and to that purpose that the poor be enabled
to chose their trustees to discover all stocks, houses, lands, etc.,
which of right belong to them and their use that they may
speedily receive the benefit thereof: and that some good improvement may be made of waste grounds for their use: and
that according to the promise of this House in your first
remonstrance care be taken forthwith to advance the native
commodities of this nation, that the poor may have better
wages for their labor: and that manufacturers may be improved
for the best advantage of our own mariners and the whole
nation."

1965

Can "More Money" End Poverty?

ROBERT LEKACHMAN

One of the more tantalizing statistics of the decade is this: for a mere $11 billion we could raise every poor American above the poverty line as poverty is currently and officially defined—an income below $3,130 for a family of four. Now, as the world knows, poverty may be a great deal more than a shortage of money and giving money to the poor may indeed amount to no more than treating the symptoms of deeper personal and social disorders with financial palliatives. All the same, even within the most sophisticated and sociological definitions of poverty, lack of money is at least part of the condition of the poor. Moreover, as every consumer of aspirin should be able to testify, symptomatic relief is much to be preferred to no relief at all.

Now $11 billion is not much, a mere one and a small fraction per cent of Gross National Product, considerably less than half of Vietnam's annual cost, just about the size of the Pentagon's *underestimate* in 1966 of Vietnam expenditure. It must also be said that of all the ways to assist the unfortunate, simple transfer of funds is the simplest, the least niggling, and the most respectful of human dignity. Either of two magnificently efficient agencies, the Internal Revenue Service or the Social Security Administration, can handle the affair with infinitely less sweat than the assembled social workers and Welfare Departments of the land who spend substantially smaller sums. No wonder then that economists of very different ideological preferences and diverging motives have come to perceive merit in some version or other of income maintenance as a part or (on occasion) the whole of the assault upon poverty.

This of course raises the question, if the New Conservatives at Chicago join New Frontiersmen at Yale, Harvard, and MIT in favor of income maintenance, why doesn't some alert, major-party politician adopt this mechanism for his very own? Why doesn't Lyndon Johnson incorporate income guarantees into his domestic program instead of merely promising to appoint a commission directed to make its report safely after the 1968 Presidential election? Some of the answer may lie in the politician's timidity before any new idea. The remainder just might be found in the sheer meanness which seems to compel so many pious Americans to deplore the prospect of giving their fellow citizens money they haven't worked for.

But even if sudden altruism swept over the national psyche, a number of issues of principle would be important, indeed rather more important than they are now in the 1967 political mood. One way to identify the issues is to list the criteria of a good income maintenance scheme. At the least these number four:

1. Money should be given to those who need it but not to those who do not (of this more later).
2. The grants should not be tokens. They must be substantial enough to achieve their stated purpose, the elimination of financial poverty.
3. Grants should be extended in ways that strengthen rather than damage the incentive to get paid jobs in the labor market.
4. Finally, the grants should be substitutes only for that portion of welfare assistance which covers goods freely

available in the market place to those with the money to buy them—food, clothing, recreation, and the like. Where welfare counsels, trains, or treats, the argument is for extension of present programs not contraction.

Broadly, these criteria describe the position of economists who are also liberal Democrats. Those to the Left will not accept the first criterion as now stated. Those to the Right will quarrel with the last one.

Without further preamble, let us glance at some of the actual proposals that have been made. Take a very simple one first. If a family's earned income is too low, why not just give its members whatever is needed to bridge the gap between its present situation and the poverty minimum? Thus, if a family of four earns only $2,000, the prescription is a cash grant of $1,130. As the family's earned income rises to $2,500, diminish the grant to $630, and when earned income touches $3,130, discontinue the subsidy entirely.

This procedure severely tests the incentives of the poor and the generosity of the just barely not poor. As far as the effect upon the poor is concerned, increasing earned income from one point below the poverty line to another, higher point means a tax of 100 per cent upon earnings, a poor impetus indeed to initiative and extra effort. Those whose incomes just barely exceed $3,130 and who are therefore ineligible for assistance will, to put it mildly, be inclined to dislike a program that differentiates little between the fully employed at low wages and the "poor." A man earning $3,200 a year is unlikely to be thrilled at the sight of his neighbor, totally unemployed and granted a cash subsidy of $3,130.

Examine next a very different scheme. Chicago's Milton Friedman supports income maintenance because he believes in freedom of choice within the free market. Cash benefits are superior to present welfare measures for reasons that Mr. Friedman summarizes in this way:

The advantages of this arrangement are clear. It is directed specifically at the problem of poverty. It gives help in the form most useful to the individual, namely, cash. It is general and could be substituted for the host of special measures now in effect. It makes explicit the cost borne by society. It operates outside the market. Like any other measures to alleviate poverty, it reduces the incentives of those helped to help themselves, but it does not eliminate that incentive entirely, as a system of supplementing incomes up to some fixed minimum would. An extra dollar earned always means more money available for expenditure.[1]

In this statement Friedman made explicit his intent: rely on free choice, substitute grants for welfare services, and preserve incentives. This last point deserves amplification, for in Friedman's view the preservation of incentives requires termination of assistance at incomes far below the poverty line.

Without necessarily endorsing this limited assistance, the Wisconsin economist Robert Lampman has described the way Friedman's plan would work. Speaking of our present structure of taxes, Lampman notes that the "present rates fall from 70 per cent at the top to 14 per cent at incomes just above $3,700 for a family of five, to zero per cent for income below $3,700." It would be easy enough to extend the progressive tax structure downward:

The average negative tax rates could move . . . from zero per cent to minus 14 per cent for, say, the unused exemptions that total $500, to 20 per cent for those that total $1,000 and 40 per cent for those that total $3,700. This would amount to a minimum income of $1,480 for a family of five; it would retain positive incentives through a set of grants that would gradually diminish as earned income rose.[2]

But the gain in incentives would entail a high cost: many families would be left far below the poverty line and some

---

[1] Milton Friedman, *Capitalism and Freedom,* University of Chicago Press, 1962, p. 192.

[2] *American Economic Review,* May 1965, p. 527.

would be placed in a worse situation than welfare now puts them in. And the emphasis upon incentives appears decidedly misplaced so far as the elderly, handicapped, or disabled are concerned in groups which form a very large percentage of the poor.

The most seriously worked out (and the most generous) version of income maintenance is that of James Tobin, a member of the first Kennedy Council of Economic Advisers and now Professor of Economics at Yale. Tobin makes a deliberate effort to compromise among incentives, grant adequacy, and financial burdens upon the community. His proposal makes ingenious use of both cash grants and tax benefits. If a family has no income from earnings at all, Tobin would pay it $400 per person. For Lampman's family of five this would be $2000 as compared to the $1,480 contemplated on Friedman's assumptions by Lampman. But for Tobin this is by no means the maximum. As this family's earned income moves upward from zero, the grant is decreased by 33⅓ per cent of each additional dollar earned. It stops entirely when family earned income approaches $1200 per person. Above that income the family continues to pay taxes at the same 33⅓ per cent rates until it attains earnings of $7963 where it begins to encounter normal tax treatment. A portion of Tobin's illustrative table will make the consequences of the Tobin arrangement plainer:[3]

How successfully does this schedule of benefits and taxes compromise among Tobin's three objectives? On the incentive side, the plan scores well. Beneficiaries of the scheme are allowed to retain two thirds of additional earnings. They receive special tax treatment all the way up to an earned income of $7963. On any reasonable computation the budgetary cost is also manageable. In the summer of 1966, Tobin estimated

[3] James Tobin, "The Case for an Income Guarantee," *The Public Interest,* Number 4, Summer 1966, p. 38.

MARRIED COUPLE WITH THREE CHILDREN

(1) Family Income before Federal Tax Allowance	(2) Present Tax (−)	(3) Tax Schedule Income after Tax	(4) Tax (−) Allowance	(5) Proposed Schedule or Income after Tax or Allowance
$ 0	$ 0	$ 0	$2000	$2000
1000	0	1000	1667	2667
2000	0	2000	1333	3333
2500	0	2500	1167	3667
3000	0	3000	1000	4000
3700	0	3700	767	4467
4000	− 42	3958	667	4467
5000	− 185	4815	333	5333
6000	− 338	5662	0	6000
7000	− 501	6499	− 333	6667
*7963	− 654	7309	− 654	7309
8000	− 658	7342	− 658	7342

* Income level at which the present and the proposed methods of calculating taxes and benefits coincide; above this income (as at the $8,000 level included in the last line) the present tax schedule applies.

gross cost to be $12.5 billion annually. However, since welfare payments would be reduced (not eliminated as under Friedman's scheme) net costs would be much lower, possibly of the order of the year-to-year increase (at full employment) of federal budgetary receipts.

Some important questions remain, even after this much is said. It is apparent that in Tobin's model, families whose earned incomes do not reach $2500 will still be below the poverty line even after they receive their income grants. Whether their lot will be improved by substituting grants for some portion (or all) of welfare payments will depend upon the political constituency in which the poor family resides. In the more ungenerous states where welfare assistance stops at a low percentage of the poverty minimum, Tobin's system would improve the lot of many families even if all welfare payments stopped as a consequence of the grants. But in comparatively liberal constituencies like New York City and Connecticut, many poor persons will actually be worse off. This is likely to be especially true of elderly widows or widowers whose sole present income derives from Social Security. A $400 grant added to a small Social Security pension leaves their beneficiary well below the poverty line. Conceivably Tobin's position may be damaged if the income grant serves as a pretext for the elimination of more generous welfare supplements to his Social Security pension.

Such points, however, are far from fatal flaws. If the public will allows, it is perfectly possible to reform welfare practices in such a way as to avoid automatic curtailment of assistance by as much or more than the income grant. But it bears repetition to say that if the objective of public policy is the elimination of poverty, no plausible scheme of income maintenance can serve as a complete substitute for other measures, including welfare, housing subsidies, retraining allowances, and unemployment compensation.

Tobin's plan raises questions at the other end of the income scale as well. As the table makes clear, families will receive actual cash grants even though their income from earnings substantially exceeds poverty minima. Moreover, some families will enjoy special tax treatment all the way up to nearly $8000 of earned income. Should we thus assist families, substantially above the poverty line, and actually above the median income level of all American families, a figure not much in excess of $6000? Or, to put the matter sharply, should the extremely prosperous subsidize not alone the poor but also the *less* prosperous?

To say "yes" unequivocally to these questions (as I do) is to make a judgment about the equity of present taxes and the fairness of the present distribution of income between rich and poor. If one believes (as again I do) that present exemptions and rates outrageously favor the affluent, then any proposal which redistributes even a small sum from rich to poor and average citizens is a good thing. It is important to recognize that any proposal which promises really substantial help to the poor (on a scale far larger than Tobin contemplates) will redistribute income and at the same time fracture the fragile alliance which now joins liberal and conservative exponents of income maintenance plans.

What finally of the rather different mechanism of income support favored by Daniel Moynihan? In his testimony before the Ribicoff Committee, Moynihan spoke strongly in favor of a family allowance scaled to the number and age of dependent children. As he noted, most industrial nations (including neighboring Canada) operate family allowance plans, so that the idea itself is less novel than negative income taxes or other forms of generalized income grants. For the United States Moynihan estimated the cost of a possible program as about $9 billion each year. Some of the relevant numbers appear in this quotation:

A family allowance for the United States roughly equivalent to Canadian or Scandinavian levels would suggest payments of perhaps $8 a month for all children under 6 years of age, and $12 a month for children between 6 and 17. At present population levels this would cost $9 billion a year, just over 1 per cent of the gross national product. For a family of four children, this would increase income by, say, $40 a month, or roughly $500 a year.[4]

Of this approach to income support, it must be said at the outset that it raises in the most direct form an issue of social policy implicit in all income maintenance schemes. A public policy which simultaneously sings the virtues of birth control and small families, and actually rewards financially not the childless but rather the parents of large broods, is, to say the least of it, confusing. The mind rather boggles at public sub-

[4] See *The New York Times Magazine*, February 5, 1967, p. 71.

sidy, say, to Senator Kennedy's 10 children. More seriously, family allowances at least on the scale presently advocated by Mr. Moynihan will not of themselves raise a very large proportion of the poor out of their poverty even when families are large. The program will evidently do nothing at all to assist the childless or the elderly.

Where do we come out at the end of this quick glance at the schemes of the well-intentioned? As now designed, no proposal is a complete remedy for financial poverty. In part this outcome is the consequence of intent (as in the Friedman proposal). In part it is the result of prudent estimates of political reality.

Here is an example of the political reality Tobin and Moynihan may have held in mind. The speaker is Senator Ribicoff, a cautious and presumably representative moderate northern Democrat:

The idea of giving the poor more money—whether it is a guaranteed income or a negative income tax—is being discussed a great deal these days. As a person with some political experience, you can recognize how hard it is to put the idea across. Instead of talking about a guaranteed income tax, suppose we talk about guaranteeing a job . . . The person earning $100,000 a year wouldn't be worried very much about someone who would be getting $3,000 a year, even though he was not working. But how about the man who works 40 hours a week for $3,500 a year and sees his neighbor get $3,000 a year for not working? I think the American people will just not be able to swallow this.[5]

Friedman set his final income after assistance at so low a percentage of the poverty minimum because he feared larger benefits would impair incentives and divert benefits to those who really did not need them. The Tobin approach has the effect of relieving a rather larger percentage of poverty but only at the cost or with the added merit (according to view-

[5] *Ibid.*, p. 68.

point) of indulging in some redistribution of income in the direction of equality. Though it is not so presented, the Tobin proposal is the most radical in its implications.

All plans seem to demonstrate that it is impossible to design a proposal which simultaneously eliminates financial poverty, stimulates incentives, and avoids "unneeded" rewards to the moderately prosperous, non-poor. It is fair then to restate a point which has run through this essay.

At least for liberals and still more for radicals, income guarantees, however designed, are an addition to the armory of social care, not a substitute for everything from job retraining to psychiatric counseling. A good income maintenance scheme will substitute for that portion of welfare now most burdensome upon both recipient and social worker, the portion which consists of grants for food, shelter, and clothing. Income maintenance will facilitate the long-overdue reconstitution of welfare as individual case work. Income guarantees, properly viewed, fit properly into a public policy design which includes more liberal Social Security programs, a full-employment level of aggregate demand, provision in public service employment for those unable to secure jobs even in time of high demand, genuine desegregation of schools, suburbs, and cities, and a serious attempt to turn our cities into livable abodes for free citizens.

1967

The War on Poverty Reconsidered

S. M. MILLER AND PAMELA ROBY

> The War on Poverty has been greeted by sharp criticism
> from those on the political right as well as those on the
> left. . . . If the war were to default, it would not be clear
> where its supporters could be found. We suspect that
> nothing succeeds like success—if the program succeeds,
> it will develop supporters. If it fails, it will be disclaimed
> by those who are already critical of its mission.[1]

These words, written in December 1964, unfortunately describe the course of the Office of Economic Opportunity and
the War on Poverty. From the start OEO lacked a constituency, and it has failed to develop one in succeeding years.
Instead, enormous dissatisfaction has emerged. We have had
a striking escalation of expectations with a very small payoff
for the poor—particularly the Negro poor. Why have the
returns been so small?

An appraisal of the War on Poverty should not begin with
the Johnson administration or the Office of Economic Opportunity. Rather, the difficulties of OEO are to be found in the
enabling legislation of the Economic Opportunity Act of

---

[1] S. M. Miller and Martin Rein, "The War on Poverty—Perspectives and
Problems," in Ben B. Seligman, ed., *Poverty as a Public Issue,* New York,
Free Press, 1965.

1964. This law, which provided the War on Poverty with very narrow boundaries, rested on a set of compromises among competing government bureaus, Congressional sentiments, and budgetary restraints. The Act had no job provisions. Housing was untouched. Economic policy was fundamentally unaffected. (Many still believed that aggregate economic policy would sufficiently increase employment and demand so as to absorb a large proportion of the poor.) There was no effort to deal with the sizable number of the poor who were dependent upon cash transfer allowances, welfare, and social security. For these reasons, the major blame should not be placed on the OEO. Only limited gains could be expected from OEO, given the limited activities it was permitted to pursue.

Under such restrictions, it was important that its activities be viewed not as final, tested programs but as probes to uncover new and better approaches. Programs which were obviously failing were to be succeeded by those whose potential had not been tested. Experimentation, unfortunately, occurred on a very limited basis. Similarly, considering the narrowness of its legislative mandate, OEO has been guilty from the start of overselling its programs. In a few short years, no program could produce stunning results. OEO's leadership refused to see that; officials from the top down took an extraordinarily short-sighted view of the poverty problem. It has been reported that an important White House aide said shortly after the OEO bill was passed, "Now that we've licked poverty, we lack issues to deal with." Because the OEO did not recognize that the poor were so starved for hope that any offer of aid would be expected to show immediate gains, the consequence was disappointment among both the poor and the backers of OEO when results were as slow as they inevitably had to be. Headlines are not programs; nor programs a guarantee of results.

Essentially, OEO was designed to coordinate and improve social services. To some extent, it hoped to build an independent school system under the guise of "training" and Head

Start, so as to compete with or prod the regular school system, and except for the participation theme, OEO was permitted little else in its early days. But social services and coordination could not provide jobs or income. Consequently, it is important to recognize that while the overselling by OEO led to many of its problems, the fundamental difficulty lay in its narrow mandate.

Although much of the political power behind the development of an Economic Opportunity Act came from the "Negro Revolution," there was a general failure to recognize that the Negro problem was largely a problem in the reduction of inequality. In Washington, however, the emphasis was upon bringing the poor, especially Negroes, up to a fixed poverty line rather than upon changing American society and its economic functioning so that the gap between those at the bottom and the affluent majority would be reduced. The targets of OEO were too low and lacked a time schedule.

Many of those involved in drawing up the OEO legislation had a very peculiar view of poverty. They believed essentially that the problem of poverty was that of a culture: it was necessary to change the practices of individuals, and then the economy would be prepared to receive them. Consequently, the legislative emphasis was upon rehabilitation, social services, and training. By contrast, there was no emphasis upon guaranteeing jobs at the end of the production line. To some extent this occurred because the Administration feared that a bill containing a direct job component would not be passed by Congress.

Many of the planners seemed to believe very strongly in the importance of changing attitudes among the poor rather than drastically expanding opportunities. Undoubtedly, some of the poor do suffer from a lack of motivation and psychological difficulties, but to argue that the problem is mainly one of motivation is misleading. Rehabilitation and training without assurance of some return at the end of the line is a dangerous political game. It is a game which might nevertheless have been played if one did not arouse large expectations from meager programs. But the combination of high expectations and incoherent programs could only produce controversy, difficulty, and dismay.

Whatever one felt about the panoply of programs developed under OEO, one thing soon became obvious: there was considerable ambiguity of goals, and this could only compound OEO's difficulties. Was the Job Corps an effort to train "hardcore" youth in skills, a device for social control over some youth, or an "aging vat" to keep youngsters out of the labor market? Did it have some other purpose in terms of vocational education? If the emphasis was upon especially difficult youth, the program lacked a deliberate screening device to guarantee that only certain kinds of youth entered the program. If it were meant to further vocational education, there was neither a definite connection between what took place in a Job Corps and what might occur elsewhere, nor a clear-cut reason for the residential program.

The Neighborhood Youth Corps was billed as a program designed to develop "human resources" by increasing the skill capacities of low-educated youth. But there was little skill development in either the in-school or out-of-school program. Indeed, many of the problems of the youths in the program were questions of how to *appear* to be working. Little skill development or supervision occurred on the job. In effect, the in-school program provided cash income to families and little training. The out-of-school program was a form of work relief with very little training. Both types of programs are eminently desirable at particular times, but the difficulty arose from their being presented as something more than they really were. This led to confusion among youth and to public disappointment. And what is still more disturbing, we have no data as to what kind of jobs these youth have six months or a year after their "training" experiences.

The Community Action Program evolved into OEO's deciding on a national level how funds should be used, rather than into an effort to promote each community's competence in deciding what it needed. One result was that communities which did not even have kindergartens began to have Head Start programs because money was available for one and not the other. In the determination of priorities, competition between localities and the national office led to incomplete and underdeveloped plans at the local level and a strain between local priorities and shifting national emphases. The result was, in many cities, hastily drawn-up programs and poorly delivered services.

But it was not these crises and deficiencies which propelled OEO into deep trouble. The theme of "maximum feasible participation" did that. OEO took a courageous stand by making a large issue out of participation of the poor in poverty programs. As a result, considerable local opposition emerged and participation of the poor became largely symbolic, though not unimportant.

The radical critics of OEO attacked the organization for its failure to push more strongly the theme of participation; but this criticism seems to reflect a misreading of what really took place. The failure was at the local level, where groups did not actively and forcefully fight to make sure that participation did occur. OEO's staff moved way beyond what one would conventionally consider the role of a federal agency in pushing localities to make real the idea of representation. No other government agency exerted anything near OEO's pressure for participation. But, as it happened, civil rights and other groups were not effectively organized to implement the OEO charter —here was the failure of participation. Nonetheless, the burden of blame was placed upon national OEO, and consequently the possibility of developing a constituency among grass-roots groups collapsed.

The enormous concentration on the participation issue began to provide OEO with a special character. With the inevitable failure of the other OEO programs markedly to affect poverty, "maximum feasible participation" carried a heavy burden.

OEO's administrative difficulties were huge at the local as well as the federal level. A coordinated, concentrated attack upon poverty did not emerge. City agencies did not cooperate with one another, nor did the federal. Agencies failed frequently even to inform each other of what they were doing. Programs did not start when they should have; funding was frequently so late that programs could only be hurriedly jammed through. The quality of many was low, especially at the start.

Since there was no strong supporting constituency, the implementation of programs depended greatly upon immediate local conditions. Where the mayor was strong—usually where he was a Democrat with both business and labor support—there was a chance of getting a program which had effective services. But at the same time, little grass-roots participation in decision-making occurred in these cities. Participation was important in cities where the mayor was weak. In some cities, such as Philadelphia and San Francisco, the local groups won out immediately over weak mayors and seemed, for a while, to gain in importance. But as services were not delivered, the mayor began to reassert his power. In the end, in cities like New Haven and Chicago, with strong mayors, there was efficient servicing but little participation. Finally, in just about all cases, participation became mainly nominal.

The broader economic policies of the federal government, concerned with growth and not poverty reduction, also failed OEO to a sizable extent. The reduction in unemployment rates which resulted from Vietnam proved that the structuralists and the aggregationists were both wrong. While the growth in the economy reduced unemployment, it did not sharply reduce unemployment among the low-educated, the unskilled, and

Negroes. (The 1967 unemployment rate for youths aged sixteen to twenty-one was 11.8 per cent for whites and 24.8 per cent for nonwhites.) The difference in unemployment rates between Negroes and whites was reduced, yet the Negro rate remained over twice the white rate: in July 1967 the white unemployment rate was 3.5 per cent while the nonwhite was 7.2 per cent. Obviously, special economic activities are necessary to reduce the Negro and unskilled unemployment rates, but these were not built into the War on Poverty. The Concentrated Employment Programs were hopefully designed to aim at the worst-off of the unemployed, but they were not created until 1967, and inadequate planning and guarantees preceded the programs in many of the cities involved.

Nevertheless, many of the difficulties of the War on Poverty might have been overcome if the economy had expanded in useful ways and poverty-reduction expenditures increased. Vietnam was the great obstacle which led to the reduction of the expansion rate of OEO's activities. The data on national expenditures are illuminating: about a twentieth of the increase in gross national product in 1965 went for military purposes; in 1966, a fifth; and in the first quarter of 1967, *two-thirds of the increase was devoted to military activities*. The projected increases in OEO expenditures are kept a state secret with the actual rate leveling off as a sacrifice to "the other war."

Nor was the impact of Vietnam only financial. It created an atmosphere, especially in Washington, which made domestic issues seem less significant. Our society seems able to concentrate on only one concern at a time. Vietnam *or* poverty could be center stage; not both. America turned outward rather than inward. Perhaps the race riots will redirect the nation's attention. But during the crucial years of OEO, concern moved swiftly away from domestic to international issues. Consequently, the War on Poverty was at best a skirmish.

The difficulties of OEO, however, should not obscure its

accomplishments. The greatest of these was its selective attention to the problems of the poor. Instead of depending upon economic growth and general national policies to improve the conditions of the poor, we instituted programs which were *directly* aimed at benefiting the poor. In this way the poor were provided not only a voice within the national establishments, but a set of programs which could be experimentally developed into something more effective.

Yet OEO has brought about few institutional changes. The principle difficulty lies within education. OEO has attempted to influence education through Head Start and job training. These efforts to build a parallel system were made because there is little expectation of directly influencing educational systems to become more relevant to students who have trouble with school. Hopefully, with more pressure, the emergence of large-scale programs may eventually have some impact on schools. Evaluations of Head Start by Max Wolff and others have demonstrated that Head Start graduates do not maintain their gains in regular school programs. This unsurprising conclusion has led to the development of a program (naturally called "Follow Thru") attempting to affect education in the early grades.

The Elementary and Secondary Education Act was perhaps the most important distillate of the poverty program. Although we do not have an adequate accounting of the use and impact of these funds, it is important that funds are now specifically allocated for the education of the poor. Behind this lies a growing acceptance of the notion that more should be spent on the education of the poor than on the education of others. And while inequalities in the distribution of educational expenditures have not been reduced, the emergence of a War on Poverty has spotlighted the need for providing more funds for the education of low-income youth.

Among other achievements of the War on Poverty are innovations in the extension of legal aid to the poor. While our society prides itself that all are equal before the law, lack of available legal aid has been one of the great inadequacies of the poor. The Office of Economic Opportunity, in promoting legal services to the poor, has reduced the disparities between the poor and the non-poor. But a gap remains.

Similarly, OEO has innovated in medical care by developing comprehensive neighborhood medical services. While this program is still in the demonstration and pilot phase, OEO may inaugurate significant changes in the delivery of medical care in this country. The War on Poverty has had a crucial impact upon Negroes. It turned the problem of Negroes from that of civil rights to poverty, or echoed the change beginning to take place. It importantly affected the transition from "Negro" to "black." The early emphasis upon the War on Poverty's great achievements rapidly escalated expectations which could not be realized. Negro discontent and frustration were heightened by the struggles over "maximum feasible participation." What followed was the expression of "white power," and then a "black backlash" toward separatism.

OEO has had some impact upon discrimination in the United States. Particularly in the South, the War on Poverty has made important steps. For the first time in many communities, Negroes are represented on official boards. In Mississippi the Head Start program had an enormous political consequence. Some parents, concerned about what was happening to their children, began to have an income base through employment in the Head Start program. They became involved in positions of importance. In effect, OEO helped push many communities toward the development of interracial groups and activities in which the poor had some influence. Although the role of the poor and blacks has frequently been token, in many cases it has actually allowed the development of new political forms and new political leaders.

OEO's most significant and lasting achievements may be political. The War on Poverty is helping to change the political structure of cities. As cities become more and more Negro, they are slowly developing new ways of getting Negro representation. At the local level, the War on Poverty has been offering Negroes means of representation and political jobs and leverage. It has also focused increasing attention upon the slowness with which cities adjust to the new citizen. With all its difficulties, "maximum feasible participation" has ushered in an important new right in this country, raising the question of the relationship of the citizen to the bureaucracies of the welfare state.

Thus the War on Poverty, despite its ballyhoo, has produced some important changes in the American scene. Although its publicity far outstrips what it could possibly have done, there have been significant beginnings, even in these brief years. How far these will go depends mostly upon the development of political support.

The character of poverty is quite varied. Poverty is a condition not only of income insufficiency but also an insufficiency of housing, basic services, education, and political and social participation. Similarly, the poor are varied. There are the poor who are young, who might be in the labor force; the poor who are aged; the poor who are female heads of households; the males who are employed but do not make enough to support their families. This diversity means that no one program can adequately deal with all the issues and people involved in what we call "poverty."

The diversity of the poor and the numerous dimensions of poverty and inequality result in first dealing more with one kind of poor person rather than another or one problem rather than another. Consequently, a War on Poverty will have phases or stages. We see three.

Poverty War I is OEO up to now with emphasis upon social services. As this approach proves inadequate in linking people to jobs and income, considerable talk has begun to arise about a job or income component in the War on Poverty. The major plank of Poverty War II, if it emerges, will be to extend new forms of welfare or transfer income to the poor. Whether these are in the form of a negative income tax or family allowances, they will probably be connected to a program which will directly guarantee jobs to the poor rather than emphasize training. After the violence of summer 1967, there seems to be hope that the government will serve as "employer of last resort." Public sentiment is growing in support of the notion that jobs are important for the poor, especially the black poor. Prominent business leaders are accepting the idea of a direct job program.

The crucial support of this program came through Congressional action rather than OEO. The Javits-Kennedy, Nelson and Scheuer amendments in the post-1964 programs pushed towards direct jobs. OEO was not at the center, as it should have been, in seeking these expansions of mandate. In part, this reluctance was due to the fact that expenditures for new programs might have meant less money for older programs. But if OEO had been willing to drop activities which seemed weak, it could have moved towards a direct jobs proposal which was believed to be unacceptable to Congress in 1964. The Office of Research at OEO did, however, support the idea of a negative income tax, and it is to be commended for helping to keep this idea in discussions.

The jobs program will probably move in two directions: the utilization of non-professional employment in the expanding public and quasi-public basic services; and the subsidization of private employers in order to induce hiring and upgrading of hard-to-place workers. In both cases, the former emphasis on "training" for indefinite, uncertain jobs will be succeeded and balanced by the much more sensible approach of "jobs first, training later."

The emphasis upon improving the income of persons who are outside the labor force or are receiving inadequate incomes from work is desirable for a variety of reasons. But it is not a panacea for the problems of the poor. Marginal improvements in income will neither solve the health, housing, and educational problems of the poor, nor guarantee a high level of participation within the society. Unless we recognize the limitations of income programs, much dissatisfaction will arise in Poverty War II. We will find that many problems are not easily or automatically eradicated by increases in income.

It will be important to turn economic policy from a concern with general growth towards specific efforts to reduce poverty and inequalities. The 1964 tax cut, for example, benefited the relatively well-to-do. It would be useful to consider the income tax not only as a measure to secure funds and to provide economic stabilization, but also as a way of reducing income inequalities. Now that inequality seems to be growing, we might develop some standard by which we could begin to use tax rates to create change.

Rather than hoping that general economic advance will be of some assistance to the poor, we need economic programs which have specific value for them. Most economists have underemphasized the importance of selective economic programs for reaching the poor who are outside the usual income streams and who now benefit only marginally from general economic expansion.

The poverty war needs to be strongly extended to poor whites and other ethnics. Otherwise, as a black program, the poverty war is unlikely to gain large funding at this time. For the poverty program to win support, it needs to be connected with a general economic program rather than being an enclave of rather minor programs which appear to be unrelated to the general economic advance of the United States.

Rural as well as economic development should be stressed in these programs. Various kinds of economic development are specifically needed in rural areas because migration cannot swiftly depopulate these areas which have high reproduction rates. Large numbers will be left behind. Consequently, direct measures should be taken to improve the economic prospects of the rural poor, who are in many ways the poorest of the poor in the United States.

Some chance of a housing program now seems to be appearing. Its shape is unclear. If it does emerge, it will most likely subsidize private enterprise for producing housing for the low income.

At this moment, the possibility of better programs rests largely on the connection of business profit with poverty reduction. Many liberals and radicals will be in a quandary about how to react. What if IBM could really do a better educational job in running the schools than the New York City Board of Education? *The reshaping of the American Society through an expanding "public sector" may not diminish the significance of business as much as change its source of funds.* Bureaucratic encrustations may be fewer and freedom of choice greater in business-operated programs. But the end result may not be to diminish inequalities.

Poverty War II, as it is developing, is narrowly economic, neglecting the political dimension of poverty and inequality. Even some humanistic socialists when they turn to political action seem now to be unable to think beyond economism. The failure of Poverty War II to emphasize participation should lead to a following wave of action (Poverty War III) in which the involvement of the poor will again be important.

In order to begin to generate support for participation, it is now time to make clear that the problem of participation is not exclusively a problem of the poor. All groups in society have difficulty relating to bureaucratic organizations today. We should broaden the principle of participation so that it benefits other groups. The poor may benefit from society's growing acceptance of the theme of participation and its consequent expansion.

Administrative simplicity is greatly needed in the War on Poverty. This is part of a broader problem in American society.

We have developed numerous techniques and regulations to insure impartiality and honesty. The extent to which our administrative techniques achieve these two goals is uncertain, but it is clear that they produce an enormous amount of red tape and difficulty. As Nathan Glazer put it in his classic title, "Is New York City Governable?" the problems of administration have outstripped our capacities to move rapidly. While these difficulties extend beyond the War on Poverty, they deeply affect the Poverty War because it extends across many jurisdictional lines in its efforts to deal with urban and other immediate problems.

As we move along in the War on Poverty, it will be important to look upon it in longer terms. Looking in these longer terms requires having some fairly specific goals or targets. It will be important to try to reduce poverty by a specified amount in each of the succeeding years.

The difficulties of OEO are filled with "ifs." If the programs had expanded as planned, would they have had more impact? If civil rights groups had organized in the ghettos, would maximum feasible participation have taken another course? The absence of achievement in certain substantial forms means neither that we should abandon our belief in the importance of a poverty war, nor that we should accept the war as we have known it.

The War on Poverty is an important, though inadequate, instrument for dealing with our present problems. Our society is now struggling to resurrect an interest in poverty and to build acceptance of the heavy expense a real War on Poverty would require. To obtain substantially more funding today probably requires expanding the poverty appeal by attuning more poverty programs to the non-Negro poor, connecting poverty programs to economic development and growth, and vitalizing local organizational groups in the United States. The efforts of intellectuals, labor, civil rights groups, radicals, liberals, and others need to be linked in building a political constituency which will permit expanding expenditures. But will this happen where there is so much disagreement simply in defining the problem? We doubt it.

Discontent with the War on Poverty has led to a variety of recommendations. Congressman Goodell and other Republicans have advocated dismantling OEO and placing its various programs in other federal agencies. We argue against this because we do not think that significant institutional change can be obtained through this approach. At the present time, we believe that despite all its difficulties, it would be best to maintain OEO as it is—a beleaguered agency playing many different kinds of roles, but centering its efforts upon the poor.

1967

Is There Really a New Poor?

STEPHAN THERNSTROM

A specter is haunting the imaginations of commentators upon the contemporary scene, the specter of the "new poor." In days of old (precise time conveniently unspecified), the cliché goes, "the immigrant saw poverty as a *temporary state* and looked forward to the day when he or his children could gain greater access to opportunity and financial resources. The poor of today are more inclined to regard poverty as a *permanent way of life* with little hope for themselves or their children. This change in the outlook of the poor can be explained by changes in the opportunity structure." (From Louis Furman's *Poverty in America*.) You can fill in the rest for yourself easily enough: the poor of old had aspirations; the poor today do not. The poor of old had a culture; the poor today have only a culture of poverty. The poor once had political machines which protected them; now they have only social workers who spy upon them. And the crucial contrast, from which so much else follows: the poor were once on the lowest rungs of a ladder most of them could climb; the poor today are a fixed underclass, a permanent proletariat.

A compelling, dramatic image, this, but is there any evidence that it is *true*? This is not the place for an exhaustive analysis of the data,* but I suggest that the answer is negative. Much depends, of course, upon just whom we have in mind when we refer to "the poor"—the semantic hazards here are even larger than in most issues of social policy. If, for instance, we insist that the authentically poor are the kinds of people Oscar Lewis describes in his studies of "the culture of poverty," it is difficult to say anything at all about whether there are more or fewer of them and whether their lot is better or worse than it used to be, because the historical record provides few clues by which to make a judgment. But such simple operational definitions as income, concentration in unskilled or semi-skilled jobs, etc., yield relatively straightforward conclusions. These conclusions will not be palatable to the kind of mindless radical who reasons "things are terrible. Q.e.d: they are getting worse," though they certainly do not, I will argue, dictate a complacent view of the fate of the other America.

First, a word on the poor considered as an income class. There has been a good deal of heated argument about precisely where to draw the poverty line, but little attention to what seem the two points of greatest significance. One is that wherever the line is drawn—$3000, $4000, or whatever—an ever-smaller fraction of the American population falls below that line. The long-term trend of per capita income in this country is dramatically upward, and the way in which that income is distributed has not shifted abruptly in a direction unfavorable to those on the lower end of the scale. The rich have been getting richer, all right, but the poor have been getting richer at much the same rate. There has been no major increase in the proportion of the national income going to those on the bottom in recent decades—a fact American liberals have

* Documentation of the claims advanced in this essay will be found in two related papers by the author: "Poverty in Historical Perspective," in a forthcoming Harvard University Press volume edited by Daniel P. Moynihan, and "Urbanization, Migration and Social Mobility in Late-Nineteenth Century America," in Barton Bernstein, ed., *Towards a New Past,* Pantheon, 1968.

been pathetically slow to recognize. But the unpleasant truth that there is no pronounced trend toward more equal distribution of income in this country should not obscure the elementary fact that the disadvantaged are now receiving the same fraction of a pie which has grown substantially larger. Admittedly they *expect* more; in some ways it can be said that they *need* more, but that it *is* more is of considerable consequence, however it might seem to those of us who do not have to worry about the grocery bills.

A second observation is that it is very important to know whether the poverty line currently in favor in Washington, or some other (presumably higher) figure preferred by those of us on the left, marks off an *entity* with more or less stable membership, or whether it is a mere category into which Americans fall and out of which they climb in rapid succession. If we can assume that some fixed figure represents a minimal decent income for a family of a certain size, and that all those below it are living in poverty, it is obviously important to know if it is pretty much the same families who fall below that line year after year, as is commonly assumed by proponents of the "new poverty" thesis, or if there is a great deal of annual turnover in the composition of the group. Some people with desperately low incomes, after all, are graduate students. Are many of the poor temporary victims? No one has any idea about the extent of continuity in the lowest income categories in the American past—say, in the nineteenth and early twentieth centuries—though there is a common and highly questionable assumption that there was little continuity then. What is more remarkable is that hardly anything is known about the continuity of low income in present-day America. I have been able to turn up only two fragments of evidence which bear upon this point, and neither does much to support the case of the pessimists.

One such fragment is the oft-cited statistic that about 40 per cent of the parents receiving AFDC in 1964 were themselves raised in a home where public assistance had been received. This may sound impressive, but not when we recall that a high proportion of these parents were presumably children in the Great Depression, when more than a quarter of the American population was on relief at some point. AFDC parents are somewhat overrepresented by this measure, to be sure, but this is not very telling proof of the persistence of hard-core poverty.

The other fragment is a set of figures which reveal that 69 per cent of the families with incomes below the poverty line in 1962 were in the same unhappy posititon in 1963 as well, with the racial breakdown of that rate 67 per cent for whites and 76 per cent for Negroes. Is an annual rate of persistence in poverty of about two-thirds a high one or a low one? It would seem to be rather low if one could assume that remaining in the persisting group from one year to the next did *not* alter one's probability of escaping it in future years, for 70 per cent persistence over two years would mean 49 per cent persistence over three years, 34 per cent over four years, 24 per cent over five, etc. We probably cannot make the assumption I have made, but clearly we need more long-term studies to see *how much* reality departs from the convenient assumption that these are independent trials. We also would want to know, of course, how much long-term persistence varies with such characteristics as race, female-headed household, unemployment or underemployment of male household head, etc. Most important, it is necessary to compute these rates using a variety of poverty lines rather than one dollar figure; obviously we want to know how many people depart from poverty or fall into it by earning $50 more or $50 less a year. There is the interesting finding that of the families who climbed above the line between 1962 and 1963, 2/5 remained under the $4000 mark, 1/5 earned between $4000 and $5000, and 2/5 pulled in more than $5000. The latter families are, of course, the really impressive ones, and one would like to know much more about how many of them ever fall back and under what circumstances. Appallingly little is known about this essential matter. At a minimum, however, one can say that those who are convinced that poverty in the U.S. is increasingly being meted out in life sentences have yet to do the homework to substantiate the claim.

If we turn to another aspect of the new poverty thesis—the assumption that it is now far more difficult for a low-skilled manual laborer to work his way up the occupational ladder than it once was—there is again a startling lack of evidence to buttress the claim. For all of the facile talk we hear about the barriers against mobility growing ever higher, the fragmentary knowledge we have about the American class structure in the past and the extensive literature on current occupational mobility patterns suggests that changes in the opportunity structure over the past century have been minimal, and that those minimal changes are in the direction of greater upward mobility today. It is clear that the educational requirements for many desired jobs have been going up steadily, but it also appears that, on the whole, the expansion of educational opportunities has kept pace with, if not outrun, this development. It may be that decisive career choices are being made earlier than they once were—that now people permanently drop out of the race for certain attractive positions when they drop out of school, positions for which there were once fewer formal requirements; but I am very doubtful that this has resulted in less recruitment from below. To some extent, it has had the opposite effect, in that the change has been part of an increasingly universalistic process of selection.

It is doubtful indeed that a new poverty has recently been created in this country because of creeping arteriosclerosis of the occupational structure. Unskilled and semiskilled laborers still do rise to a higher occupation during their lifetimes, in at least a minority of cases; their sons still make the jump more frequently than their fathers.

Impressive though it is, the evidence on rates and patterns of occupational mobility does not entirely dispose of the arguments of the pessimists. They would emphasize that the demand for unskilled labor, the capacity of the economy to absorb raw newcomers and assure them steady wages, is not what it was when the Golden Door was open to all. That could be true without lowering the rates of occupational mobility, of course. This has become a received truth in discussions of contemporary poverty without the benefit of the slightest critical examination, it seems to me. It is indubitable that the demand for unskilled labor is not what it used to be, if we take as our measure the proportion of jobs that are classified as unskilled; and indeed, discussions of this point often allude to the shrinking of the unskilled category in this century and the mushrooming of the white-collar group, as if that proves something. But what about the demand relative to the supply? To say that this relationship has changed in a way unfavorable to the unskilled is to assert that the pool of unemployed laborers—the Marxian industrial reserve army—is characteristically larger now than it was in the past; and that wage differentials between unskilled and other types of work are now larger. Neither of these propositions can be substantiated.

As to the first, we have a decent times series on average annual unemployment only back to 1900, and one broken down for specific occupational groups—which is really what we want—only since 1940. But you needn't dig at all deeply into historical data to arrive at the conclusion that, however hard it may be for many people to find steady employment in our society today, it was often still harder in the past. Robert Hunter's 1904 study *Poverty* pulls together a few chilling fragments we might profitably recall. In the year 1900, 44.3 per cent of the unskilled laborers in the United States were unemployed at some time; of a sample of Italian workers in Chicago, for example, 57 per cent had been out of a job some time during the previous year, with the average time unemployed running over seven months! The fact that horror stories like this become increasingly difficult to duplicate as we approach the present, plus the mild but distinct downward trend in the overall unemployment time series since 1900 makes me feel very skeptical about the common assumption that things are getting worse for those on the bottom.

It is possible, of course, that the unskilled labor market now offers fewer employment opportunities to certain kinds of people, and greater opportunities to others. The most obvious case would be the aged, who once were free to die with their boots on and now suffer compulsory retirement. But few of them lived *past* what we now consider retirement age, so that isn't much of an argument for the good old days. The case of the Negro naturally leaps to mind here. It is perfectly clear that the labor market today is not color-blind: at comparable skill levels the Negro receives lower wages, is more often unemployed, etc. If we are assessing trends, however, there is a question as to just what we compare this grossly inequitable situation with. If we compare Negro-white differentials in the past, the only way of arguing a long-term deterioration in the Negro position would be to assume that the sharecropper was better off than the urban laborer. Perhaps, however, a more fruitful point of comparison would be with the most recent immigrant group at other points in the past. Was the gap in wages and employment security between Irish and Yankee laborers in the 1850's or Italian and Yankee laborers in the 1890's as large as the racial gap today? Probably not, though no one has proved it yet.

To the extent, then, that in talking about poverty we really have in mind the problem of the Negro, the historical trend is open to debate (depending on the point of comparison we think most reasonable). With that exception—admittedly not a small one—I see no basis for the common cliché about the sluggish unskilled labor market.

As to the argument about wage rates and differentials, I have found no evidence which indicates any sharp decline, absolute or relative, in the position of the unskilled relative to the skilled. The long-term trend, indeed, has been towards a diminution in wage differentials between these two groups. There have, however, been some changes which have made things tougher for those on the bottom of the ladder and which have been responsible for some of the distress and discontent which have been mistakenly attributed to the supposed tightening of the occupational structure and the presumed glut on the unskilled labor market.

One of these has to do with the costs and rewards of having a large brood of children. We are now acutely aware that the rich get richer and the poor get children, so much so that we tend to forget that there ever was a time when kids were an economic asset. In nineteenth-century America the earnings of young children were of decisive importance in enabling laboring families to secure a property stake in the community, and there is evidence that much the same sort of thing happened elsewhere well into the present century. This, of course, no longer holds true. The extension of compulsory school attendance has steadily narrowed the span of years in which a youth is old enough to work but too young to set up a household of his own. Furthermore, it appears that youths who are working and yet living at home are less likely today to turn their earnings over to daddy: the shift from the CCC practice of sending a lad's wages home to his parents to the Job Corps practice of paying members directly is a revealing symptom of a larger social change which weakened the economic viability of the working-class family. Having multiple wage-earners, all of whom felt that what they earned was not their own but the family's was not only a means of generating a surplus for the savings account; it was also a kind of primitive unemployment compensation scheme, in that even in very hard times, it was unlikely that all six wage-earners would be thrown out of work. This benefit was available in only one phase of a man's life cycle, of course—it is not very common to have a steady stream of children throughout one's entire life—but if a house could be paid for during that phase, the reduction in income that came with the departure of children would be tolerable.

The other major change which demands attention is the steady erosion of the subcultures which defined the expectations of workingmen in the past. There were once working class *enclaves*—often with ethnic boundaries, but not necessarily—within which the mobility values of the larger society were redefined in more attainable terms. The workingmen of nineteenth-century America whom I described in my study *Poverty and Progress* toiled with remarkable dedication to accumulate the funds to pay for tiny cottages of their own and were amazingly successful at it. There are some contemporary analogues to those cottages, as books like the Middletown volumes, Chinoy's study of automobile workers, and Berger's *Working Class Suburb* make clear. But everything about contemporary America conspires to make both copping out entirely and lowering one's sights more difficult. Television is the prime symbol of the change I have in mind, though not necessarily the prime agent. Certainly there are great expectations abroad in some quarters. When a Negro leader in San Francisco greets the news that a few hundred new jobs paying $1.25 an hour have been opened up with the comment that "if you're working at the minimum wage, man, you're still unemployed," we certainly cannot assume that he is speaking for the Negro working class. But it is significant that in the past a reaction like this would be utterly unimaginable. One of the clichés about the new poor is that their aspirations are lower than those of the old poor—they are a defeated bunch, living in a system "designed to be impervious to hope." But the point to stress is surely the opposite. Many of the poor today *expect more,* and they will take less from others in order to get it, precisely because the enclaves of old have been leveled, with all of the docility and deference which they fostered.

I see no reason to mourn the passing of these enclaves of
old. I find it hard to believe that those poor bastards breaking
their backs in the industrial city I studied were receiving their
just reward, even though they seemed to have believed it. Their
conception of "making it" seems a pathetic delusion. But it
was, of course, a delusion which made many of them behave in
ways which kept them out of trouble, and it is quite possible
that the more we do to improve their worldly lot, the more
trouble they'll make. Even if we gave them all the cash necessary to put them above the poverty line tomorrow, their incomes would be a little less than half the median family income
in the United States. Why *should* they be content with that?
One thinks of Samuel Gompers' famous reply when pressed
as to the objectives of the labor movement: MORE. In reading
Arthur Dunmeyer's extraordinary testimony before the Ribicoff Committee, I kept thinking of that, and of Bukharin's
dictum: "in revolutions, appetite grows with the eating." It
would be premature to descry an incipient revolution around
us, but there are hints at least that fundamental questions
which have been left to the market place—the core question
of income distribution—will be increasingly open to political
conflict and decision. A recent analysis of the poverty problem
by the U.S. Chamber of Commerce concludes comfortably
that the objective situation of the poor is so encouraging now
that "the old socialist tradition in discussing income (distribution) is dying out. Conditions no longer call for deep-seated
and widespread social change. Rather, the discussion now is
on helping the poor. Expropriation of property is no longer
seriously considered as a remedy." The enlightened capitalists
and the economists they hired do a surprisingly intelligent job
of describing the extent and character of contemporary poverty,
I grudgingly admit; but they naively assume that to disprove
the law of increasing misery is to assure that no one on the
bottom will ever want to rock the boat. We need only note the
creative ferment which has been provoked by the current Ad-

ministration's version of "helping the poor" to see that this is by no means the case.

I do not, in sum, see any grounds for believing that this country is now threatened by a mass of "new poor" whose objective situations, especially their opportunities to rise out of poverty, are much worse than those of earlier generations. The real changes I see are generally encouraging, or at least mixed. Some families are worse off today because they can't reap the benefits of child labor: but in the long run, presumably, their children are better off.

I think that one can be clear-headed about what is happening without being complacent about the status quo. I have never understood why so many Americans believe that to assert that things are bad you must insist that they are getting worse. I would argue that they could well be getting a little better— as the situation of the poor in America is, on the whole—and still be intolerably bad. A little less unemployment can still be too damned much unemployment, in a culture where people have become civilized enough to understand that recurrent unemployment is due not to the will of God but to the inaction of man. To conjure up a Golden Age from which to judge the present and find it wanting is quite unnecessary, and as de Tocqueville pointed out long ago, it is even slightly un-American, for the American way is to reject the achievements of the past as a standard for the present or future; Americans, he said, use the past only as a means of information, and existing facts only as a lesson used in doing otherwise and doing better.

1967

Initiation for Whitey: Notes on Poverty and Riot

JEREMY LARNER

As I write (in the Summer of 1967) the slum areas of several dozen large American cities have been ravaged by Negro rioters and by the cops and guardsmen who put them down. For urban Negroes, the pull-back of the poverty program may have been that final straw which broke down their habitual patience and resignation. The ballyhooed War on Poverty was sabotaged, according to the burgeoning number of left ideologists, by an essentially racist country conducting an imperialist war in Asia and bent on holding down exploited dark-skinned masses everywhere. Whether or not such generalizations are justified, the hysteria which prompts them finds ready symbols in the bombing escalation in Hanoi and toward the Chinese border, in the photos of "Vietnam-type" tanks rumbling through the streets of Newark, in news broadcasts announcing that Viet Cong are flushed out of tunnels with "anti-riot" gas.

There are others on the left, myself included, who still see America as less than monolithic, who insist that there are forces available in this country to change both foreign and domestic policy. For us, American resources have been tragically misspent, aims deflected and purposes misguided. We still insist that there is a fight worth fighting on the battleground of American politics—in the interests of not only the Negroes but all the people.

For the time being, however, the argument has been vacated by a cycle of paranoia, wherein the lies, chauvinism, sweeping historical analogies, self-righteousness, and violence of American policy-makers are reflected in perfect miniature by the demagogues of American racism, off their rockers black and white alike and ready to give no quarter until their pain and rage are satisfied. Political emotion bounces from far right to far left, with no room anywhere for the constructive analysis so desperately needed if American democracy is to survive in any viable condition.

Stokely Carmichael is in Cuba, singing loon-songs of world-wide guerrilla warfare. But Richard Hughes, the liberal Governor of New Jersey, is warning that we must draw a line to separate us from "the jungle"; and the disgraceful 90th Congress passes legislation which only punishes the cities and prolongs the horror in Vietnam.

Yet when the poverty program began it drew thousands of previously disenfranchised poor people who saw in its pitifully inadequate funding an opportunity to create institutions of social equity, and who insisted they were all the more American to do so. Everywhere poverty funds were available, new elements who had never been active in politics came forth to struggle with traditional power groups and in many cases to make space for themselves in the political structures of their communities. Anyone but the most rigid determinist would have to acknowledge positive possibilities in the ferment created by the beginnings—and the idea—of a war on poverty.

Still the ghettos remained, Vietnam drew off funds, and local party hacks acted swiftly to eviscerate programs. The gains of the poverty program, like the gains of the civil rights movement, have led mainly to bitterness and a sense of promises betrayed. In an atmosphere of frustration, anger, and expanded freedom, desperate alternatives are quickly put forward. One is the idea of "Black Power"—which at its best involves developing the ghettos (now partially gutted) as economic and political "power bases," at its worst reinforces the existing stalemate of separation and racial mistrust and drives away the liberal forces who are needed to speed the dissolution of that stalemate. Frequently connected with the Black Power slogan is the idea of revolutionary violence—for some a religion, others a therapy—which seems in this moment of rioting and backlash an inevitable but hopeless development.

All of which presents problems, to put it mildly. Even before the rioting, the poverty program had raised serious issues in relation to the welfare state and the problem of democratic participation. Now, as violence raises the ante and there is no sign of slackening pressure abroad, there has emerged among radicals and liberals an apocalyptic yet personally exculpating world view in which the United States stands revealed as having been all along the representative of total reaction—history's antithesis, as it were, which in the throes of self-annihilation will liberate humanity.

If this is gospel truth, then speculation is mere distraction. But once one does indulge in thought, monistic historical and political assumptions won't go very far toward describing or explaining the rather complex set of circumstances which surround American poverty and our various attempts to cope with it. Let me propose the virtues of a double-minded attitude—for purposes of action as well as analysis.

II

Most radical and liberal commentators are quick to condemn what they correctly describe as America's "two-faced" attitude toward poverty. On one hand America recognizes that certain elements among the poor cannot be absorbed into the world of steady, responsible work. It therefore gives them the dole—but under extremely degrading circumstances. On the other hand America perpetuates the myth that it is an open society in which all can find honorable work. For those who have fallen by the wayside, it provides "social services."

The activist critics of the poverty program often try to resolve this situation by urging that poor people are just as capable and self-sufficient as anyone, and that all they need to set them on a level of social and economic equality is a regular dole—as a matter of right, not charity. They also insist that the poor themselves should be the main administrators of poverty funds—an idea which influenced the O.E.O.'s original concept of Community Action Projects. (For these liberal theorists "community support" is a negative term, because it involves "condescending liberals." "Elected officials" are anathema to these middle-class poverty leaders, because they inevitably "serve the interests of the middle class.")

There is much truth in these strictures. Anyone in contact with the inhabitants of urban slums cannot fail to be impressed with a kind of realistic wisdom which, while not propelling its possessors up the ladder of American success, manages to provide sustenance, pleasure, and in some cases a version of affluence. Slum-dwellers may not run their affairs in accordance with the standard models, but they are capable of running their own affairs. And the investigatory, punitive system of welfare only hampers them. To cite only the most glaringly destructive feature, it may force a husband to leave or pretend to leave his family so that his wife may collect Aid to Dependent Children.

Yet for all its saving graces, its toughness, flexibility, and hard-boiled humor, the culture of poverty is self-defeating and self-perpetuating. One thing the poverty program has proved is that simply turning over funds and programs to the poor does not in itself enable them to transform the circumstances that keep them poor.

Among these circumstances is the deep-grained philosophy

of the hustle, which sees society and personal relations as a series of power games. Granted, there is truth enough to such a view—especially when one is looking up from the bottom. But hustling as an outlook or as a mode of activity finally cannot comprehend the various problems which have to do with learning, training, saving, postponing—and other attitudes necessary to achieve full economic participation in an increasingly technological society, whether one is "middle-class" or not. In some cities—though no one likes to admit it—the hustling view of life has caused Negro youngsters to turn down decent jobs in favor of a more free-wheeling style of livelihood. The philosophy of hustling must be undermined and destroyed by any poverty program worthy of being taken seriously. Hustling will be given up only when it is the least useful defense —which is to say, only when jobs with futures are provided, jobs which involve a meaningful connection with the larger society. Furthermore, job-holders must be trained to see and use that connection, probably while they are on the job. There are some respects in which it is not enough merely to pay the poor.

HARYOU in New York is one of the many Community Action Projects which suffered from a too-loose distribution of funds, resulting not only in shortages but in cases where a few hustlers were accused of taking up to 100 per cent kickbacks from the kids they hired. Perhaps the most uncomfortable aspect of HARYOU was its hiring of black nationalist youths in sinecures designed to keep them from touching off riots. For at least one summer this end was achieved. But what do you teach a kid when you pay him a government salary to threaten the government or to spread mindless propaganda? Precisely that life is a hustle—that might not only makes right but is identical with it. Since he has the pay-off already, why should he bother with any form of education or self-discipline? And finally, how could political or social ideals be anything more to such a youth than expressions of class or race or personal drives for power?[1]

Yes, we have failed to make our American representative system truly representative—we have left a segment of our population powerless and impoverished. Yet poverty programs turned over entirely to "local" groups were often at least as corrupt as programs run through the standard political bureaucracies. And often they were even less representative of the people in the neighborhoods. Nepotism flourished, minority factions usurped whole organizations, and an inordinate amount of money was siphoned into plans, studies, staff, and equipment.

Where do we go from here? Somehow programs have to involve linkages with the mainstream of society—for the benefit of all concerned. It is not enough to turn the slums over to the slum-dwellers: that is too much like what they already have, whether you call it "participation" or penury. Real participation would involve openings beyond the ghetto into areas of massive economic opportunity and retraining. The culture of the ghetto must be absorbed and utilized—which is not the same as being destroyed. The ghetto itself must be destroyed.

Some radicals unwittingly contradict themselves in calling for welfare reform. Basically they insist on the dole in recognition of the fact that the poor are not fully employable. Fair enough. But at the same time they maintain that poverty funds must be turned over exclusively to the poor. What makes them think that people who are not fully employable are fully capable of administering poverty funds? Even in cases where they are, the most successful local programs plus a steady dole would not by themselves break up American poverty; they

[1] Andrew Kopkind echoes this attitude in *The New York Review of Books* (August 24, 1967), where he states that "Morality, like politics, starts at the barrel of a gun." Presumably he learned this from "the underground press, the speeches of Malcolm, the works of Fanon, the songs of the Rolling Stones and Aretha Franklin," which he cites as "the important literature now."

would at best be no more than the mainstays of an isolated community in an inferior economic position. More important than either the dole or subsidized autonomous projects is the need for a full-scale national economic program, without which local projects are doomed to dry up from lack of umbilical connections.

If the issue is reduced to whether there should be a guaranteed income or not, of course there should be. But work is even better. To speak realistically, people on dole will not have "dignity," no matter what. We can and should eliminate the abuses, the condescension, the costly and degrading check-ups. But surviving on a welfare check or an income subsidy is not the same as having a future. And for most people, it's not necessary—not when there is so much work to do in this country. People who are now battling the welfare inspectors increment by increment could be staffing hospitals, rebuilding cities, providing services, perhaps creating whole new communities.

If such an overall effort were under way, it would be matched by individual efforts to participate in it. The worker looking above him would see opportunity and not merely a closed corporation. He would have an incentive to become skillful. I am mindful that the American ideal of making one's self has been for some a vicious myth. But channels for doing just that have always been open, and remain some of our most valuable social possessions. We need more channels, more representation, a larger, fairer dole—and nationally planned work programs involving both middle-class and poor people engaged together in meaningful reconstruction of their own country.

We cannot hope for a magic resolution of our double attitude toward poverty, since poor people are in fact burdens as well as honorable victims. Perhaps the most productive stance would be an open acknowledgement of ambiguity—so that we may simultaneously proceed with an improved welfare system *and* an economic program which could free every individual capable of being freed. These efforts are not mutually exclusive.

III

One problem for the boy growing up in the ghetto is that models are lacking to show how one might successfully enter the world of trade and technology in which most American males are employed. The young Negro who is successful in "straight" employment is apt to move away—and become identified with the larger world, which is seen from the ghetto as a white world.

The power who remains "on the street" (or parked in his Cadillac) and thus available for identification, is the hustler. I have already mentioned the hustler's credo of might equals right, but there is another aspect of his makeup worth underscoring in terms of its educational implications. Which is simply that the hustler knows all the answers. He picked them up—as Malcolm X did—by watching and listening all day long to power-plays. He is shrewd about the use of force, at least within his own precincts. But when it comes to knowledge, what he mainly wants is a ready-made line, a set of hard-nosed aphorisms—so that he will have a quick answer in any threatening situation. He wants not to be caught short verbally, for he knows a sharp retort is another form of power.[2]

[2] " 'John,' I said, 'how many degrees in a circle?'

"He said, 'Three hundred and sixty.'

"I drew a square. 'How many degrees in that?' He said three hundred and sixty.

"I asked him was three hundred and sixty degrees, then, the maximum of degrees in anything?

"He said 'Yes.'

"I said, 'Well, why is it that Masons go only to thirty-three degrees?'

"He had no satisfactory answer. But for me, the answer was that Masonry, actually, is only thirty-three degrees of the religion of Islam, which is the full projection, forever denied to Masons, although they know it exists."

(From the chapter "Satan" in *The Autobiography of Malcolm X*.)

Like Malcolm, Stokely Carmichael lays great stress on "the power to define." Here is an excerpt from a speech to the students of Morgan State College, as transcribed in *The Movement*, June 1967:

The trouble is that street knowledge can't risk unsureness, can't risk leaving questions open. So that if something can't be picked up in a quick formula, it will likely be banished from consciousness. Malcolm, for instance, with his razor wit, had at any point in his life—whether as zoot-suit hipster, Black Muslim, or pan-African nationalist—a complete set of consistent answers which turned complexity into a captivating simplicity. After a speech of Malcolm's, his followers repeated his answers by rote—as they still do in the junior nationalist "five-percenter" groups, where youngsters are given a catechism to memorize, full of anthropological and historical absurdities.[3]

No doubt poor people are not the only ones susceptible to the all-or-nothing concept of learning. But for poor boys such a misconception is fatal, because it means that training and education are seen as initiation—as into a club, or a secret society—rather than as an open process. There are sad stories among poverty workers of Negro youths who approach, say, psychologists, and announce, I've seen what you do, man: why can't I take your place? On being told they must go through a specific training process over a period of years they throw up their hands.

"Now then we come to the question of definitions. We will talk about that for a while. It is very, very important because I believe that people who can define are masters.

"I want to read a quote. It is one of my favorite quotes. It comes from *Alice in Wonderland*, Lewis Carroll. . . .

" ' "When I use a word," Humpty Dumpty said in a rather scornful tone, "it means just what I choose it to mean, neither more nor less." "The question is," said Alice, "whether you can make words mean so many different things." "The question is," said Humpty Dumpty, "who is to be master." '

"That is all. That is all. Understand that. . . . the first need of a free people is to define their own terms . . ."

Note that Mr. Carmichael, unlike Mr. Carroll, identifies uncritically with Humpty Dumpty.

[3] ". . . if you started with a black man, a white man could be produced; but starting with a white man, you never could produce a black man— because the white chromosome is recessive. And since no one disputes that there was but one Original Man, the conclusion is clear."

(From the chapter "Saved" in *The Autobiography of Malcolm X*.)

What happens these days to the large majority of boys who aspire to be "street-wise"—who in fact *must* be, simply to survive—but who can't make it big as hustlers and who lack some lucky talent that would enable them to rise in the world unassisted? Naturally they resent the white establishment, whose official members they see as licensed hustlers—licensed, in some cases, to treat Negroes brutally. These boys don't want training—they *want in right away*. If Whitey won't give them an initiation, then they'll initiate Whitey.

If he goes into the Armed Services, a Negro boy may get his desired initiation. But if he stays on the street, the young Negro is likely to collide with another type—exemplified by Carmichael and LeRoi Jones, among others—the successful middle-class Negro who can't bear the torment of perceiving himself a part of "white" society while masses of his people are left behind. He solves his identity problem much as does the hustler—by adopting a set of absolute answers, in this instance those of the apocalyptic black revolutionary. He offers this identity to drifting youth—an identity of innate bravery and superiority and dedication and solidarity. It is only reasonable that many a young Negro will prefer this conception of himself to that of the disadvantaged student, fighting a lonely struggle to educate himself and keep his bearings in the face of discrimination and poverty. An interaction goes on between demagogue and potential rioter not unlike the traditional interaction between Negro preacher and potential lamb of Jesus.

A white man may argue that Negro violence is not politically efficient; he may deride the intellectual inadequacy of the new black ideology; but he cannot legitimately tell a young Negro that his allegiance to the catchwords of Black Power does not make him feel better on the inside.

What of the white civil rights and poverty workers—the idealistic students, the increasingly radical social workers, the impassioned ministers—who in past years have gone into the ghettos to unite themselves with America's most urgent cause?

I am afraid that many of them—at least the ones who project onto the Negro their longing for a noble savage—must share with Congress and other officials, and with society at large, a responsibility for the riots. For in many cases, *seen in terms of a might makes right perspective*, the poverty workers have been fawning—allowing themselves to be conned and worse (sometimes much worse). And this too confirms the desperate identity of superiority. The young militant has no respect for those who come to his neighborhood to tell him how great he is. If I'm so great, he thinks, then I will take what you have.

IV

Interesting that so far the rioters have attacked mainly police (with bottles and bricks and words, seldom bullets) and property. They have fire-bombed white stores, loan offices and adjacent housing. In retaliation, guardsmen in Newark smashed black-owned stores, and troops and police shot up Negro dwelling-places. Supposedly they were shooting at snipers, but one has to wonder about the existence of snipers who hit so few targets. If there were organized Negro assassins at work, it's hard to believe they could have aimed so badly. Perhaps they had reasons for aiming to miss. At any rate, the vast majority of those killed were Negroes, and in most cases few people were killed until the order was given for official triggers to be pulled. Reporters have confirmed that in both Newark and Detroit, the cops and guardsmen shot at each other and at the sparks of their own bullets striking houses. In some cases, they waited in ambush to shoot up cars which failed to stop at unmanned roadblocks.

It seems clear that regardless of Black Power rhetoric— "burn this town," "shoot honkies," etc.—the main motives of those who joined in were economic. Some inhabitants of the ghetto felt they were entitled to loot white-owned stores, and that the police and troopers were agents of hostile forces. Their actions examined apart from rhetoric said very simply and explicitly, "we will not endure these circumstances. You owe us more than you can ever give us."

And we do.

v

The militant—the creator of and the believer in black rhetoric—is deeply dependent on the very world he is scorning and threatening. He's not abandoning America—he can't. He wants to punish America. Far from aloof, he's deeply hurt at having been snubbed and used and moved away from. He wants America to pay attention; when he gets no response, he feels himself nothing. And he is very American in the way he goes about creating his position.

First he has an "image"—a militant image, a black image, a unique image without which one does not have access to the media. The young militant shares and feeds the American appetite for image. Already this gives him a role to play—destructive, threatening, but nonetheless part of the scene. It's better than nodding out on junk. If people are afraid of you, you exist, you know who you are.

If he relies on ideology—well, certainly the Jews, Irish, and Italians protected themselves with cynical philosophies about American opportunity (and their own superiority)—and certainly they developed their share of hustlers and hoods. I am told that the Irish riots of the nineteenth century were bloodier than anything we've yet seen from the Negroes. And righteous free-lance violence is hardly an exclusive property of Negroes, as an evening with your TV set will confirm.

As far as looting is concerned, the Negroes are small-time compared to American businessmen—and I don't mean the little shopkeepers either; I mean the swingers on Wall Street and the WASPs who head up our huge corporations. Which costs Americans more—riots or oil depletions? Riots or drug mark-ups? Riots or market manipulations?

In their roles as true believers, as masculine upholders of

honor and right, unafraid to take violent action, even to die, in behalf of their beliefs, the Black Power cultists are more classically Western than the white flower ideologists out to transform human nature with drugs, youth, love, colored lights, pop music, and polysexuality.

It's even possible to understand why some historians see the riots and the talk of guerrilla warfare as symptoms of the inevitable disruption that occurs whenever a new class or group forces its way into the mainstream of American society. Some years from now, their argument goes, the racial conflict will have resolved itself, and the usual variety of opinions and loyalties will flourish among a more relaxed Negro population.

Maybe so. But in the meantime it is a terrible thing to see whites and blacks locked into oratorical abstractions which only reinforce hatred and guilt and violence. It seems obvious that the Negroes will be hurt most, even as in every riot they make up a large majority of the dead and wounded. Surely of all the segregated groups that have fought against social stigmata, the Negroes, brought to this country against their will and subject to slavery, lynch-law, and emasculation, have the toughest fight on their hands. For that reason they are prey to the most self-destructive temptations. But for that reason also they of all people can least afford any kind of self-deception.

It is frightening to see a cycle in operation: a cycle of poverty and rhetoric, violence and backlash. American society has a tremendous job to do in terms of creating genuine economic and educational opportunities; yet apparently this job will get little more than peanuts allocated to it as long as our President is escalating the war in Vietnam. With every escalation a portion of faith is torn away from this country. The black man in the ghetto stabs at his own heart, which is also the heart of our cities, and as the ghettos burn, one hears loud crackings all around, as if the whole crazy country were on fire.

1967

The Poverty
of Aging

BEN B. SELIGMAN

Americans are proud of the fact that the nation is becoming young. Nearly half the population is now under twenty-five years of age and about a third under fifteen. While this may mean crowded colleges or teen-age unemployment, the problems of *senior* citizens, who are increasing in numbers, do not diminish because older people become a smaller portion of the population. In fact, in an industrial society the position of the aged tends to worsen. The long-run decline in death rates, signifying greater longevity, coupled with the inability of older persons to compete for jobs, makes the problem of the aged more visible, despite a desire on the part of the rest of us to push them out of sight and out of mind.

The final stages of human existence can be a protracted period of human obsolescence. As in so many other societies, we would prefer simply to discard our aged. While we do not burn the villages of the aged dead, or fill the air with cries of joy over the departed,[1] we do stuff our aged into institutions to let them await death slowly. There they are given care of a sort. Unfortunately, as Jules Henry has revealed, such care is of the order that might be accorded to an inanimate object.[2] Often, the names of the inmates are not known to the staff that takes care of them. Institutions for the aged are likely to be tombs for those still alive, and as in a tomb, silence prevails.

A resident of an old age home must foster the illusion that he is among the living, although awareness that he has been discarded by relatives, friends, and society is not uncommon. In some private profit-making homes, the inmates ". . . suffer most from [a] sense of being dumped and lost; [from] the . . . vacant routine, the awareness of being considered a nuisance and of being inferior to the most insensitive employee."[3] Soon ordinary human functions are distorted, so that the resident of an old age institution undergoes a "pathogenic metamorphosis" akin to that experienced by characters in the tales of Franz Kafka. If he reaches pathetically for reality, the inmate is apt to be rebuffed by a staff member: the latter do not want reality, for the transformation of their charges is the only reality available to *them*. Ordinary human dignity would represent too serious a challenge to the apparatus of the institution, the main purpose of which is to create hopelessness. When this has been achieved, persons of sound mind and body can then withdraw from the aged without qualms of conscience. The sense of doom that the aged suffer hastens their passage through the vestibule to death.[4]

The aged may be among us, but they are not part of us. The aged are simply an embarrassment. They are poor, unable to

---

[1] Cf. J. Campbell, *The Masks of God: Primitive Mythology,* New York, 1959, p. 118 ff.

[2] J. Henry, *Culture Against Man,* New York, 1963, p. 391 ff.

[3] *Ibid.,* p. 407.   [4] *Ibid.,* p. 437.

provide medical care for themselves: they violate the canon of self-help, and so we dishonor them. Irving Rosow has demonstrated that a secure position for the aged can exist only under conditions that cannot be found in a modern industrial society. If the aged owned or controlled property on which younger persons depended, if they were transmitters of culture in possession of key blocks of knowledge, if they provided significant links to the past, if the extended family were still central to our mode of life, if our society were tradition-oriented, and if the output of the aged were in any way economically useful, then they would still be honored.[5]

An older person has a chance for a fruitful existence if he is married and living with his spouse, but many of those over sixty-five years of age have no spouse and widowhood increases with age at the rate of 20 per cent with each decade after sixty-five. An old person has a chance if he is still at work, but most of the aged do not work. Today only a third of persons sixty-five years of age or older are in the work force, as contrasted with two-thirds at the turn of the century. Escape from poverty and hopelessness is possible if there is no loss of income, but the data show a drop of as much as 50 per cent in income after retirement. Life might be meaningful if one's health were good, but most of the aged suffer from a large assortment of illnesses. Says Rosow, the chances of a man over sixty-five having a favorable rating on all four counts is seven in a hundred, for a woman over sixty-five, one in a hundred.[6]

To be sure, there has been some improvement in institutional homes in recent years. The recognition that the aged need to have a choice in living arrangements has been growing, and some better homes have been provided by religious denominations and fraternal organizations. The private proprietary institutions, though they are proliferating, rarely set up respon-

[5] I. Rosow, "And Then We Were Old," *Trans-Action*, Jan.–Feb., 1965, p. 21.

[6] Rosow, *ibid.*, p. 25.

sible lay boards to review both policy and day-to-day operations. With social security payments as a base, the aged poor
can turn to private services when no others are available; yet
few of these institutions tie their services to a medical-care
system or rehabilitation effort that would minimize the "disuse
syndrome" among their clients. In the final analysis, proprietary
homes are commercial enterprises and generally isolated from
community health services.[7]

Living with relatives has not been a viable solution either.
In one study two-thirds of the persons interviewed were opposed to having aged parents live with their children.[8] It was
evident that little contact or understanding between the generations existed. Only 13 per cent of the respondents in this
study saw virtue in some semblance of an extended family.
The higher the educational level, the more undesirable did
joint living appear to be: educated persons were less likely to
provide a home for their older relatives. A similar attitude prevailed among the aged: older persons with incomes of at least
$5000 a year expressed preferences for separate domiciles.
And older persons in states that provide higher Old Age Assistance appear to live alone more frequently than in states where
OAA is minimal.

How difficult living alone must be is underscored by the
income data for the aged. The largest proportion of aged
married couples—79 per cent—derive their income from social
security payments. Other government retirement programs,
such as railroad retirement systems, provide income for 12
per cent, while private retirement schemes lend support to
16 per cent.[9] Earnings were a source of income for somewhat
more than half the aged couples. For the non-married aged

[7] Senate Committee on Aging, *Developments in Aging: 1959 to 1963*,
Washington, 1963, *The New York Times*, July 19, 1966.

[8] J. N. Morgan, *et al.*, *Income and Welfare in the United States*, New
York, 1962, pp. 158 ff.

[9] L. S. Epstein, "Income of the Aged in 1962: First Findings of the 1963
Survey of the Aged," *Social Security Bulletin*, March 1964.

this ratio dropped to 24 per cent. More important is the size of the income: the median for married couples was $2875; for non-married persons, $1130. Almost all of the latter had incomes under $3000 a year: this was also true for 54 per cent of the married couples. Set against the standards of "modest but adequate" budgets, these data suggest that at least two million couples and six million unmarried aged are in dire straits.

It is often argued that older persons do not need as much as younger ones, because the aged spend less for clothing, housing, food, and medicine. But as Harold Sheppard has said, this reflects a curious reversal of logic, since the aged spend less only because they have less.[10] The patent fact is that those aged who do not sustain a loss in income do consume as much as anyone else in their income level. No doubt the aged would be worse off were there no social security payments. Yet a large percentage of social security beneficiaries still require public assistance, mainly because the benefits are too small to maintain them at even low levels of existence.

Families headed by older persons represent one-third of all poor families, a ratio substantially higher than the one in seven for the total number of aged in the general population. As we have suggested, the non-married are worse off than couples: they tend to be older and poorer, so that one in six requires old age assistance, as contrasted with one in twelve for the married aged. A large number of social security beneficiaries receive the minimum benefit: women who select "early" retirement get even less.

There may have been some improvement in the income position of the aged in recent years; yet as late as 1962, 5 per cent of aged married couples and 44 per cent of aged non-married persons had incomes of less than $1000 a year.[11] While the

[10] H. L. Sheppard, "The Poverty of the Aging," in B. B. Seligman, ed., Poverty As a Public Issue, New York, 1965, p. 98.

[11] H. S. Gordon, "Aging and Income Security," in C. Tibbitts, ed., Aging and Society, Chicago, 1960, p. 212.

proportion of all families and individuals in dire poverty has
decreased since 1900, the proportion of the aged in such circumstances has not decreased markedly.[12] Nor do they have
accumulations of savings on which they can fall back. The
aged may have homes with mortgages fully paid, some insurance, and some liquid assets; but in 1960, 30 per cent of
spending units with heads over 65 years had no liquid assets,
and 20 per cent had such assets amounting to less than $1000.
And more than half the home equities were worth less than
$10,000. Such assets are not available for the usual emer-
gencies that afflict the aged.

Of course, there have been improvements in the last few
years. Amendments to the Social Security Act have helped,
and the beneficiaries now coming onto the rolls with better
earnings records than those in past years have added to
average benefits. Yet in December, 1964, the average social
security payment was $79 a month. At the end of 1964, there
were 13.7 million aged persons receiving such benefits; on the
average this represented 3 out of every 4 aged persons in the
nation. In 1965 it was estimated that 35 per cent of all social
security recipients were poor and that another 38 per cent
would fall below the Social Security Administration's poverty
standard in the absence of social security payments.

Of course, social security encourages withdrawal from the
work force.[13] The proportion of the aged who work appears to
have fallen sharply in recent years, although it is conceivable
that illness or changes in attitudes toward retirement may have
accounted for the decline.[14] Curiously enough, social security
is structured in such a manner that the income transfers flow
from lower-middle-income groups to lower-income groups,
with upper-income groups contributing very little. In effect,

[12] *Ibid.*, p. 211.

[13] C. D. Long, *The Labor Force Under Changing Income and Employment,* Princeton, 1958, p. 163.

[14] M. Gordon, *The Economics of Welfare Policies,* New York, 1963, p. 35.

support of the poor comes from those quite close to them in the income scale. Further, because of the retirement tests, the law limits beneficiaries in supplementing benefits in any effective fashion. Furthermore, widows must surrender part of their benefits if they marry another beneficiary, leading to "the St. Petersburg sin," couples living together to overcome loneliness, but in an unmarried state.[15]

After some years of agitation, improvements were made in 1965. Monthly cash benefits were increased by 7 per cent, so that the range is now from $44 a month to $136 a month, with the maximum scheduled to rise to $168 a month in future years. The tax base was raised to $6600 a year and the tax rate stepped up to reach 4.85 per cent by 1973. For a family the maximum benefit may reach $368 a month. The retirement test was altered, allowing earnings up to $1500 a year. Benefits were continued for children still in school up to the age of 22. Disability allowances were liberalized and the standards made less restrictive. Widows could receive benefits at age sixty on an actuarially reduced basis. These changes do indeed offer some improvements, but whether they will take the aged poor out of poverty remains to be seen.

All too often an aged person receiving benefits must ask local authorities for additional help. And for the aged poor who do not have recourse to the federal program there is no alternative to Old Age Assistance (OAA). Yet more than half the states fail to make OAA payments sufficient to meet their own income tests. The Senate Committee on Aging noted numerous cases of local agencies reducing their aid when other sources were made available.[16]

As with all forms of public assistance at local levels, OAA is conditioned by the perennial clash between proponents of low taxes and those who express a concern for the poor. Yet assistance to the aged, as well as other categorical forms of

[15] *Ibid.*, p. 44.
[16] Senate Committee on Aging, *op. cit.*, pp. 69–70.

aid, has become much too severe a problem to be handled by private charity, as is frequently suggested by low tax advocates; moreover, the private agencies have developed their own specialized clientele and they are now reluctant to become involved in aid programs rooted in economic distress. They prefer to deal with such matters as family counseling, leaving economic need to public authorities.[17]

So large is the bill for public assistance that on occasion a local authority throws up its hands in frustration and simply closes down its program. When Clermont County in Ohio cut off aid in 1961 because the voters rejected a tax levy for public assistance, the burden was simply shifted to landlords, grocers, doctors, and other agencies. Debt in the county rose 54 per cent in a fifteen-month period, and evictions increased alarmingly. Clearly, cutting the aged and other needy off the rolls was no solution. On the other hand, neither does increased aid make the problem disappear. Although survivor's insurance may lighten the widow's burden and help the orphans, no one anticipated that illegitimacy and desertion would in turn crowd the public assistance rolls.

While 2/5 of the total public assistance burden goes for OAA, its distribution is quite unequal. A higher proportion of the rural aged are reached through OAA than the urban aged. Yet there is no consistent pattern among the states: Louisiana reaches 49 per cent of its aged poor; Delaware only 3 per cent. But this doesn't mean that Delaware's level of aid is munificent—its average monthly payment is $63. In actuality, there is no rational economic explanation for the sort of benefits the individual states bestow on their aged poor. Worse yet, the state-run programs are frequently conducted in an irregular manner. Confidentiality requirements may be flouted or recipients classified on some arbitrary basis other than need.[18] The eligibility standards usually mean emotional agony

---

[17] G. Y. Steiner, *Social Insecurity: The Politics of Welfare,* Chicago, 1966, p. 11.

[18] *Ibid.,* p. 84.

for the recipient who is willing to run a bureaucratic gauntlet to obtain aid. All too often the public agency tends to blame his situation on the client himself.

Recipients, especially those on OAA, cannot influence the level or administration of the programs that serve them. As Gilbert Steiner says, farmers have their lobbyists, publishers express their views on mail subsidy to Congress, and trade associations speak for industry, but the aged—or for that matter, any recipient of public assistance—are not asked what they need. (Some change in this regard is being sought by some civil rights groups.)[19]

One might think that private pension benefits would relieve the situation of the aged. In 1960 total payments to retirees from private pensions were about $1.3 billion, four times larger than a decade before. The various plans cover over 20 million workers, or about 43 per cent of the employed private work force, almost double the ratio in 1950. Much progress had been made in ten years. Nevertheless, the income derived from private pensions represented less than 6 per cent of the income of the aged. And most of the recipients could be classified as "higher-income aged." Less than 3 per cent of social security beneficiaries who receive under $1200 a year obtain any income from private pension plans.

To rely on private pension income to relieve the condition of the aged poor would be disastrous. Small firms are less apt to have pension arrangements than large ones. Low-wage industries, in which many of the aged poor have spent their working lives, have not instituted pension programs in any widespread fashion. Federal tax regulations are so cumbersome that entrepreneurs in these industries are discouraged from even trying. The most serious problem is the lack of airtight legal protection for pensioners. Despite some improvement, stemming from the Welfare and Pension Disclosure Act, it is still possible for an employee to discover that he really has no pension. For in the last analysis, the contract is between the

[19] *Ibid.*, p. 153 ff.

employer or trustees and the carrier, and all too often trustees can escape penalties for negligence or misconduct. Many private plans have poor vesting—an absolute right to a pension—or none at all; and in the absence of portability—the transfer of pensions from one company to another—a feature conspicuous by its rarity, workers lose years of accumulated rights when they change jobs.

Meeting health costs is a major problem for the aged. Private insurers could not solve the problem of offering adequate benefits for a high-risk, low-income population, nor were they especially interested in doing so. Despite the American Medical Association's crude effort in 1960 to demonstrate that the aged weren't suffering from sicknesses and could easily meet their health bills, the fact was that 4 out of 5 aged persons had chronic ailments as contrasted with 2 out of 5 for younger persons. Mental, as well as physical illness, was a problem for the aged: first admissions in mental hospitals were two-and-a-half times greater than those for patients under sixty-five. The aged stay in hospitals longer; they need more home care and more drugs; they visit the doctor more often. Set against this record the mounting hospital costs—an increase of 27 per cent between 1960 and 1962—and it is patent that the health problem of the aged has been indeed serious.[20]

The demand for health insurance as part of the social security system grew without abatement. At the eleventh hour, private insurance companies sought to offer plans for aged health coverage within their underwriting perspective, but these were inadequate. They were almost all hospital-oriented and did not deal with other medical needs, i.e., they were not comprehensive. The industry failed to convince anyone—not even itself—that it could do the job. In 1959 hospital insurance coverage for the aged covered 46 per cent of that group as compared with 67 per cent in the total population; surgical coverage was 37 per cent, a little over half of what everyone

[20] Senate Committee on Aging, *op. cit.*, *passim.*

else had; and only 10 per cent of the aged had insurance for doctors' visits, as contrasted with 19 per cent for the general population. The lower the income, the less coverage: only a third of the aged with incomes under $2000 a year had hospital insurance.

All too frequently the insurance the aged did have provided lower benefits at higher premiums.[21] Furthermore, the shift from a community rating basis in setting costs to an experience basis tended to force up rates. In any case, the usual commercial coverage offered fixed dollar benefits according to some predetermined schedule rather than in terms of need. And the deductible corridors—that part borne directly by the insured—placed a substantial part of the cost on the policy holder. Ordinary health insurance did not meet more than 7 per cent of the total cost of the aged's health requirements.

Nor did the Kerr-Mills Act in 1960 solve the problem. Admittedly passed as a substitute for health care through the social security system, it asked the states to develop their own medical aid programs for the aged as a condition for obtaining federal grants. Numerous restrictions were instituted—means tests and family responsibility—which severely limited coverage. The administrative costs were inordinately high. Moreover, since most of the states had failed to provide even adequate general assistance to the aged, it was unlikely that they would assume the added burden of Kerr-Mills. By 1962 only one in every 200 eligibles was receiving aid through Kerr-Mills. Many refused to utilize the "service" when they discovered that they would have to pauperize themselves. Quite simply, Kerr-Mills was a failure.

It remained for Medicare—medical aid through social security—to make the first sensible step toward an adequate health scheme for the aged. While Medicare, as passed in 1965, fell short of the original proposals, it was a significant advance,

21 *Ibid.*, p. 15.

one that took twenty years to achieve. Its impact will probably go far beyond the 10 per cent of the population for whom it has been devised. It is more than likely that private health insurance plans for younger persons will be altered and Medicare will no doubt affect proposals developed through collective bargaining.

In brief, the 1965 amendments to the Social Security Act provide hospital and medical insurance for beneficiaries. The hospital plan is financed by a separate earnings tax and separate fund. Enrollment in the medical plan is voluntary, paid for by a monthly premium of $3 to be matched by the federal government. Benefits include a maximum of 90 days hospitalization for each illness, post-hospital, extended care for 100 days, and outpatient diagnostic services. The law also stresses the need for community health planning.

Opponents apparently have accepted Medicare as a *fait accompli,* and indeed are getting on the bandwagon. Medical practitioners are helping the government to set up the necessary standards, and the AMA, after spending almost $1 million in the first three months of 1965 to forestall the passage of Medicare, is now urging its members to cooperate. Nevertheless, it was reported that some 20,000 physicians have decided not to participate. Private insurance companies, on the other hand, are cooperating. No doubt it was their influence that resulted in all of Medicare's deductible corridors, for these allow dove-tailing private plans with government plans. There is still some business they hope to get. A query remains: will not those aged who do not buy private "dovetailed" policies continue to suffer a financial burden by virtue of the deductible corridors?

It was predicted that Medicare would enforce vast changes in hospital administration. Fees for some services provided by hospitals would be raised; the prices of other services would be reduced. Thus, charges for rooms, X-rays, and medicines were expected to fall, whereas service costs for obstetrics and pediatrics might increase. New arrangement might be worked out for staff doctors, and it was hoped that Medicare would speed up integration in Southern hospitals. In any case, it was expected that the aged of the nation would flock into the 7200 hospitals across the country and overtax already limited facilities. No one thought that the deductible corridors would provide some restraint.[22]

While plans for Medicare were being formulated, most observers overlooked Medicaid—Title 19 of the 1965 amendments to the Social Security Act. Unnoticed for months, attention was called to Title 19 when New York State took advantage of its provisions by adopting enabling legislation in April, 1966. This amendment is a liberalized and expanded version of the 1960 Kerr-Mills law. Financed by general revenues, not through social security, it provides for certain kinds of health care for the aged poor, but on a broader scale than Kerr-Mills. In fact, Title 19, sponsored by Rep. Wilbur Mills, offers benefits through matching grants to the disabled, ADC families, and to those who may have enough for other needs, but not for medical care. In effect, funds would be made available to all medically needy persons under twenty-one and over sixty-five and to the blind or disabled and ADC cases between those ages. By mid-1966 seven states had obtained approval for their programs and a number of others had applied for approval. It was expected that Medicaid would eventually reach some 35 million people. The initial cost to the Federal government was expected to be more than $350 million. Quite significant too was the marked easing of eligibility rules, residence requirements, and family responsibility regulations. Further, there was a prospect that some of the deductible corridors under Medicare would be covered.

When it was suddenly realized that New York's plan alone would cost over a billion dollars a year in combined federal,

---

22 *New York Times,* May 29, 1966; June 13, 1966; June 19, 1966; *Wall Street Journal,* June 15, 1966; *Baltimore Sun,* Dec. 21, 1965.

state, and local payments, the legislators in Washington were
stunned. They hurriedly tried to amend the law, but it seemed
too late—the welfare state had barged through the cautious
legislative barriers with a resounding crash. For the members
of Congress had left the definition of "medically indigent"
up to the states, and some of the latter were prepared to be as
liberal as New York had been. Under the latter's program up
to 40 per cent of its inhabitants could qualify for Medicaid.
Moreover, the states were not permitted to substitute Medicaid for existing welfare programs in order to prevent new
federal monies from paying for old state welfare programs,
thus encouraging liberality.

Senators and Congressmen were chagrined at their extraordinary *faux pas* and tried to scale down the generous program.
Yet by October, 1966, some 24 states and Puerto Rico had
taken advantage of Title 19. Although most of the state plans
were modest, California and Massachusetts had devised fairly
ambitious ones, and their representatives in Washington made
it known that they would not tolerate any changes in the law.
Congress proposed to bar able-bodied adults whose children
were receiving assistance under other welfare programs, but the
income standards were still open doors for aid to such adults.
Only $80 million would be cut from the estimated half-billion-
dollar federal cost in the year beginning July, 1967: the
original estimate for federal contributions had been $238
million a year. It was feared that Washington's Medicaid bill
would reach $2 billion annually.[23]

For all these improvements, social security remained inadequate. It was clear that much remained to be done if the country
was to catch up with standards elsewhere in the West. One
problem was the erosion that resulted as prices continued their
upward drift. Somehow social security benefits would have

[23] *New York Times,* May 29, 1966; *National Observer,* June 20,
1966; *Boston Globe,* June 5, 1966; *Wall Street Journal,* July 11, 1966;
October 20, 1966; *Business Week,* June 25, 1966.

to be tied to a "cost of living" formula if the retired were not to lose ground. It was obvious too that the structure of social security taxes, which provided the "trust fund," could not be expected to do the whole job. Sentiment increased for recourse to the general revenues, although a sharp increase in the tax base—perhaps up to $15,000 a year—was not unthinkable. It has been argued that the steep increase in payroll taxes that this entailed would generate resistance, and discourage firms from increasing their work force because of rising costs. Further, no matter what the base limit, a payroll tax remains regressive: with the present $6600 limit, those receiving income under this figure pay proportionately more than those whose income exceeds $6600 a year. The prospect seems to be that social security benefits will come less and less from direct contributions to a special fund.

The aged need decent housing as well as adequate income, yet the limitations from which they suffer in income impose severe restrictions on what they can purchase in shelter. This was underscored by the Senate Committee on Aging in 1962, and despite existing legislation little genuine progress has been made. Local housing authorities have available certain instrumentalities under the Housing Act to allow the construction of special facilities for the aged: by the end of 1962 about 8000 such units had been built. New rental housing for the aged can be supplied through government-insured mortgages: by 1962, about 26,000 units had been built. Direct loans are also available to non-profit organizations sponsoring housing for the aged: by 1962, about 8800 such units had been constructed. It seems obvious that these programs have provided a tiny fraction of the need.

Even in the one agency primarily concerned with poverty—the Office of Economic Opportunity—the aged have been relegated to secondary status. For months during 1965–1966 a bureaucratic battle raged in OEO on whether the aged poor should become a prime target group or remain a minor concern of the agency. Budgeting outlays in OEO through 1966 for the aged were about 2 per cent of the total. Said some bureaucrats in justification of the policy: "We're a youth-oriented nation." Yet Congress made it clear in 1965 that OEO was to consider the special problems of the aged "wherever possible." The only program for the aged to which OEO gave any priority was "Medicare Alert," under which older persons were given temporary jobs at $1.25 an hour to brief other aged on the benefits available under Medicare. Their job was done by March 31, 1966, the deadline for registering for Medicare. While President Johnson specified in August, 1965 a many-sided crash program for the aged poor, only one of these, "Foster Grandparents," a program to train older persons to serve as "substitute parents" for neglected children, was in operation six months later. The program was small in scale, employing about 1200 elderly persons in March, 1966; in the meantime, OEO's original allotment for this venture was cut back from $10 million to $5.5 million; and total OEO funds for aged programs were cut in half.

Yet there are numerous services the aged could be trained to perform—library assistants, recreation aides, school crossing guards, toll collectors, helpers to shut-in persons, and sub-professional social work are just a few. The cost-benefit philosophy that had begun to infect many federal agencies, however, impelled some OEO officials to question the pay-off of investment in the aged. The brutalizing habits of the larger society seemed to have undermined what would appear to be the moral obligations of an agency concerned with poverty.

The outstanding feature of such an effort as "Foster Grandparents" was the remarkable reliability and sense of responsibility of the participants. After eight months one could detect no demonstration, no dropouts, no absenteeism in the project. While the lives of hundreds of rejected children were brightened for a brief time, a sizable group of aged men and women, all poor, were given a new interest in life. Even Congressmen who had expressed some doubts were pleasantly surprised at the results. Some children's institutions were horrified at the prospect of "caring" for older persons in addition to what they had to do: within weeks of the inception of the program they were asking for more "foster grandparents."

If one suggests an utter failure of imagination on the part of OEO in dealing with the aged, he would not be far from the truth. All Sargent Shriver could do was to tell a Senate Committee that little could be done for the aged: older persons, said Shriver, had low educational levels, are in poor health, and cannot compete for jobs. Besides it was more difficult to get local communities excited about the aged poor. Other agencies, insisted Shriver, had a greater responsibility for the aged; OEO could at best play a minor role. The only way to help the aged seemed to be direct cash benefits. Perhaps in *our* society this may be the only way—give the aged poor money and let them stand aside, silent and unseen.[24]

1967

[24] *New York Times*, Dec. 22, 1965; Jan. 20, 1966; *Washington Post*, May 13, 1965; Jan. 20, 1966; *Chicago Tribune*, May 1, 1966; *National Observer*, March 7, 1966.

Head Start or Dead End?

DEBORAH MEIER

The photograph of Negro children looking at an attractive young teacher while she intently reads them a book has become a symbol of the War on Poverty. It conveys a commitment to the innocent and forgotten child, concern for small and unglamorous details, and a one-to-one relationship between the middle-class reformer and the victims of poverty.

The Head Start program has been termed the one unmixed blessing of the War on Poverty and LBJ's pride and joy. Since it deals with the education (and not integration) of the very young, it is subject to fewer complications than programs dealing with employment, retraining for adults, and housing.

Yet even in this deceptively simple area the basic difficulties of the Poverty Program reflect themselves in a hodge-podge of conflicting ideologies and interests. Patronage politics, Negro nationalism, middle-class reformism, bureaucratic bungling, and the highest idealism and self-sacrifice—all make themselves felt in the new nurseries.

The Philadelphia Get Set project was perhaps the first to extend the Head Start concept into a year-around program. After the success of one summer's Head Start, it was assumed that a year or two of pre-kindergarten enrichment would help disadvantaged children compete with their middle-class peers. For this purpose the federal government contracted with the Philadelphia Board of Education for a program involving 5,000 three- and four-year-olds for a minimum of one year beginning in the fall of 1965. It is of course too early to make any final judgment as to its success. Some of its problems are unique to Philadelphia, but many others are certain to appear wherever the program gets under way.

While Get Set teachers are hired by the Board of Education, they are not required to satisfy normal certification or substitute requirements. As a result, the program has attracted many men and women who otherwise would not make their way into public school teaching. On the whole, these are people of *greater* general intelligence than their elementary school counterparts. A minority of course is attracted by the special hours possible, or by the relatively good pay. Probably a third of the staff is Negro and about a tenth male. But by and large these people demonstrate a greater interest in the problems of deprived children than would ordinary school teachers.

The 200 teachers were given a two-week training program which proved essentially chaotic and confusing. Within a few weeks, after having lost some of their original self-confidence, they were thrown out into the field. Their only support from then on came from the eight well-meaning but harassed supervisors who had to divide their limited hours among eight or nine different "schools" scattered throughout the city. Thus some teachers had as many as three different supervisors during their first five months. Basically, however, the supervisors, who are the only experienced pre-school personnel in the program, are without any power and perform the functions of messengers and clerks. All problems, both weighty and petty, must be cleared by the Director, who looks upon teachers and especially supervisors as threats to her prestige and power.

Get Set classes are held in churches, recreation centers,

and settlement houses. Lack of classroom space is typical in areas where, at present, many children are deprived of even kindergarten. (One of the ironies of the program is that Get Set offers pre-kindergarten services to three- and four-year-olds, whose five-year-old siblings must remain at home.) Perhaps the most shocking aspect of the program for most new teachers has been the physical state of the centers. While some are in lovely spacious churches, most are in dark, dingy rooms, with poor lighting, inadequate toilet facilities, no yards or gyms, etc. In a general effort to fill up the enrollment and spend the money provided by Congress, supervisors were instructed to put as many teachers into the centers and as many children into the rooms as possible. Where rooms were ample and airy they were divided in half with makeshift partitions. Some rooms are as small as 200 square feet, and sometimes two classrooms operate side-by-side in one room of 500 square feet, with only chairs or tables separating the two groups.

Despite the presence of elected Community Action Councils, the Get Set program is run in accordance with normal school procedures—from the top down—and is aimed towards eventually integrating the program into the school system rather than the community. The teachers were somewhat dismayed at first to learn that most of the mothers had heard that Get Set would be opening day care centers, thereby enabling the mothers to get jobs. They were disappointed that the hours we could provide were at maximum 9:00 A.M. to 3:00 P.M., and that for most children we could offer only morning or afternoon programs for only four days a week. Few were aware that a family-means test excluded children whose parents earned over $6,000. Naturally the criteria encourage cheating by both parents and teachers.

Despite these shortcomings, the demand in most communities was immediate and overwhelming. In the heart of the more crowded ghettos the centers were besieged. In marginal areas the response was slower and many centers remained half- or even quarter-full. The administrators wavered between relenting on income ceilings in order to increase enrollment and cracking down on the ceiling limitation in fear of exposure. Some children were admitted, expelled and readmitted as rules changed. Teachers and supervisors coped with contradictory rules that changed from day to day, always ready, if not willing, to take the blame for having made the wrong guess. Meanwhile they were bombarded with threats and slogans from higher-ups, such as "dedication can conquer all," and "if you don't like it, quit." If they suggested innovations, they were told that "we're part of the public school system, and it's not done that way." When they complained during the early months about the absence of blocks, dolls, paints, paper, etc., they read in *The Philadelphia Bulletin* that their director considered this a blessing: "I don't care about tables or chairs. I'm interested in dedicated teachers who want to work with children. Sometimes I wish I didn't have a whole lot of equipment. It can get in the way of teaching."

They had only to pick up *The Inquirer* to learn that the director, a Negro and a former elementary school principal, considered herself an expert on the parents whose children they were teaching: "If they didn't have children at home, they'd spend more time in the beer gardens than they would at work. I know this community. Personally I wish we could take children from these mothers all day long." At a Friday training session, the director informed the teachers that the Board of Education was impressed with the "special, unique and unusual quality" of their teamwork, which she attributed to an atmosphere in which every teacher felt free to punish any child, even if it weren't "her" child.

II

Demoralization aside, teachers were most confused when they tried to comprehend the purpose of the program and the specific means by which they were supposed to carry it out. Consultants from the federal program had talked during the early training period about the importance of visual, sensual, concrete materials, about free play and non-teacher-dominated activity, about the concept of "play as child's work," about activity appropriate to stages of maturity, and so forth. But a list of what was to be "taught and learned" was handed out and mimeoed sheets were periodically distributed listing techniques quite the opposite of those recommended by the consultants.

Friday training sessions were supposedly the asnwer to the lack of experience with which most teachers came into the program. But they soon deteriorated—starting late and ending by lunchtime. While children are expected to sit and learn for over five hours a day in our school system, it was generally conceded that only two to three hours could be asked of teachers. Pep talks and introductions from the director took up the first hour, sometimes extended by group singing or amateur talent shows. At one session, the director and her husband, who was in charge of cultural enrichment (which has so far meant a trip to see a worn-out Santa Claus at a downtown department store), played a violin-piano duet of "Danny Boy." A speech on the glories of marriage, including coy references to her own marriage, and reminders to share our adventures and talents with "our one big happy family," rounded out the director's concept of training.

Meanwhile, back in the classroom, the teachers and children carry on. The caliber of the teachers and supervisors and the present cautious enthusiasm of the community has produced a superficial impression of success in many centers: children seem happy, parents satisfied, and teachers feel some children have changed for the better. Since an organized program of research appears to be in the hands of thoroughly inexperienced personnel—without background in early childhood or research methodology—it may be a long time till we can properly evaluate the program. One type of "research" consisted of requiring every teacher to list one way in which each of her students had improved under her care in the course of one year. This study indicated that 99.99 per cent of the students "improved." In the absence of a controlled and overall evaluation, one is forced to conclude that almost everything is occurring somewhere and sometimes.

Most supervisors—insofar as they have an effect on the educational practices of their teachers—favor non-authoritarian classrooms with controlled but extensive free play in the general tradition of nursery school practice, with perhaps some extra emphasis on language development. On the whole, they agree with Martin Deutsch, the most eminent expert in this area, that these programs must aim at reinforcing whatever self-confidence and positive self-image deprived children bring to school. But at least one supervisor has advocated spankings for disobedience, water over the head for tantrums, and still more medieval techniques.

The teachers are baffled. Most are open to persuasion and eager and willing to learn at this stage. In a year at most they will have settled into patterns which will be hard to alter. They are skeptical about traditional nursery school values and techniques. They do not know why middle-class children should go to nursery school or why early childhood school experts have advocated the nondirective, freewheeling environment. They tend to equate a child-centered nursery school with baby-sitting, and a teacher-dominated room with "learning." They settle for gimmicks which will meet the outward appearances of "play," while in fact they really are teaching counting, "nice" words, better pronunciation, the alphabet, phonetics, colors, shapes, better manners, please and thank you. They are constantly on the look-out for a didactic message to impart to their charges.

"What have I done today to prepare these children for kindergarten or first grade," is the latent worry in the minds of many teachers. And while most have raised their own children in an environment of considerable freedom, they wonder if deprived children don't need greater discipline. Shouldn't "getting them ready" mean preparing them for the harsher aspects of reality? If they have to stand in line to go to the toilet, or say the Pledge of Allegiance in kindergarten, maybe we should introduce them to such practices now?

It is often the best intentions that lead teachers into such attitudes: they want to "do something" for these children and it is difficult for most teachers to avoid translating this desire into an imposing and manipulative classroom approach. They are restrained by the emphasis given in the training period on free play and by their sensitivity to the children's reactions to manipulation. Their manipulative techniques are generally nonpunitive, and, in contrast to many ghetto public school teachers, they demonstrate much warmth and affection for their charges.

On the other hand, they are encouraged into stricter and more dominating techniques by parents and community laymen, who feel that their children have been short-changed in ghetto schools in the past and who tend to equate harsh discipline and the three R's with Real Education. The parents are eager for their children to adapt, and willingly support strict discipline and high conformity. They have been told their children fail because they misbehave, don't listen, squirm and cause trouble. Since this is what the public school teachers have told them, this in turn is what they tell the Get-Set teachers, who hardly know what to believe and who are hardly in a position to make up for the lack of a consistent educational program.

III

From top to bottom the purpose of this pre-school program is almost never squarely faced. No one stops to examine the nature of the educational failure which has occurred in our poverty schools. Everyone agrees rather glibly that the children of poverty—and particularly of ghetto poverty—are performing badly in the lower grades and dropping out of high school at an alarming rate. And everyone notes that these children show their most symptomatic failure in the areas dealing with reading and the "language arts." While it is agreed that ghetto schools are incompetently staffed, under-equipped and overcrowded, most observers feel that something even more basic goes wrong with ghetto children. The notion is that they *come* to the schools with too many educational handicaps. In view of the fact that middle-class children often have one to three years more actual formal schooling by the time they are six, not to speak of the informal educational advantages of more prosperous, motivated families, it is natural that they should do much better in school. If poor children, the theory goes, could get some of this additional formal and informal "head start," they too would enter school better prepared for success.

But this is an insufficient and in fact misleading statement of the problem. It ignores the evidence that Harlem children enter school with less of a handicap than they have six years later—after the school system has "enriched" them. It ignores the fact that 25 per cent of the children in North Philadelphia schools at the end of first grade seem to be college-bound on the basis of achievement and IQ, compared to only 4 per cent at the end of sixth grade. It ignores the fact that most poor children do learn the mechanics of reading and compete more or less successfully until the fourth grade where they reach an early and final plateau. It ignores the fact that in the early years poor children are more conforming, quieter, and more amenable to school routines than children in schools with high academic achievement levels.

Each of these facts points to deep rifts within the general society in regard to the purposes of the War on Poverty. And the teaching methods that each individual teacher tends to fall back on are likely to reflect his feelings about social change in general.

IV

In their attitudes toward education, teachers fall into three roughly defined groups which we shall imprecisely label (1) public school traditionalists, (2) reformers, and (3) radicals.

Those whom we call public school traditionalists want to continue the standard patterns of dealing with poor children, but to start earlier. There is no question in these teachers' minds where the fault lies: with the poor themselves. Such an approach emphasizes discipline, rules, morality, authority, and the three R's. This outlook would have it that poor children cannot afford the luxury, too rampant among middle-class "brats" anyway, of a free and child-centered classroom. Only through a willingness to learn by old-fashioned methods (which worked so well for the poor in the past), will they develop the necessary know-how. Some hold these views with considerable sophistication. Others are merely ignorant of historical fact (the poor of the past rarely received an education beyond the sixth grade and were considered successfully schooled if they had mastered the mechanics of reading and arithmetic). They are ignorant as well of the nature of ghetto schools (which are *already* authoritarian and nineteenth-century oriented), and of the kind of problems that poor children produce in schools (severe discipline problems are not any more common in the very early grades than they are in middle-class schools). Many teachers naturally but incorrectly assume that lower-class parents are belligerent. In fact, while hostility and fear toward the school is common among the disadvantaged, they generally defer to the school on all matters of discipline, and back the school against their own children in times of conflict or trouble—in contrast to middle-class parents. (This attitude, however, is gradually changing.)

If the argument were to go on in the arena of theory, problems of fact would not worry us. But given the malice or ignorance of many of those who direct this program, the primitive physical conditions teachers are faced with, and a general downgrading of the need for serious training, the ideology of traditional school thinking may win out by default, as it has in our city grade schools. The more independent, sophisticated and forceful teachers who want to help children and are sensitive to their pains are rapidly driven out of the program or forced to make so many compromises that they soon bring only a small part of their original spirit to school.

In opposition to this trend are the "reformers" in the field. Unlike the traditionalists, they have few rigid answers, and hold many diverse viewpoints. But on the whole they accept the idea that "deprived" children lack a home environment conducive to learning, and that good pre-school experiences of the sort middle-class children naturally receive are necessary to academic success. They seek enthusiastically therefore to remake these less fortunate children into something more akin to the successful middle-class five-year-old.

The reformers claim that the greatest difference between deprived and middle-class children lies in their respective language abilities. The deprived child is said to be held back by inadequate or nonexistent experiences out of which language skill might develop, and an environment where little verbal or written interchange exists that can serve as an example or as a laboratory for the child.

Reformers usually favor an environment of security and pleasure in which children could identify new experiences with warm, happy associations. The new experiences fall into two classifications: (1) good and consistent examples of politeness, middle-class articulation, vocabulary, and neatness; and (2) a planned program to introduce the children through experiences, games, drills, etc. to various habits, manners, skills, and language arts already familiar to the middle-class child entering kindergarten. They will play house and, as they do so, learn how to set the table, say "please pass the butter," answer the door or phone politely, etc. They will take trips to the farm and play farm lotto so that they are familiar with words like "duck" and "sheep" (which appear so often in IQ tests and primary readers). As far as possible, the teacher is to present the children with an attractive picture of what life could be and is like in the larger world, as differentiated from what it is like in their own dismal communities.

The "radicals," while they share many reforming values, would rather remake the school than the child. They are likely to question whether lower-class children *really are* lacking in the rich experiential base for good language development or in long-run goals for success. They are likely to point instead to the special abilities which lower-class children have developed to cope with hardship and uncertainty. They argue that such strengths have in the past led to withdrawal in the face of certain threatening situations, such as school. The very strength of lower-class children has of necessity—the necessity to survive—produced resistance, apathy, fatalism, and superstition. Attitudes which help one survive in a community closed off from escape can be weaknesses in a world where intellectual growth and creativity are rewarded—though the rewards may be too far in the future for ghetto children to appreciate, while the pressures which cause resistance are immediate. The "culture of poverty," however, cannot be eliminated by pretending it doesn't exist for four hours a day—which is what setting the children a nice, middle-class example amounts to.

As a first step, ghetto schools must realize that change begins with self-acceptance. They must find ways to utilize the "culture of poverty" itself, to begin with the child's own experiences, good and bad, to involve his parents and his community, and to let each child's growth develop from his already functioning personality rather than cut off from it and rootless. Only a child who comes to school as himself is capable of going beyond mechanical learning skills. The child who shifts upon entering to a special personality, a shell divorced from all meaningful life experience, will leave both the shell and what he learns through it at the door when he goes out again.

Even with the best of intentions, a school that eliminates all that is familiar to a young child will be perceived by him as a threat to his self-esteem and identity. Radical teachers argue that we must find ways of teaching these youngsters based on their own backgrounds, families, language abilities, and experiences. Further, these circumstances must be accepted without the intrusion of moral judgment. If the child is truly given a chance to grow in terms of his own awareness, he will eventually be able to decide for himself what kind of world he wants to live in and what kind of person he wants to become.

V

Education alone will not resolve the issues at stake in the War on Poverty. And as long as the public permits widespread discrimination in employment, housing, and public services, it is not likely to spend the money to equalize educational opportunity. Under such circumstances the poor will continue to receive much of their more creative education from informal educational institutions that arise within the ghetto and that will arise tomorrow in new forms—through the civil rights movement, community organization, political movements, etc. But since much education does take place, for good or ill, within the formal framework of our publicly-supported schools, and many of tomorrow's choices will be determined by the way the schools educate, the alternative methods of pre-school education pose a critical choice. The ideals of childhood education can be translated for lower-class children with the emphasis on democratic purposes and respect for the child's integrity, or they can become tools to mold the poor but essentially keep them in their place. Education can accept society's need to reform itself or simply pretend to reform the child. It will never be argued so crudely, but these are the issues at stake. And, ironically, if those in control fail to learn anything, or if we fail to produce the kind of pressure that will force them into new paths of educational effort, the addition of two vulnerable years to the present school tenure may simply produce an exaggeration of the benumbing and depressive effect that ghetto schools are already having. Under such circumstances the highly vaunted Head Start will only be a head start into a dead end.

1966

Morality and Tactics in Community Organizing

PAUL BULLOCK*

Though many of the young and idealistic radicals of this generation may be convinced that "participatory democracy" is a revolutionary concept of their own making, a re-reading of Saul Alinsky's *Reveille for Radicals* will remind us that the essential idea has been around for at least a quarter of a century. Alinsky's work, first published in 1945, is replete with detailed descriptions of the varied ways by which a People's Organization can be built, offering as its most concrete example the Back of the Yards Neighborhood Council, organized in Chicago in 1939. The history of this movement in the intervening period is sobering and instructive: the Back of the Yards community is today a bastion of conformity and segregation.

In 1967, almost every urban area where radical and cultural minorities are concentrated contains at least one organization which purports to represent the needs of the traditionally unrepresented poor. Organizers of such groups fall roughly into four categories: (1) Alinsky and his staff of professionals, through the Chicago-based Industrial Areas Foundation; (2) civil rights organizations, predominantly Negro; (3) New Left

* The author is grateful to Mr. Wycliffe Mutsune for research assistance in the preparation of this article.

organizations, predominantly white; and (4) certain labor unions, working independently or in conjunction with other groups. Socially conscious unions such as the UAW and the Packinghouse Workers, and some staff members of the AFL-CIO's Industrial Union Department, are actively promoting the formation of "community unions." Jack Conway and Woodrow Ginsburg of the IUD have suggested that a community union "could merge traditional trade union functions with modern community center functions. For example, a community union could bring tenants together to bargain collectively with slumlords."[1] Incipient forms of community unionism have already appeared in Chicago, Los Angeles, and Newark.

The sources of the current movement for community organizing are thus diverse. Alinsky is a professional, coldly realistic in his approach to tactics, fascinated by power, temperamentally suited to the public role of "trouble-maker," contemptuous of amateurish do-gooders. Civil Rights groups are uncertain and uneasy in their new roles as urban organizers, seeking with limited success to move from the task of organizing in the rural or small-town South to the immensely complex arena of the sprawling big-city ghettos of the North. The New Leftists, many of them Anglo-Saxon youngsters from middle-class family backgrounds, bring with them an uncompromising rejection of the prevailing value system but often very little in the form of a definable program. The unions have a cadre of experienced organizers, but again the techniques of organizing in a factory are only partially applicable to a wider community, and organized labor itself is ambivalent because it is at least partly within the "Establishment."

The common thread which binds the groups together philosophically is a belief in democracy and in the capacity of rela-

[1] "Extension of Collective Bargaining to New Fields," *Proceedings of the 19th Annual Winter Meeting,* Industrial Relations Research Association, December 28–29, 1966, p. 308.

tively uneducated people to represent their own interests effectively. This implies a freedom of choice, a freedom from manipulation. The paradox faced by community organizers is, however, that the achievement of their goal—a functioning and independent organization—seems to require at least a measure of conscious manipulation of motivations and attitudes. Alinsky is explicit on the point that organizers always talk and act in terms of the interests and experience of those being organized. A judgment must be made as to the motivations of people in the community and of "leaders" whose decisions may influence the success of organizing; and in turn this judgment becomes the basis for trying to channel their actions.[2]

Alinsky is impatient with his younger and more impulsive contemporaries in the field of community organization. "It requires a certain degree of sophistication in terms of tactics to organize a community and some of the younger civil-rights leaders don't have it. It's like putting kids into a lion's cage. . . . The problem with those kids is that they always want the third act—the resolution, the big drama. They want to skip the first act, the second act, the tediousness, the listening. Actually you do more organizing with your ears than with your tongue."[3]

The professional approach to organizing demands a heavy investment of time and personnel in the process of listening to grievances. The organizer must not impose his own preconceptions upon the community; his role is initially passive, focused on an objective ascertainment of the feelings, institutions, and indigenous leadership in the area. Once having acquired this knowledge, he must evaluate it in terms of how best to build an organization out of the raw material already present in the community. He moves from passive listening to

[2] "The Professional Radical: Conversations with Saul Alinsky" (Part I), *Harper's*, June 1965, p. 45. See also *Reveille for Radicals, passim*. (See footnote 4.)

[3] "A Professional Radical Moves in on Rochester: Conversation with Saul Alinsky" (Part II), *Harper's* July 1965, p. 56.

active work with that material, using his experience and organizational sophistication to draw residents into the process of organizing together. As local participation and leadership increase, the organizer's function again recedes into passivity and finally withdrawal.

Presumably the organizer has fulfilled his function: a community organization has been built. But how does one define a "community organization" in practical terms? How much of a given community must be involved before it is possible to say that the "community" has achieved representation? Is a community organization genuinely independent and indigenous when a major part of its funding comes from outside the community, whether from a foundation, a church group, or government? How is it possible to guarantee that the organization's executive board is responsive primarily to the needs of the total community and not merely to its own individual or collective interests? Can uneducated and unsophisticated people administer a mass organization so as to avoid the omnipresent traps set by politicians, bureaucrats, and other members of the "Establishment"?

Alinsky himself raised the question of organizational representativeness in *Reveille for Radicals,* and his answer further emphasizes the complexity of the issue. A five per cent participation in any community, he then said, "is a tremendous democratic phenomenon."[4] If any organization really represents only a small minority, in a direct sense, the possibilities of *mis*representation are numerous indeed. The initial listening process implies a conscious or accidental selection of informants; the people who are most verbal about "problems" are by that very fact unrepresentative of a community which is not oriented to frank discussion in the presence of outsiders. Fur-

[4] *Reveille for Radicals.* Chicago: University of Chicago Press, 1945, p. 201. Obviously neither Alinsky nor any other organizer will adhere closely to a quantitative standard, but the point is simply that no organization directly represents more than a relatively small minority of the community.

thermore, communities are rarely homogeneous, even though they may be segregated. Attitudes and interests vary sharply from one person to another, in low-income Negro areas as well as in the less alienated parts of the city.

The experience of organizing the Watts Labor Community Action Committee, in Los Angeles, is revealing. Promoted in early 1965 by a combination of Watts area residents, union representatives, and UCLA staff, the organization was to be constructed around a nucleus of union members living in the Watts area. The organizational experience and leadership potential of union members would presumably offer a strong base for organizing. But one factor that soon became evident as the work proceeded was that in an area like Watts active union members are an "elite." As persons with steady work, cars, property of their own, and insurance policies, their attitudes and motives often diverged from those of the self-ordained ministers, ambitious local "politicians," and those with various personal gimmicks who were mixed in among the poor people attracted to the meetings.

Led by a dynamic and aggressive UAW shop steward, a long-time resident of Watts, the organization achieved some public recognition and community status in 1966, when it was active in an apparently successful drive to secure a new county hospital in the area. When substantial federal funding for a summertime youth program in Watts became available in midyear, WLCAC was selected to administer it. The resulting program, later renewed and expanded and still in operation, has received praise even from such respectable sources as the *Los Angeles Times,* usually not known as a friend of organized labor. The committee's activities, highly meritorious in most respects, have therefore been well within the conventional framework of public policy, and its role has been primarily that of a program administrator and not an abrasive critic of institutions.

The experience of WLCAC reflects both the potentialities

and the limitations inherent in community organizing. Any community organizer confronts the dilemma that the people of the area expect visible results within the reasonably near future, or they will see little point in supporting the organization. Yet such results can be obtained, as a rule, only by working within the "system," even though some sort of direct action (demonstrations, boycotts, etc.) may be involved. The opponents of the system, therefore, are confounded by the fact that if the Establishment produces results satisfactory to the residents, it merely increases its strength in the community —while if no results are forthcoming, the organization will probably die.

The problem of finances similarly complicates the task of an organizer. Poor communities may sometimes lack the economic base to support organizations of their own, with paid staff. Hence they must rely upon volunteers or seek outside funding. Though Alinsky has publicly set down a general rule (perhaps not to be taken literally) that the organizations he promotes should become self-supporting after three years, he found it necessary to abandon the rule in the case of The Woodlawn Organization in Chicago, considered to be his outstanding achievement. TWO has subsequently sought and obtained government contracts to administer training programs and so forth. It is difficult to run an organization on a strictly volunteer basis and without a reliable source of funding. Yet when paid staff positions are created, the internal competition among candidates may become bitter and intense. Poor people are not immune from the selfishness and careerism which pervades our society; indeed, the daily struggle for survival leaves little room for any other concern.

These dilemmas are particularly acute for the idealistic and youthful radical organizer. Alinsky, however, does not glorify or romanticize the poor: "Too often I've seen the have-nots turn into haves and become just as crummy as the haves they used to envy. Some of the fruit ranchers in California steam around in Cadillacs and treat the Mexican-American field hands like vermin. Know who those bastards are? They're the characters who rode West in Steinbeck's trucks, in *The Grapes of Wrath*."[5]

The youngsters are more likely to enter the community with preconceived idealistic notions, usually commendable in themselves but often unrelated to the realities of organizing in a slum ghetto. Certainly they cannot be satisfied when the result of their efforts is reflected only in a greater enlistment of Americans into the detested middle class. Yet the psychology of the ghetto itself militates against a too ambitious and large-scale perspective in community organizing. The ghetto resident, in the poorest and most alienated category, is the product of a cruel environment, and this hardly increases his patience and forbearance. Essentially he is interested in only one thing— escaping from poverty. He is not at all concerned about a mass redistribution of income, long-run social revolution, or any other concern of the young radical. He has no objections to being "corrupted" by money; quite the contrary, he yearns for the opportunity.

Ghetto life breeds a deep cynicism about human motivation; to many a ghetto resident, all life is a "hustle," and everyone has his own "bag." The world is divided between the "takers" and the "taken," and one purpose of living is to stay in the former and out of the latter category. When strangers come into the community, spouting unfamiliar philosophies and claiming to be altruistic in motivation, they will be eyed with extra suspicion. The first assumption is that the stranger is motivated in the usual way: he is probably a policeman, a bill collector, a researcher, a dope peddler, a welfare investigator, a salesman, or a reporter. Without necessarily abandoning this suspicion completely, the ghetto resident may next assume that the newcomer is a "patsy" who is exploitable as a source of occasional or frequent loans, influence with probation officers,

[5] "Conversations" (Part II), *op. cit.*, p. 56.

training allowances, and so forth. Only after a long period of time, and after the newcomer has been tested in many ways and found reliable, will the basis emerge for a genuine rapport and trust.

Above all else, the ghetto resident is pragmatic. The fight for basic survival makes him realistically skeptical about rhetoric and promises, however appealing they may seem in various ways. Despite the obvious emotional strength of "black nationalism," a proposal by SNCC for incorporation of the Watts area into a separate city has never aroused broad support. The objection of Watts residents is directly to the point: "How can a poor community like this finance a city government of its own?" The history of Negro political activity is also instructive. Despite the status of Negroes as the most exploited group within the economy, and theoretically a likely target for Communist appeals, the Communist party has had remarkably little success in enlisting recruits or sympathizers from the Negro community.

The issues with which a community organization will concern itself normally fall into the practical, short-run, bread-and-butter category which some New Leftists would condemn as "reformist," "compromise," "half-measures," "liberal palliatives": school lunches, tutorial projects, crossing guards, urban renewal, community improvement, training programs, employment, and so on. From his own viewpoint, of course, the New Leftist is wholly correct: none of these measures fundamentally alters the prevailing social system. Each one, in fact, fits easily within, even as it slightly modifies, the framework of American capitalism. Yet the best a community organizer can expect, usually, is to help move the residents from the traditional stance of apathy and preoccupation with personal survival to a concern with those issues which, with good planning and some luck, can be resolved with tangible benefit to the entire community. Most ghetto residents do not trust the "revolutionary" any more than do the more affluent members of society.

Some of the young radicals, especially those who have had experience in attempting to organize urban ghettos, are aware of these realities. Tom Hayden, who has organized in Newark, describes his aims as "rent control, play streets, apartment repairs, higher welfare payments, jobs."[6] Others may be so blinded by their internal emotional conflicts that they respond more to their own needs than to the interests of the community. They identify themselves with those who share neither power nor affluence within American society, but often find themselves in the anomalous position of belonging by background to the "exploiting" rather than the "exploited" class. They feel oppressed and frustrated, but can usually express these feelings only in behalf of other groups—Negroes, farm workers, welfare recipients. Their "revolutionary" experience is mainly a vicarious one, seen through the eyes of the actually exploited. Most have tasted the presumed joys and advantages of middle-class life and now consciously reject them; their revolution is essentially a personal one, manifested most clearly in the material self-denial which they not only accept but exalt. Needless to say, their ascetic philosophy is not shared by the poor.

No wonder, then, that the youngsters welcome Paul Goodman's description of American education as "mere exploitation."[7] In revolting against the college bureaucracies, they assert their own feelings and values; if they achieve power on the campus, they achieve it presumably to advance their own ideals. Their "revolutionary" experience is no longer vicarious, and there is no danger, as there always is in community organizing, that the genuinely deprived will reject their radical values.

Because most of these young organizers are intellectuals, their belief in participatory democracy coexists uneasily with an elitist strain. They strongly disapprove of popular opinion

---

[6] Quoted in "The New Radicals," *Time*, April 28, 1967, p. 27.
[7] Paul Goodman, "Berkeley in February," *Dissent*, Spring 1965, p. 162.

and mass rule in the prevailing forms. What the New Left appears to espouse is "participatory democracy" for certain defined groups which either share its values or engage its sympathy. At times, this becomes analogous to a civil libertarianism which defends only the rights of left-wingers. The young radicals would answer that the more affluent communities are already organized, and they would merely extend that power to the poor. While this is partly true, nevertheless the principle they advocate is a two-edged sword. They fail to recognize, in addition, that the basic ambitions of the poor and the rich are similar; the communities differ only in the extent to which those ambitions can be realized.

The New Leftists thus make ambivalent organizers because they suspect that successful organizations develop bureaucracies of their own and tend to join the "Establishment"— that vast complex of institutions, including most labor unions, college administrations, governmental programs, corporations, and the military services, which establish rules designed to protect their institutional interests and exploit those outside their framework. Furthermore, the quasi-anarchism of the New Left organizers, added to the diversity of interests within the community, makes it difficult for them to develop concrete affirmative programs in ways that can be related to the exercise of power. Alinsky has noted the importance of having any identifiable enemy (such as Bull Connor in Alabama and urban renewal in Chicago's Woodlawn area) as a stimulus to organization; apparently people will organize more quickly to repel the threats or defeat the plans of others than to advance their own spontaneous ideas and proposals. The reason, in part, is that the diversity of interests and personalities is reflected more readily on the "positive" than on the "negative" side. Thus it is easier to organize in Woodlawn, where there appeared to be a common enemy in the University of Chicago, than in Watts, where the enemy is more amorphous and harder to define.

The young New Leftists are valuable in their willingness to unsettle the more comfortable bureaucrats and to challenge the pretenses of the traditional "leaders," including many of the liberals. They are inclined, however, to develop a new set of clichés and stereotypes ("middle class," "Establishment," "participatory democracy") which can only obscure the complexity of the issues involved in organizing poor communities and even reduce the effectiveness of those intent upon building viable organizations. Yet the effort to organize previously unorganized (and supposedly unorganizable) communities has substantial merit in and of itself—even if it achieves only limited goals within the framework of a considerably less-than-perfect society. Thus, the sit-down strikes of the 1930's failed to usher in a brand-new social system; indeed, they resulted in the creation of labor organizations which, in the view of some New Leftists, have become part of the Establishment. Nevertheless, it would be difficult to sustain the argument that the unions have not been of tangible benefit to groups which were previously unrepresented within the industrial structure. No one can be sure that sometime in the future, The Woodlawn Organization in Chicago will not go the way of the Back of the Yards movement or that the striking farm workers in Delano, California, will not concentrate on bettering their own economic and social status instead of focusing on the development of a new society. For the moment, it may be enough to assure that they have some freedom of choice, and that they are not simply the victims of manipulation.

The unpleasant truth is that many of the potential "indigenous" organizers seek mainly to smooth their own path to what the radicals might define as middle-class status. It is precisely this kind of person, in fact, who is most likely to gravitate to leadership positions in any new organization, because he is the one most sophisticated about the available opportunities for advancement and most motivated to pursue them. The complex task of the outsider who wishes to help build an effective community organization is to assure, as much as possible, that the leaders coincidentally serve the broader interests of their community in the process of advancing their much narrower and more personal aims. This requires a certain Alinsky-like toughness, combined with a genuine commitment to both the desirability and the feasibility of creating a community-based organization. The ousider, of course, can usefully provide technical knowledge and political support, but he must remain sensitive to the delicacy of his relationship with the community.

In sum, the poor should be free from the tyranny of the bureaucrats and the dogmatic militants alike. They should be manipulated neither to serve capitalism nor to destroy it. Their rights as individual human beings, with a diversity of values and personalities, should take precedence over the administrative demands of the bureaucracy *and* the emotional or ideological needs of the community organizers. One may hope that "the poor don't want to be middle-class," but clearly a great many of them will settle for a secure job and a comfortable house in the suburbs; and after all, don't they have the *right* to choose that option, however irritating it may be to both conservative suburbanites and leftist militants?

Hopefully, in the course of their rise to higher economic levels, their own cultural and personal values will permeate the larger society and generate changes for the better. Perhaps their group identity will be sufficiently preserved that they remain at least partly resistant to the temptations of conventional middle-class living. Nothing can be judged certain or predictable in this process. The critics of capitalism may or may not take comfort from the fact that social revolutions often occur at the "wrong" place and the "wrong" time, for the "wrong" reasons. Meanwhile, we should keep striving for the less ambitious victories of the moment.

1967

The Politics of Housing

CHESTER W. HARTMAN

There is a great deal of ferment in the housing field at present, but not much action. Rhetoric has far outrun (and in a sense can be said to divert attention from) any corresponding commitment to allocate resources. The housing problem is shaking down to an easily identifiable form, following resolution of the anomalies caused by the Depression and War. Those with adequate income by and large are getting adequate housing, and the private sector, strategically assisted by the government —notably via FHA and VA mortgage insurance and urban renewal—works moderately well to satisfy the housing needs of middle- and upper-income groups. The vestigial housing problem, although by no means trivial—at a minimum, some twelve million U.S. families are living below minimum standards—is composed of specific "types": families and individuals who lack and have little hope of earning adequate income; non-white minorities (with and without adequate income); the elderly; rural slum dwellers; and the vague catchall category, "multi-problem families." What is now absolutely clear to all but the most resistant is that the vast majority of these twelve million families are not going to secure decent housing through the processes of "normal" mobility, and that existing government programs to aid this sector of the population are hopelessly inadequate to the task, qualitatively as well as quantitatively.

At the present we are being bombarded with new ideas, some good, some not so good, some really innovative, some merely rehashes of old proposals. Model Cities, rent supplements, instant rehabilitation, "turnkey," Percy Plan, Kennedy Plan, Ribicoff Plan are but a few of the terms flying thick and fast over conference tables and speaker's platforms. But it is still a time of rhetoric, not of results, nor even of realistic plan-making. The issue is primarily one of money. The costs of achieving the National Housing Goal, established nearly twenty years ago ("a decent home and a suitable living environment for every American family") are big, and as a nation we just don't seem to want to spend big money these days for anything but killing Vietnamese. We don't even have any good estimates on the costs of attaining this goal (in part due to the vagueness of its definition). But based on 1960 Census data on the incomes of families presently living in substandard housing and using 1959 Bureau of Labor Statistics figures on the costs of obtaining "modest but decent" housing in metropolitan areas, a program of housing subsidization for all families in the U.S. who cannot afford decent housing on the private market might cost an additional $7–8 billion a year. (This figure would be somewhat higher if housing subsidies were also to be made available to reduce housing costs for families living in standard housing who are devoting an excessive proportion of their income to rent.) This looks awfully large when compared with present expenditures for housing the poor (less than $400 million annually, plus whatever portion of welfare payments is used—generally speaking, wastefully—for housing), but it represents only about 1 per cent of the nation's GNP and less than four months of warfare in Southeast Asia. Needless to say, there is no immediate prospect of having anywhere near the amount of money required to implement current proposals, except on a token or pilot-project scale. This is the basic political fact which must underlie any discussion of housing.

But even if the problem of resource allocation could be solved, there would still be an imposing array of fundamental problems, conflicts, and decisions to be faced. It is these areas and the ways in which they are dealt with under existing and proposed programs that form the hub of this essay.

Race: Any housing program must face the fundamental fact that the overwhelming majority of white Americans are afraid of and do not want to live anywhere near non-white Americans, and that at least a substantial portion of the non-white population, if not the majority, does not consider integration into white America (at least on the majority's terms) a very high priority. This situation can only intensify as non-whites increasingly experience and suffer the effects of second-class citizenship, and as resentment of and insurrection against this status takes ever more hostile and violent forms. It seems quite probable that we have passed the point where massive integration of the races can be an element of a housing program that will improve the lot of the vast majority of slum dwellers, black as well as white, in a relatively short time span (say, within five to ten years). Existing residential patterns are too firmly fixed, the population shifts and disruptions required would be too massive, and popular resistance to any program of this nature would be staggering. In the December 17, 1966, *New Republic,* Frances Piven and Richard Cloward argue that stress on racial integration as a necessary component of housing programs has drained support for these programs; as a result of a policy of "either integrated housing or no housing," those most in need of better shelter have been denied the benefits of potentially helpful programs, in effect paying the price for goals and ideals which are less important to the poor than they are to the reformers. What has undoubtedly been true in the past for relatively meager programs (*viz,* Congressional curtailment of the rent supplement program, and local opposition to public housing projects) will *a fortiori* be true of programs of the magnitude that have recently been suggested by more radical and impatient reformers. If, instead of producing 30,000 units of low-rent public housing annually, we embark on a program which will provide new or rehabilitated housing for a minimum of 800,000 low-income families each year, the specter of massive racial shifts would create insurmountable problems with regard to financial appropriations and site selection.

One need only look at current government low-rent housing programs to gain insight into the future. The Federal government and many local authorities are now insisting on an end to lily-white public housing projects. In combination with more systematic forces (Negroes apply to public housing in disproportionate numbers because of lower incomes and a narrower range of housing choice), this policy is turning public housing into an all-Negro program, and not too gradually at that. Nationally, 53 per cent of all families in public housing are non-white (an increase from 43 per cent in 1954), and in many cities there are virtually no white families living in housing projects. As projects lose their all-white character, the number of white applications decreases and white families move out of the projects in increasing numbers, frequently to worse and/or higher-priced—but "safe"—housing. As Negro families apply in ever larger numbers (in Boston, where 26 per cent of public housing families are Negro, over half of all applications are now coming from non-white families) and as more and more projects "tip"—a process which is surely irreversible—the program will become in fact a Negro institution.

While the Department of Housing and Urban Development is trying to induce localities, albeit with much difficulty, to move away from the project approach to public housing (in order to increase the possibility of racial integration, as well as for other reasons of a social and aesthetic nature), these newer forms of publicly subsidized housing (leasing of private units, public rehabilitation of substandard units, joint public-private developments) are meeting a great deal of local resistance, in no small part due to the possibility of invasion of "good" neighborhoods by "problem" (i.e. Negro) families. Depressing as it may be to white liberals, the truth must be faced: to insist upon racial integration as a *sine qua non* of housing improvement is to consign millions of American families, white and black, to their present slum conditions for years to come. This is not to say that a housing program must proceed on a strictly segregated basis: ample opportunity and protection must be provided for those minority-group families who value integrated living highly and are willing to endure the hardships this course may entail. But if we persist in the illusion that improvement of urban living conditions can and must be accompanied by racial integration, ten years from now we will discover that we have not progressed very far at all in solving the nation's slum problems, just as there has been but little improvement in the past ten years.

Among the newer programs and ideas, the Model Cities Program seems to have accepted this argument, at least implicitly. The program rejected a true "model city" approach that had been initially proposed (attempting, on a pilot project basis, to provide solutions to all urban problems in four or five prototypical cities) in favor of a "model neighborhood" approach—providing these same solutions for an area of the city housing no more than 15,000 persons (or 10 per cent of the population in the case of large cities). While this shift was made in part to permit existing funds to go farther in political terms (more cities would get something from the program, thereby increasing its potential support), it also had the effect of allowing cities to compartmentalize the race issue. Most large cities chose one of the worst Negro slums as their model city target area, and given the program's general mandate—to improve conditions *in* the demonstration area *for* the area's residents—the program in effect has become a "gild the ghetto" program (save in those smaller cities where poor white neighborhoods were chosen as target areas and in the one or two larger cities where a principal objective of the program was to provide open housing opportunities for the area's Negro residents). Not that this critical feature of the Model Cities program has been universally lamented: in fact the more progressive newcomers to the upper echelons of the HUD hierarchy see it as a sound development. More help will go to those most in need of government assistance, and if integration is ever to come about it will be only after the ghetto and its residents have developed their own economic and political strengths.

Social and Economic Integration: Related to the problem of racial integration is the question of social-class integration, or heterogeneity vs. homogeneity. A good deal of overlap exists here, because Negroes tend in fact to have lower incomes and occupational and educational attainments than whites, and also because most whites tend to see most Negroes as lower-class, regardless of objective economic and social indices. But the problem is distinct from the racial problem: it comes up as an issue among white families of different social classes and among Negro families of different social classes; and at least among some segments of the population, educational, occupational, and financial attainment are sufficient to erase most barriers imposed by race. In policy terms, the issue comes down to this: should housing subsidies require the grouping of low-income families together, apart from unsubsidized, higher-income families, or should programs be developed which permit or require mixture of subsidized low-income families with families of higher income who do not receive a housing subsidy (or at least the same kind of subsidy, since in our peculiar folk logic such things as FHA insurance and urban renewal land write-downs for middle- and upper-income housing are not regarded as subsidies). The arguments for and against "mixing" are fairly simple, although they seem to be based more on assumption and ideology than on concrete evidence. It is held by some that the grouping of low-income families creates stigma and reinforces deviant or pathological living patterns, whereas mixing low-income families together with families of higher socioeconomic status (usually conceived of in terms of a marked disproportion, with the subsidized families representing 10–30 per cent of the total) will offer incentive, status, and alternative (and assumedly more desirable) models for behavior. Generally, the heterogeneity argument is also buttressed by terms such as "more democratic," although why this one manifestation of inequality is chosen as a symbol of non-democracy in a society with such wide income disparities and such unwarranted poverty is unclear. Arguments against social and economic integration range from those of the economic conservative worried about the effects on incentive of having persons of different incomes, paying different rents, living in essentially identical quarters, to those of the sociologist, concerned that differences in life-style, child-rearing patterns and the like will in fact exacerbate interclass tensions and conflict rather than create mutual understanding and a "rub-off" effect. There is also a large group to whom such thinking represents a form of cultural imperialism and an attempt to destroy valuable forms of unity and vitality among low-income groups.

Most of the newer forms of public housing, as well as the new rent supplement program, represent an attempt to eliminate the worst forms of isolation and stigmatization that have characterized traditional public housing projects. The so-called "scatter-site" type of development focuses on the problem of scale: projects should be small, located in viable neighborhoods, and designed so as to blend with existing buildings. Rehabilitation programs developed by local housing authorities rely on purchase and remodeling of substandard private buildings and offer public housing that is architecturally no different from housing that remains in the private sector. The so-called "turnkey" approach to public housing, in which site development and construction is done by private developers, who then sell the completed project to the local housing authority, also represents an attempt to avoid institutional design. This reliance on the private construction industry is purported to offer significant cost savings, too, but claims to this effect are at present of dubious validity, and if true, may derive from use of non-union labor paid at less than union scale—a "saving" that may not be in the public interest. The leased public housing program, under which individual privately owned units, usually in multi-family buildings, are leased by the housing authority at market rents and then subleased to public housing tenants at reduced rents, is one of the most far-reaching attempts to blur the public-private distinction. The buildings are privately owned and managed, and restriction on the number of public housing tenants in any one structure makes it likely that there will be some form of economic and social mix (although this depends largely on the character of neighborhoods in which the housing authority leases its units). And nascent projects which combine public and private sponsorship of developments with mixed middle- and low-income occupancy also carry the integration idea to an extreme form, relegating the public presence to the background, so as to create no invidious distinction between the subsidized and the unsubsidized. Finally, the rent supplement program carries this idea one step further in bypassing the housing authority altogether as agent for choosing apartments and tenants: in this program the private developer directly contracts with the Federal Housing Administration to accept a certain number of low-income tenants, and in return receives the difference between the rent established for the low-income family (25 per cent of family income) and the market rent for the unit.

A close look at the operations of these new programs provides some insight as to how we can expect the issue of heterogeneity vs. homogeneity to develop in the future. In virtually all cities where these newer programs have been tried, the amount of meaningful social and economic integration has been minimal, in some cases non-existent. In brief, where the private sector has been drawn into the public housing program and where mixing has occurred, the utmost care has been taken in tenant selection to choose only the most "worthy," midde-class representatives of the poor: intact, small families at the upper levels of the public housing income range, usually white, employed, and educated, with no suggestion of social problems which might cause conflict and resentment among their neighbors who "pay their own way." These programs attempt to skim the cream off the top of the public housing population and in effect provide no information (except, by inference, negative information) about the impact of and prospects for this kind of mixing. (An ancillary effect, of course, is that by drawing these families away from the housing projects, the remaining public housing population becomes all the more atypical and deviant from the rest of society.) The average family simply is not inclined to live near low-income families which exhibit any "deviant" attributes, such as having no male head of household, having too many children, living on welfare, causing or demonstrating any of a variety of social problems. Sensing that landlords—particularly in the sellers' market that presently exists in the housing field—will not participate in a public program that risks having to rent to lower-class tenants, and that political pressures from unsubsidized families of higher income will lead to extraordinary controversy, administrators of these newer public housing programs have taken the path of least resistance and have avoided any meaningful socioeconomic integration. An inescapable conclusion seems to be that, desirable as some amount of heterogeneity may be (and whether and in what ways this may be true is still not absolutely clear), political pressures, both overt and internalized, will be such that local administrators will avoid difficulties wherever possible.

The only way in which low-income families—at least those who wish to do so—will be able to integrate themselves successfully with families of higher socioeconomic status is through a type of program that has not yet been developed: i.e., through creation of sovereign consumers by widespread use of rent or income supplements. The income subsidization approach does not seem feasible at present. Even if we were to achieve a guaranteed annual income (or some version thereof through a negative income tax), the levels presently being discussed would be totally inadequate to secure decent housing at present market rents. The income floors being discussed are on the order of $3100 for a family of four; yet, using the 20–25 per cent rent/income ratio yardstick, decent housing costs at least twice that much in urban areas. (The Bureau of Labor Statistics' 1959 model budget for a family of four in Boston required $6100, over $1200 of which went for rent, in order to achieve a "modest but decent" standard of living; and that figure has undoubtedly risen in eight years.) A direct and adequate subsidy of the housing expenditures of poor families, through a device such as rental certificates, available for new or rehabilitated standard housing, might permit social and economic heterogeneity, providing mechanisms existed to ensure non-discrimination against certificate holders by private landlords. Such controls over landlords and developers might be secured via incentives to participate in the program in the form of low-interest construction and rehabilitation financing or assistance in site acquisition, in exchange for which the private developer would agree to accept as tenants a certain percentage of certificate holders on a first come, first served basis. The present rent supplement program bears some similarities to this suggested program, but has several critical features (apart from its recent Congressional curtailment) which make it unlikely to produce any meaningful residential mixing. Although the program is tied to the government-assisted market-rate 221(d)(3) program (for moderate-income families), there is no corollary requirement that developers who build with the aid of these government-assisted loans also participate in the rent supplement program. Inclusion of low-income families is at the option of the private developer, and, in order to induce participation, private developers are given complete discretion in tenant selection, a policy which insures that only the "cream" of the poor will get in. Furthermore, FHA has set no upper limits on the number of rent supplement families which may be included in any one project, with the result that many of these projects (the majority of the first batch to be approved) are using rent supplements for 100 per cent of their units, thus creating low-income concentrations similar to those in public housing projects.

Clearly, existing programs are avoiding the issue of economic and social integration (even though there is a nominal attempt in this direction). Current efforts at least make clear the fact that unless low-income families have the effective buying power and concomitant freedom of choice of their more affluent brethren, and unless ways can be found to guarantee that private landlords will in fact treat subsidized tenants in a non-discriminatory way, government housing programs will produce no significant amount of meaningful heterogeneity. A massive program of rent certificates tied to an equally massive program of low-interest development loans will of course meet with substantial political resistance from those who recognize and oppose this potential for social and economic mix; but should such a program be passed, it is fairly automatic and self-sufficient in operation and will not meet the repeated political pressures and battles that the local public authority must face each time it wants to move ahead with a new project.

Public vs. Private: One of the most salient political issues currently under discussion in the field of housing and urban development is the question of private sector vs. public sector: to what extent and in what ways can and will the private building industry meet the pressing housing needs of the country's low-income families? While it is indisputable that the realities of land and construction costs have made and will continue to make it impossible for the private sector, unaided, to meet the housing needs of this segment of the population, it is also becoming quite evident that provision of low-rent housing through the public sector has a great many fundamental and inherent defects. It would be fruitless to go into any great detail about the failures of the public housing program. The litany of social, aesthetic, and administrative defects is already widely known and acknowledged. Many of the program's shortcomings might be effectively remedied through some of the newer forms of public housing described earlier. But it seems virtually impossible for the program to live down the reputation it has acquired over three decades. The very words "public housing" are anathema to too many people, including the program's clientele; the words evoke images of massive, ugly projects, located in the most undesirable parts of the city, teeming with problem families, governed by harsh and arbitrary regulations. The legacy of thirty years of failure is that people are simply turned off to the notion of public housing, no matter how creative and subtle the form in which the public subsidy comes wrapped.

Similarly, we are beginning to recognize the failings of the administrative mechanism through which low-rent housing has traditionally been supplied to the city. Many housing experts are questioning the efficacy (and even the good intentions) of the local public housing authority. We are beginning to see that many of our cherished "good government" institutions (like draft boards, welfare boards, housing authorities), putatively governed by disinterested civic types, above politics, with only the public interest at heart, in fact consist of a quite biased segment of the population, with their own values, class interests and preconceptions—all of which render them quite unrepresentative of (and possibly unsympathetic to) the clientele and segment of population served by these programs. In short, local public housing authorities (with very few exceptions) have not been aggressive advocates of a vastly expanded and improved low-rent housing program, have not been true spokesmen for the interests of persons in need of better housing. Nor should we have expected this: although systematic data are not available as of this writing (the author is currently making a survey of the local housing authority commissioners), it is generally known that local housing authorities are governed by boards that are overwhelmingly white (whereas over half of all families in public housing are Negro); upper-income (persons in the $10,000 and up income range); heavily weighted toward business, real estate, insurance, and other occupations that suggest an inherently conservative outlook. In many communities these boards act as a restraint and control on the number, type, and location of low-rent housing developments. Because of who these people are and whom they owe allegiances to, it should not be surprising that they have not been a force pushing for more low-rent housing (in Boston, for example, a city where 20–25 per cent of the population lives in substandard housing, not a single unit of family public housing has been constructed in thirteen years). Further, there seem to be few, if any, forces in the community that are assuming the advocate role which the local housing authority has abjured.

The local housing authority also builds crucial geographic limitations and distortions into any program for housing reform. With few exceptions, the jurisdiction of these authorities is confined to a single municipality. The clearly metropolitan character of housing problems and housing markets thereby finds no corresponding administrative mechanism for dealing with these issues. The most rational approach to providing decent housing will often involve use of outlying vacant sites, dispersal of families throughout a metropolitan area; yet at present planning and control must stop at the municipal boundary. A study commission of the Illinois legislature has just submitted a remarkable recommendation for abolition of local housing authorities in favor of metropolitan- and region-wide authorities and programs, yet the plan is given virtually no chance of passage, due to the complex vested interests in the present fragmented structure. Since the Federal low-rent housing program has traditionally and painstakingly allowed for maximum local autonomy and discretion, there seems little hope of restructuring the present system of local housing authorities. Rather, ways must be found to bypass what has become an administrative roadblock.

It is in large part due to above-mentioned shortcomings that proposals have evolved for "unleashing the private sector," bringing the profit motive back into the low-rent housing field. The argument is based on the need for increased activity and motivation; on the private sector's freedom to maneuver and reduce red tape and political constraints; and on the potential that American corporative know-how offers for innovation in the production and marketing of housing.

There is unquestionably a severe shortage of expertise in the housing field, and a large part—if not most—of the technical capabilities regarding all phases of residential development is to be found in the private sector. This expertise refers to questions of financing, land acquisition, legal procedures, design, construction and management. In a field as complex as real estate development, with as many resources involved—financial, human, and technical—delay and inefficiency become exceedingly costly. The paucity of entrepreneurial talent in the public or quasi-public sector has been amply illustrated in the difficulties which non-profit organizations have experienced in developing housing under several

current government programs. Any program of housing subsidization that can make maximum use of existing talents in
the private sector, particularly considering the shortage of
these talents (or their subservience to other considerations)
among public housers at the local level, will clearly be that
much better a program.

What is needed is a government agency with the power to
operate over an entire metropolitan housing market area,
which will give private developers—operating on a limited-
profit basis—maximum freedom to use their talents within
the broad program and planning objectives established by
public policy. The new rent supplement and moderate-income
FHA Sec. 221(d)(3) programs, which were designed to cir-
cumvent the local housing bureaucracy in favor of direct
negotiation between FHA and the private developer, offer a
form of controlled freedom that, with some changes, would
seem to be amenable to private developers and at the same
time capable of meeting desired policy objectives. The stip-
ulation of limited profit (which, in fact, with entrepreneurial
slight of hand, turns out to be considerably above the presumed
6 per cent maximum) will not be a significant deterrent to the
private developer, if unnecessary red tape is eliminated, if a
built-in market is assured (through some form of rent supplement or rent certificate program), and if the system provides
rewards for demonstrated ability to produce (in the form of
lowered initial capital requirements, for example). Adherence
to a general set of public policy controls would become a
quid pro quo for receipt of government aid, in the form of
low-interest loans and land acquisition assistance. Public controls must relate to site selection (to encourage and insure
metropolitan planning and solutions), and to adequate protection of the interests of those moderate- and low-income
families who can secure decent housing only through government assistance. Specifically, the public agency will need to
insure that an ample number of low- and moderate-income

families are being accepted as tenants (and as owners—for there is no reason why outright ownership, cooperatives, and condominiums should not be included as options under programs of public subsidization), and that they are being accepted and retained in a non-discriminatory way (i.e., without prejudice as to race, welfare status, family composition, and other social criteria).

It should be recognized, however, that part of the motive underlying this move toward the private sector is traceable to some very unrealistic notions regarding the comparative costs involved in public vs. private production of housing. In many person's minds—back or front—lies the notion that if the private sector can be induced to do the job, this will reduce the need for public funds. Most of the recent private-sector approaches to the housing problem in fact obfuscate the cost issue by underestimating the quantity of public subsidy needed or by offering a deceptive picture of which income groups will be aided by these programs. Thus, Senator Kennedy's much heralded plan for Bedford-Stuyvesant envisions producing housing that rents for $85–90 per month. Even using the rule-of-thumb that families should pay no more than 25 per cent of their income for rent, these rent levels would require an annual income in excess of $4000 (in excess of $5000, if one uses the traditional 20 per cent ratio). There are literally millions of families in the country who are unable to afford these rents. One basic fact must be understood, then, in the public/ private debate: there is no magic to be achieved—existing income levels and the costs of providing sound housing are "givens" (with little immediate alteration to be expected from programs of job creation and cost-reducing technological innovations in the building industry). If all families in America are to be housed decently (a National Goal set by Congress that will soon have its twentieth anniversary), the gap between these two "givens" must be bridged, and it must be bridged by government subsidies. No amount of "plans" for the private sector, however ingenious, is going to alter that basic fact. It is axiomatic that if incentives are made sufficiently attractive, the private sector will produce. The infamous FHA Sec. 608 program of the postwar period made this abundantly clear, at the cost of great amounts of jerry-built housing and much bilking of the public. Maximizing profit opportunities can only lead to increased housing costs (and hence to increased public subsidies) and to irresponsible development. The private sector can and should have a crucial role to play in an expanded government housing program, but only if it is willing to accept moderate profits and adhere to necessary public controls.

Finally, we must refer to the issue of popular participation and control—that is, who makes and carries out decisions regarding housing programs and conditions for low- and moderate-income families. This issue ranges from broad questions of participation in the planning process to more specific issues regarding changing concepts in the landlord-tenant relationship. There are few areas where it is more imperative to have active and ongoing participation of the prospective clientele than in the area of housing and neighborhood planning. Clearly, questions of preference, life-style, patterns of spatial usage are all crucial to the proper planning of residential areas. Yet there has been a traditional gap between the purveyors and users of housing programs for lower-income groups. There is hardly a housing authority in the country, for example, that includes on its board a resident of a public housing project or a person eligible for residency there. It should not be a matter of great wonder that public housing projects stand as a monument to the insensitivity of program designers to the needs and satisfactions of the program's clientele. The newer, private-enterprise approaches to community development similarly overlook the issue of popular participation and control, or fail to realize the implications of the concept. Thus, Robert Kennedy's two-pronged plan for Bedford-Stuyvesant envisions an indigenous community corporation which is to assert effective control over housing and community facilities planning, plus a "blue-ribbon" board (on which sit men like C. Douglas Dillon and Thomas Watson of IBM) responsible for bringing in the industrial base which will support the community's economic renascence. The Kennedy Plan speaks of the necessity for the community to "create the conditions" under which private corporations and lending institutions will be willing to locate in Bedford-Stuyvesant. Yet there almost certainly will be conflict and contradiction between the set of preconditions demanded by the private sector and the wishes of the local community; if the economic basis of the Bedford-Stuyvesant Plan depends on satisfaction of the investment conditions set forth by the private sector, it is clear that one can speak of meaningful citizen control in only the most limited sense. The new Model Cities approach, which arose out of experience under the urban renewal program, likewise lays great stress on "citizen participation"; yet in only very few places is there the possibility that this will mean true control— the right ultimately to approve or disapprove locally any plan for the area, backed up by a commitment of funds to permit a democratically selected local decision-making body to retain its own professional planning staff to assist in the evaluation of official agency plans and the development of alternative plans.

One of the more advanced notions in true popular control of development programs is the community foundation, a combined governing body and development corporation, to which all local residents would belong. This corporation, or foundation, is responsible for the administration of government programs for community development and builds up the economic strength of the area by bringing in new employment opportunities and increasing local ownership of housing, stores, and other economic assets. The idea, originally developed by Milton Kotler of the Institute for Policy Studies in Washington, is getting its field test in an area of Columbus, Ohio, and was warmly received and well publicized during the 1966 session of the Ribicoff hearings. If the community corporation, or some variant thereof, became developer of new and rehabilitated housing in the area, hiring professional contractors and making maximum use of employment opportunities for local residents, the proper sensitivity to residents' needs and desires would be structured into government programs of housing subsidization.

The importance of housing and housing programs now encompasses far more than the traditional realms of health and safety, those basic considerations which so strongly motivated the slum fighters of an earlier generation. Dangers to physical well-being are still a notable part of slum living (ranging from rat bites, fires, and household accidents to certain housing-related diseases such as dysentery and skin ailments). But the issue has now broadened to include the social conditions under which people live: issues of status and dignity; the relation of design to behavior; control over the decisions that affect one's life and over one's own living conditions; location and character of community facilities; real choice with regard to residential location and housing type; and a host of other considerations that have not traditionally been defined as "housing" issues *per se*. Any housing program for the 60's and 70's must involve more than a bricks-and-mortar approach, must be prepared to deal with the entire set of living variables that make up residential and community life.

1967

Discrimination and
the Unions

WILLIAM B. GOULD

As the protests of 1963 and '64 with their picketing of "Jim Crow" construction projects begin to fade into history, so does the unequivocal blessing the AFL-CIO gave to the 1964 Civil Rights Act and its fair employment provisions. Certainly, no leadership has been so far in advance of its constituency as that of the labor movement on the civil rights issue. The CIO unions, particularly, pushed hard for civil rights legislation when the issue was far more moral than political—as it was 20 years ago. Large Negro memberships have also made it less difficult for them to speak out, for instance, against formal racial exclusions and the separation of Negro workers in segregated locals.

Yet, although the labor movement continuously reminds us of its support for anti-discriminatory legislation, its somewhat defensive repetition of this point indicates that something has gone wrong. This is not George Meany drawing away from the 1963 "March on Washington" for fear of a tactical error. It is something more fundamental, suggesting that organized labor is out of step with the general drift of job advancement for Negroes when that advancement tampers with established union policies and procedures.

What was said by the Civil Rights Commission in 1961 still

holds: "within the labor movement . . . civil rights goals are celebrated at the higher levels but fundamental internal barriers tend to preserve discrimination at the workingman's level." Moreover, as some of Walter Reuther's recently expressed frustrations with the craft unions reveal, the resistance to institutional change has also begun to emerge more clearly at the international level.

This refusal to abide with civil rights legislation penetrates the union's own bailiwick and tends to disrupt efforts by those in both the civil rights and labor movements who still seek to fashion a Negro-labor-liberal coalition that will be a vehicle for effective reform. For while liberals like Gus Tyler talk about the need for such an alliance (see his recent book, *The Labor Revolution*), the unions seem unwilling or unable to take the initiatives which could make such a pact beneficial to *both* sides.

A number of recent disputes are representative of what I would describe as an unyielding response on the part of labor to certain fundamental Negro demands. The first arises out of civil rights agreements negotiated in 1964 and 1966 between the Hotel Employers Association of San Francisco and various civil rights organizations. Under federal law a union which is designated by a majority of the employees bargains as exclusive representative for *all employees* within the unit. On the basis of this doctrine and certain hiring hall provisions in their collective bargaining agreement, the Culinary Workers Union challenged the validity of these agreements. The case was decided by arbitration in November 1966—in a hearing held without any of the civil rights groups that had negotiated the agreements in question. Although the courts are divided on whether a minority rival union has the right to engage in limited negotiations where certain employees prefer such representation to their own exclusive bargaining representative, the arbitrator ruled flatly that ". . . the civil rights group had no right to represent or purport to represent employees of the hotel with respect to terms or conditions of employment since the Union was the authorized bargaining representative."

The opinion neglected to mention the above referred-to decisions on rival unions or to note that a civil rights organization should be far less disruptive to the concept of an exclusive representative than a rival union. Moreover, the arbitrator held that the contractual obligation to hire more Negroes was unlawful "preferential" treatment, a theme which is being used against minority employment in many contexts. While portions of the civil rights agreement appeared to contradict the collective agreement negotiated by the Culinary Workers Union and were perhaps therefore void, the arbitrator's decision was so wide-sweeping in its exclusion of Negro representation that it provided the basis for justifiable furor in the San Francisco Negro community.

As might be expected, the right-to-work advocates have attempted to capitalize on the mood of outrage and to convince the Negro community that unionism, as an institution, is hostile to the aspirations of colored workers. The more sensible Negro approaches, however, do not express opposition to the union *qua* union but rather seek to limit the arbitrary uses of union power. Where this sort of conduct makes it impossible for Negroes to work within the established structure, some form of independent action may be the only alternative. Thus, Herbert Hill, labor secretary for the NAACP, came to San Francisco in December 1966 to call for the decertification of unions "that are engaged in anti-union practices" i.e., racial discrimination; and perhaps more important, Hill asserted that the NAACP would support new "black unions" whenever the "AFL-CIO fail in their legal duty to provide fair and equal representation to minority group members and also where they refuse to organize in Negro ghetto areas. . . ."

Used as a bargaining lever to gain concessions from the labor movement, the "black union" concept may have something to commend it as a temporary measure. But it is doubtful whether such unions can provide Negro workers with resources, financial and otherwise, to improve their work conditions substantially. It is not probable—nor desirable—that black and white unions will engage in competition for the loyalty of Negro workers. Where the AFL-CIO unions are in default, however, "black unions" can be a useful thorn in the labor movement's side.

In February 1967, there was another visitor to the West Coast—Bayard Rustin, of the A. Philip Randolph Institute —who pointed out that "right to work" legislation meant "destroying the institution of collective bargaining and thus keeping Negroes and other minority members at the bottom of the economic ladder." Rustin went on to say that

there is still discrimination in a minority segment of the American labor movement. This is a scandal, however, that is being vigorously fought by every unionist, black or white, who is worthy of the name. I myself am, in my own capacity, committed to end the vestiges of discrimination in the trade union movement, but I absolutely refuse to conduct the battle along lines that will ultimately injure the labor movement. I could not do this and still remain convinced that Negroes have a need and responsibility to make that movement stronger and more effective.

One finds the Rustin line appealing, premised as it is on the coalition theory, until one ponders an essential question which he leaves unanswered: must it always be the labor movement itself which determines what is injurious to its interest? If the answer is yes, then clearly the price of coalition is too high and, at least for the time being, the Hill approach becomes a plausible technique for extracting concessions.

One example of this trend is the Maryland Freedom Labor Union, which is staffed by Negro workers and serves as a bargaining agent for employees—practically all of whom happen to be colored—in a small number of retail establishments in East Baltimore. MFLU has recently negotiated a contract with

Roth's Supermarket in East Baltimore in which wages were substantially increased. The AFL-CIO has not paid sufficient attention to this segment of the work force and has thereby missed an opportunity.

In Columbus, Ohio—where the Justice Department brought suit on April 13 against Local 683 of the International Brotherhood of Electrical Workers for engaging in a "pattern or practice" of discrimination (the first such suit under the 1964 Civil Rights Act)—some government contractors are being forced to hire Negro craft workers through an organization called the Independent Alliance of Skilled Crafts. Negro workers—who, after all, were forced out of the crafts by white employees after Reconstruction—have formed the Independent Alliance to fill the needs of employers who are fearful of having their government contracts revoked because of the absence of Negro workers and who, at the same time, cannot get Negro labor from the craft unions in Columbus. In Columbus and in many other cities, there is untapped organizing potential in Negro craftsmen who work outside the union structure, sometimes on a part-time basis, on any job they can obtain. The significance of this potential is underscored by the much publicized recent decision of *Ethridge v. Rhodes* where the Ohio District Court has held that the State of Ohio cannot enter into construction contracts with parties that will not "obligate themselves and be legally eligible and prepared actually to secure a labor force only from sources that will reasonably assure equal job opportunities."

Both the MFLU and the Independent Alliance are representative of increased organizational cooperation and racial pride among Negroes—as distinguished from racism or "black power" insofar as that term signifies an anti-white philosophy. While it is foolish to regard phenomena like the Maryland Freedom Union as a serious threat to the established order, such groups may make the AFL-CIO sufficiently uncomfortable to encourage a more responsive attitude toward Negro demands.

This cannot come too quickly. For even the Workers Defense League—which has received cooperation from the craft unions in recruiting minority youngsters in New York and preparing them for apprenticeship entry tests—has begun to run into resistance from the Sheet Metal Workers Local 28. In 1964 there had been litigation before the New York State Human Rights Commission and the New York State courts concerning the union's traditional father-son rule which gives preference for apprenticeships to the son of a member; this litigation broke down the barrier of nepotism. The ranks were then opened up and tests given. In 1965, the WDL was able to place 11 Negroes in an apprenticeship class of 65. But the Union decided that the scores registered by Negro applicants were too high to have been legitimately obtained, and the State Commission was required to go to court before the Union was restrained from voiding the results of the tests. This flimsy pretense grasped at by Local 28 leaves a lasting impression. Even where sophisticated organizations like WDL intervene, there is no predicting the roadblocks that can be erected.

II

The most fundamental and serious controversies, however, involve the Equal Employment Opportunity Commission (EEOC). EEOC was established by Title VII, the fair employment practice provisions of the Civil Rights Act of 1964. A growing discord between Negroes and the unions is graphically reflected in an article which appeared in the *Daily Labor Report* on April 3, reprinted from the monthly magazine of the United Association of Plumbers and Pipefitters and written by Peter T. Schoemann, its president.

Schoemann was responding to the EEOC's stepped-up offensive against the exclusion of Negroes from the skilled trade unions which regulate the apprenticeship programs and hiring halls and therefore control the supply of labor for some of the more lucrative jobs in the economy. EEOC is embarking upon a program of record-keeping and reporting; this will permit appraisal of the number of minority-group people within the membership and the apprenticeship programs. Schoemann's first line of defense against what he considered an unwarranted intrusion into the private economy was that the Commission's experience over its two years of existence indicated that industrial and not craft unions should be singled out for special attention. Reporting requirements for the crafts were unjustified, said Schoemann, because "there are few complaints of actual discrimination relating to building trades apprenticeship and hiring halls." Schoemann made it clear that the *raison d'être* of the Commission's program was even more distasteful:

And what kind of report would be required? An enumeration of apprentices by racial groupings, naturally. How about that?—a practice odious to our membership and completely foreign to our traditions. If they want to inspect the jobsites for members of racial minorities, why don't they do it themselves? Or get the Bureau of Apprenticeship and Training to do it? Or maybe the Bureau of Labor Statistics or the Census Bureau—both of them experienced at nose counting? It's their hot idea, not ours. . . .

. . . is there something indecent about giving reasonable preference to sons of union members on apprenticeship entrance? Is there something unclean about a contractor taking his own son into his own job in preference to a Negro boy whom some academic liberal in a Washington office thinks he ought to take instead? This is a big part of our fight. Perhaps rather, since people are going to do what I described anyway, the real issue is their right to do it honestly and aboveboard, without the need for becoming ingenious experts at manipulating gobbledygook.

In another part of the same article, Schoemann, with apparent melancholy, says that:

We helped get Title VII into the Civil Rights Act and so bring the Commission into being. Rightly used it could be the most powerful instrument in our national life for promoting equal employment opportunity. Our support for strengthening the Commission's powers will not be automatically forthcoming in the future, and it will not be forthcoming at all if the Commission demonstrates a healthy measure of bias on its own part towards building trades and apprenticeship and the hiring halls.

In other words, one might say, "we will support Title VII only so long as it is not enforced against us."

That characterization of Schoemann's remarks, however, is a bit unfair. For the Equal Employment Opportunity Commission, by establishing the reporting requirements to which the crafts so vigorously object, is for the first time on a collision course with a dominant philosophy in the labor movement—a philosophy which becomes particularly operative where internal union problems are concerned. Employers, of course, have already submitted to the very same questionnaires which are now required of the craft unions—but if the unions objected to this practice, their protestations were not very audible. Now, unless the White House decides that 1968 is too near and that the crafts are more likely to stray from the Democratic fold than are Negro workers, the Commission—which has been relatively inconspicuous thus far in terms of forcing institutional changes—will be undertaking a major confrontation.

In retrospect, it is curious to recall labor's unanimous endorsement of Title VII, Schoemann probably envisaged EEOC as an agency to be molded along the lines of state commissions which have waited for complaints to come to them. While it might not be fair to place the entire AFL-CIO in the Plumbers' compartment (but see AFL-CIO Secretary-Treasurer William F. Schnitzler's recent statement that accusations of racial discrimination against building trades unions are "unadorned bunk"), it would seem that their view is the one expressed by the first Justice Harlan dissenting in *Plessy v. Ferguson;* i.e., a necessary prerequisite to equal protection under the law is color blindness on the part of governmental agencies.

One must be careful to note that the craft unions were not

the first in the labor movement to take this type of position. For years it has been known that qualified Negro trade union-ists could not be elected to the UAW Executive Board because Negroes were not in the majority in any single UAW con-stituency. Until 1962, when a vacancy was created with the understanding that it would go to a Negro, Reuther stated that the selection of a Negro to remedy this situation would be racial discrimination in reverse. In a situation aggravated by the allegation that white leaders *were being chosen* for a ma-jority of black workers, Gus Tyler of the ILGWU characterized the notion that Negroes would want to elect a Negro business manager as establishing a "racist" rather than a "unionist" basis of voting. While one could hope for the day when racial and ethnic background are completely irrelevant to the selection of union leaders, the plain facts are that in most instances Ne-groes can only be elected if they apply pressure as an organized group. This is what happened in the UAW, where Reuther's new policy seems largely due to the efforts of the Negro Amer-ican Labor Council.

The charge of "preferential treatment" is leveled against ef-forts to get Negroes into skilled jobs "through affirmative action" by the Commission. But color *consciousness* is going to be a necessity if Negro workers are to make meaningful ad-vances. Even Professor Ray Marshall of the University of Texas—whose recent report to the Department of Labor, *Negro Participation in Apprenticeship Programs,* is quite char-itable of the building trades—has said:

Preferential treatment for Negroes is opposed, of course, because it might discriminate against whites. But *special* programs for Ne-groes need not discriminate against Negroes or whites. For exam-ple, apprenticeship sponsors who have not recruited among Negroes in the past and who have no Negro employees, trainees, or mem-bers might make special efforts to recruit Negroes or to help them acquire training. This would be special treatment to include Negroes in the pattern, *but it would not be preferential treatment because*

it would extend to Negroes benefits which whites already enjoy.
[Emphasis added.]

Quite obviously EEOC cannot bring into play sanctions of
the Civil Rights Act which may encourage recruitment unless
it knows where Negroes do not participate. All too often there
is not enough information available about even the apprenticeship program—information which might get to the Negro community and thus trigger a complaint. Schoemann makes it
clear in his article that, regardless of what information the
Commission obtains, his union will defend the father-son apprenticeship policy which serves as a "grandfather clause" in
keeping Negroes out of some of the most lucrative jobs in the
country. Curiously enough, this same principle is rationalized
by Gus Tyler in *The Labor Revolution* on the ground that
the same practices are followed by business people. Tyler
overlooks the fact that nepotism is on the sharp decline in
management circles (see Heilbroner, *The Limits of American
Capitalism*). Moreover, even if one unabashedly engages in
preferential hiring, the deliberate selection of Negroes and
other minority groups has a more rational basis for public
policy than does the selection of a member's son.

The building trades make two points, however, for which
a great deal more can be said.

One is that the aggregate unemployment rate in the period
1961–65 in the construction industry actually exceeds the unemployment rate for Negro males during the same period of
time. This factor not only limits the number of apprenticeship
openings but leads to a little-publicized corollary: entry into
apprenticeship programs, though it may provide the Negro
community with a small cadre of sophisticated civil rights leaders, is hardly the answer to job inequality, let alone to the
frighteningly high rate of Negro unemployment. Unless the
Negro community begins to appreciate the very small gains
that flow from the tumbling of this barrier, insoluble frustra-

tions will remain. In any event, both the Negro community and the unions should be cooperating in support of legislation which will increase employment opportunities for both black and white workers. A recent proposal by Senator Robert F. Kennedy for the employment of slum residents on construction and renovation projects is a good starting point.

The second point made by the craft unions is that the industrial unions—which do not control hiring but influence such on-the-job rights as promotions—do not have clean hands. If the problem were not so serious, it would be amusing to note that both sides of the AFL-CIO blame each other for failing to treat the Negro worker fairly; and they are both correct. Indeed, the AFL-CIO has been resisting, albeit in a much more quiet and subtle fashion, a less stringent reporting system which EEOC is imposing upon "non-referral" unions. Some of the industrial unions, along with AFL-CIO representatives, have gone straight to the White House in an attempt to head off the establishment of "guidelines" by EEOC in an area of vast importance to many Negro workers—the discriminatory impact of seniority contractual provisions. Actually, these extraordinary efforts, viewed from the AFL-CIO vantage point, are quite necessary; for, as Peter Schoemann wrote in the article noted above, there have been a large number of complaints filed with EEOC alleging racial discrimination attributable to seniority provisions. The explanation for this is that the Negro worker, once on the job for a number of years, becomes more sophisticated about how the system operates than is the teen-ager who wants to get into an apprenticeship program.

For the moment, the Commission continues to rely on a "conciliation" process which attempts to persuade parties to sign settlement agreements. Former Chairman Stephen Schulman is quoted in the January 5 *Wall Street Journal* stating that "[we] have no policy on seniority as such . . . [it] doesn't lend itself to a proclamation." While the seniority dispute may not lend itself to a "proclamation," it certainly does warrant a policy.

This controversy arises out of segregated job patterns. Historically, in many establishments—especially in the South, where the practice was carried out on a *de jure* basis—Negro workers were consigned to the lower paying, less desirable jobs. Although these practices normally antedated union recognition, unions and employers negotiated collective agreements which established seniority districts around each racial group. There is hardly a person who seriously contends that this practice is lawful. The dispute concerns the remedy to eliminate what is unlawful.

The AFL-CIO Civil Rights Department contends that a remedy that disrupts negotiated seniority procedures would break faith with the interpretation of the Civil Rights Act which they have given to their members. In the AFL-CIO document, *Civil Rights: Facts vs. Fiction,* distributed prior to the passage of Title VII, these assurances are given:

The law will properly put an end to discrimination in employment —including discrimination in seniority systems. *But it does not in any way interfere with existing job rights.* [Emphasis added.]

This statement—completely unsupported by the legislative history of Title VII—has been used to get the unions off the hook with their white members who have profited from job segregation. The unease with which the labor movement addresses itself to this subject is reflected in the manner in which the question is posed in the November 1966 issue of *The American Federationist* (the official monthly publication of the AFL-CIO) by Professor Ray Marshall:

The seniority problem is complicated by a number of factors. Some unions fear the interests of white union members will be ignored in order to compensate Negroes for past discrimination. Civil Rights leaders argue, on the other hand, that preferential treatment of Negroes is necessary because merely eliminating discrimination will not permit Negroes to advance rapidly enough.

Note how that emotive phrase "preferential treatment" creeps back into any discussion which may lead to sacrifice on the part of white workers to compensate Negro workers for lost opportunities. As one who has attended EEOC discussions with civil rights organizations (and also with the AFL-CIO and some of the larger corporations), I must say I have never heard any civil rights spokesman advance a remedy which could objectively be labeled as "preferential treatment." On the other hand, I have seen "conciliation agreements" between EEOC and Negro workers which accord the latter far less than Title VII requires. And I have heard labor leaders say that EEOC should sit on its hands and wait for the remedy of full employment to wipe out seniority grievances.

In essence, unless a Negro worker is given some seniority credit for the purpose of future promotional opportunities and security layoff based upon time worked in the formerly segregated job, he is just as effectively denied equality through a "grandfather clause" as is the Negro applicant to a father-son apprenticeship program. But collective agreements often establish departmental or job classification seniority which designates the department or classification as the seniority unit. Outside of this unit, an employee loses all seniority and is subject to immediate layoff and loss of promotion rights.

Without racial considerations, there would be nothing inherently meritorious in one seniority system as opposed to another. Younger workers, for instance, might legitimately fence themselves into a narrow seniority unit out of fear of displacement by other workers with more plant-wide or company seniority. But it is obvious that a narrow unit, department, or classification, is detrimental to the Negro worker who has been denied the right to accumulate seniority, in the unit to which he now advances, because of a discriminatory promotion policy. A remedy must take into account the seniority previously accumulated and attempt to compensate for what would have been obtained but for discrimination. Without such an approach, the Negro worker's present employment status continues to embody within it past discrimination.

At a conference between EEOC and the AFL-CIO in May 1966, no union leader would risk the ire of his white members by proposing some type of compromise on this issue. The one-sided response to what is admittedly a difficult question was that the Commission is not authorized to reform labor contracts involving "vested rights" of white employees.

Now anyone familiar with the process of collective bargaining knows that the unions themselves alter these "vested rights" on many occasions and that the courts have upheld such modifications. I therefore sugested in both a report to the Commission and in an article in the Winter 1967 issue of the *Howard Law Journal*—that an accommodation be arrived at between the competing interests of Negro and white workers. For the latter group has built up reasonable expectations, even if predicated on segregation, as to the future of its employment status.

In brief, I said that under practically no circumstances should Negroes *displace* whites; that where a valid "line of progression" exists—where it is truly necessary to learn one job before proceeding to the next—Negro workers should go to the bottom of the line just as the whites had done, unless it could be shown that a Negro's presently existing skills entitled him to more. I proposed that Negro workers, once having entered this formerly all-white line, could exercise seniority accumulated on the "Negro job" *after a "residency" period was completed* during which the skills of the job could be learned. The purpose of the "residency" period would be to avoid promotion of the Negro employee with two weeks' experience on the job but more seniority than the white employee already on the job for two years. I suggested that this residency period be devised through collective bargaining between labor and management, a proposal which my civil rights friends caustically regarded as a loophole for evasion. However, my proposal included review by EEOC and the courts, if necessary, to determine whether evasion of Title VII had taken place.

This plan was too radical for the unions. It impinged upon the cherished concept of free collective bargaining. It was of little use to make the simple point that Congress had passed a statute prohibiting racial discrimination in employment regardless of whether collective bargaining agreements sanctioned the bias in question. And apparently this fact has been lost on EEOC which, as former Chairman Schulman says, has no "policy." It would seem that this agency—which cannot walk much faster than the pace prescribed for it by the White House —does not want to jostle the labor movement, at least the industrial union side of it, as 1968 approaches.

III

Is the Negro to be assigned the subordinate role in the coalition? For the time being this would appear to be the case. More talk will not change the trade union positions which have been referred to above: only court action could do the job. As John E. Hutchinson writes in *Employment, Race and Poverty:*

Most union leaders are unexceptional men, and their behavior is in some fashion predictable. They are agencies of protest and protection; but grievances have priorities and racial discrimination is not high on the Caucasian list . . . the interests of their members come first. The majority of their members do not like to be disturbed. Race questions disturb.

That generalization, like all others, does not tell the whole story. Two years ago, New York City's District 65, Retail, Wholesale, and Department Store Union went out on strike in order to upgrade Negroes and Puerto Ricans. A labor leader like Harry Van Arsdale of the New York City Labor Council has opened up apprenticeship opportunities for minority youth in his own Local 3, IBEW. Moreover, Van Arsdale has been instrumental in the placement of Negro workers with other unions. But the conduct of District 65 and people like Van Arsdale is simply not widespread enough.

The cry of "black power" may be nonsensical rhetoric. (Insofar as it means self-defeating separatism rather than organizational solidarity, I believe that it is.) But for the time being, Negroes may well be justified in organizing more "black unions" in areas where the established labor movement will not tread, and by seeking effective representation for Negro workers where AFL-CIO unions are not providing it. Congress and the courts have established a duty for the unions to treat their members without discrimination. The judges may now have to direct more attention to strike action and walkouts by Negro workers in protest against discriminatory policies where the union supports neither their position nor the stoppage itself. Until Negroes have a say about the basis upon which any coalition is to be formed, it is not likely to thrive. In the meantime, the unions are losing the support of some of their potentially most valuable allies.

1967

Federal Food
Programs and Hunger

HOWARD THORKELSON

A life of poverty is a life of hunger. This is true for the vast majority of the poor (about four-fifths) who receive no federally aided public assistance,[1] as well as for those who do receive aid. The most glaring inadequacy of the ameliorative programs is the diet of the poor. Only recently has anyone undertaken to measure the extent of hunger, malnutrition, and their health consequences in the nation. Some of the reasons that hunger is a national problem emerge from a look at the patchwork of food assistance that supplements public assistance programs: first surplus commodities, now also food stamps, both administered by the U.S. Department of Agriculture (USDA). These are not milk-and-honey programs; their operation reveals a deep ambiguity in the government's commitment to guarantee the right to a life free from hunger.

Direct distribution of federal surplus food began on a regular basis in 1933. Direct distribution was devised to avert mass starvation in the Depression while simultaneously dis-

[1] Report of the Advisory Council on Public Welfare [to the Secretary of Health, Education and Welfare]: "Having the Power, We have the Duty" (June 16, 1966). Additional numbers of persons receive general assistance, which is not federally aided, but general assistance varies widely in availability and level of payments from state to state.

posing of the food stocks acquired by the government in the initial farm price-support program. Responsibility for administration was confused, and shifted from the Federal Surplus Relief Corporation to the Agricultural Adjustment Administration. Now the responsibility lies with the Consumer and Marketing Service of USDA. From the beginning, the federal agency has distributed food, not directly to needy persons, but to public welfare and private charitable agencies. Distribution began with three commodities made available by price-support purchases: pork, butter, and wheat. It later included fruit, vegetables, eggs, fish, and other products, but the presence of a surplus almost always determined the selection. When perishable foods in surplus were distributed locally, well-off people complained about pampering those on relief—which amounted usually to no more than a surfeit of grapefruit in school lunches. The success, either in relief or farm price support, of this early direct distribution is in doubt, because local welfare agencies would often cut cash relief payments by the amount taken to be the value of the food distributed; the family would therefore end up with even less money to buy food. However, as many as 13 million persons received food in 1939.

A third program also developed in this way to provide free or below-cost lunches to children in school. In 1946 Congress enacted the School Lunch Act,[2] which made the program permanent and based it on appropriations rather than on the availability of surplus foods. Now USDA makes matching grant payments to state education departments on a one-for-three basis. The state agency is to distribute the money among elementary and high schools, both public and non-profit private, but federal appropriations specifically for free lunches were only $2 million in the fiscal year 1966–67.

A close look would probably reveal that the school lunch program discriminates against the very poor. The legislation

[2] 42 U.S.C. §§1751 et seq.

does little, and USDA less, to protect the child who can't pay. Federal money goes to the state, which may make its own allocation (within limits) between poor and rich schools. In Mobile, Alabama, elementary school children pay thirty cents for a lunch which has a federal subsidy of about five cents. At a prosperous, largely white school, which in 1966 had not had a request for a free lunch in over two years, the federal money buys a better lunch, while at a school where 500 children a day need free lunches, federal money buys each child one free lunch a week. The children at the rich school also get better lunches, because the county allocates the higher-quality commodities (which USDA provides for school lunches) on the basis of the number of lunches sold.

Investigation would also reveal favoritism and arbitrariness in teachers' and administrators' selection of which children need not pay. In some areas of the South the unavailability of free lunches at white schools discourages Negro children from exercising their right of transfer under freedom-of-choice desegregation plans.

The distribution of food acquired for surplus reduction was authorized by the first Agricultural Adjustment Act of 1935,[3] which has remained the principal basis of the direct distribution of food ever since. This prescribes no means of administration, but clearly authorizes complete federal operation. Nor does this provision prescribe any standards for determining who may receive food, or even any limitation on standards that could be used by the distributing agency. These decisions were left to the Secretary of Agriculture.

The decision was that the program should be operated locally, not by the federal government, but by the various state departments of public welfare which in turn used the office of

[3] §32 Act of August 24, 1935, 49 Stat. 774. Typically, the special provision for low-income persons was an afterthought, not added until 1939. 53 Stat. 975.

their county branches. In the post-Depression period, and today, whether families could get surplus food depended upon which county they lived in (and economic and political conditions in that county).[4] In the Deep South the divisions within states were sharp. In Georgia in 1967, 100 out of 159 counties neither distributed food nor sold food stamps. In Alabama in 1966, 36 of the state's 67 counties had neither program. These 36 Alabama counties were mostly southern, that is, the poorer counties where black people live in larger proportions. These are also the counties in which arbitrary personal and political standards are most likely to prevail in the administration of public assistance.

From 1933 to 1943, FERA and WPA provided operating funds which enabled states to conduct statewide distribution, as did Alabama, for example. Since the government now allows the states to make counties bear the cost of storing, transporting and distributing the food[5] and does not require that the state insure the statewide operation of a program, the choice for the people of any county is made by its governing body. In 1967 thirteen states shifted all such costs to counties, and others transferred some portion. Thus the general poverty of some counties encourages the white leadership to refuse the surplus food program.

Probably no county, however, has too small a tax base to pay the costs of distributing food. Yet many county officials in the South must believe that it's not worth it, since the labor of poor families is no longer necessary to agriculture, and free food would only delay their departure for the North. In Hale County, Alabama, in 1966, about half the population of 19,-000 would have been eligible for surplus foods. The probate judge told some local people that if they were poor they should go to work or leave the county. They obtained OEO

[4] Mississippi is an exception in that federal funds paid the operating costs of one or the other food program in every county.
[5] 6 CFR §503.6 (i).

funds for operating costs of a surplus food program and applied to USDA to begin it; but although USDA has authority to distribute food through local agencies other than the welfare department, USDA officials referred the Hale County Negroes to the probate judge, who, they said, would have to administer the program. Thus USDA confirms the sovereign prerogative of local leadership.

The advantages of the program probably become an open issue in the South only where Negroes are significantly represented among local leadership, as in Macon County, Alabama. There, after merchants praised the food stamp program, the county Board of Revenue voted to change from surplus commodities to food stamps. But one of the two Negro members of the Tuskegee City Council, which had supported the surplus commodities program, said about the proposal: "This is an insidious attempt to move in and exploit the poor."

Where food is available, a person must be "needy" to get it; USDA has complicated this requirement and added other artificial ones. While the "need" standard might have been applied by a simple declaration, USDA requires the states to put people through the archaic ritual of the means test (unless they are already getting public assistance), showing that their income and property are within the limitations. The income limitations are rigid. In New York State a family of four with an income of $280 a month is eligible but a dollar more disqualifies them. "Hardship" provisions, optional with the state, often require a natural disaster, such as a flood or hurricane, rather than a family illness. Then the applicants must meet USDA's definition of a "household," which it applies in both the surplus commodities and food stamp programs. "Household" is defined as people living together in an economic unit, sharing the purchase and preparation of food. This rarefied concept serves to cover almost all families, but when a person lives alone and eats with a relative nearby or when two old people live in the same house but buy their food separately,

they are denied food. In early 1967 people living in a Freedom
Camp in the Mississippi Delta, having been evicted from their
farms, were denied food on the ostensible grounds that none
of them comprised a "household," because the families were
cooking and eating in communal style.

For the rest, the states are free to impose their own limitations, within the tolerance of USDA. Thus in Arizona, for
example, a man living alone cannot get his portion of boiled
beef, rice, flour, etc., "unless it is established that he is unemployable . . ." Arizona will not feed him even if he is working
and his property and income are below the maximum standards. Nor can any farm labor family get food if there are two
or more able-bodied men over the age of sixteen and the welfare department finds that work is available in Arizona, California, Utah, Nevada, or New Mexico.[6] In other states,
including Mississippi, food is denied, during the crop season,
to men, women, and children who might be able to work in the
fields.

Once a family does qualify to receive food, it faces the problem of how to get it. In New York City it may go to one of
a number of distribution depots, which are open on a staggered
schedule. In Manhattan there are eleven. But in the rural
South getting the food often entails paying one's neighbor or
boss man to drive him into the county seat on the one day a
month when food is distributed. Someone may go *for* a family
or a sick person, but this must be arranged in advance or authorized in writing. At the depot one joins the line and waits
to be handed the bundle of food. In 1966 in Alabama the
bundle was worth about $19, and in New York its composition
and value were about the same.

For more than thirty years the issuance of canned meat,
cheese, flour, beans, dry milk, and lard was part of the routine
of survival for millions of persons. But in 1964 this routine
was threatened by the enactment of the Food Stamp Act,

[6] Arizona Manual of Pub. Welf. Admin. §3-1002(A) (1966).

which was intended to phase out the surplus commodities program. This Act was based on the operation of pilot food stamp programs, which President Kennedy had initiated in 1961. The participant, after showing that he doesn't have too much property or income, gives the amount of his income and is told how much he must pay for the stamps. If he buys them he receives "bonus" stamps in addition.

With the gradual and increasing replacement of surplus food distribution by food stamps, certain well-advertised advantages are supposed to accrue: better food, such as fresh meat and eggs; a wider selection of food; not a give-away but a supplementation of the family's food budget; and use of the existing channels of commerce. The poor consumer soon discovers, however, that merchants raise prices and put forth inferior foods. The selection does not include any food marked imported and so discriminates against Puerto Ricans or Italians who commit their food budgets to stamps. Some families in large cities will have to go to supermarkets instead of small markets and *bodegas,* some Negro families in the South to larger white-owned markets instead of Negro merchants, who are deterred from participating by inertia or bureaucratic obstructions. And since food stamps come only in two denominations (two dollars, and fifty cents) and merchants are not allowed to give change, they will cheat on the credit record; and they will tear off additional stamps.

In Louisiana civil rights workers found that food prices shot up with the adoption of the food stamp program. In rural counties some farmers, who had to borrow money to buy stamps during most of the year, made an arrangement with the grocer. He advanced the cash for the stamps, and they bought them and turned them over to him for credit. The grocer was then free to overcharge to the extent of the credit. Of course USDA regulations prohibit discriminatory price raises but provide no means for consumers to enforce the prohibition.

USDA spokesmen have told representatives of welfare groups that the purpose of the food stamp program is not to aid the poor but to maintain farmers' incomes. USDA has several means of using the program to maximize consumption. One is the regular-participation requirement, which punishes a family for failing to buy stamps for two, or perhaps three, months in succession. The family suffers exclusion from the program for a period and must reapply to participate again. Another means of maximizing consumption is the prescribed scale which determines how much a family must pay to buy stamps. The scale discriminates against the very poor in that it requires the commitment to food spending of a disproportionately high share of the income of a family which has *little or no* income. In Mississippi a family of four with monthly income between $0 and $29.99 had, at least until July 1967, to pay $8 (for $48 worth of stamps). In Illinois a family of four (not receiving public assistance) with monthly income between $0 and $69.99 had to pay $28 (for $68 worth of stamps). USDA approves a state's giving out (non-federal) general assistance in the form of special checks for food stamps; in some counties in Illinois, if the amount of aid to which the family is entitled is less than the amount of the food stamp charge (as is entirely possible), the family must commit some of its minimal earned income to food purchases in order to gain any general assistance benefit at all. The food stamp standards usually allow participation by people above the income levels of the surplus commodities program.

For any person who has received surplus foods the most important fact about food stamps is that they cost money. They often cost an amount so much higher than what the family would otherwise spend for food as to make it difficult or impossible to participate in the program.

This appears in the sharp drop in the number of people benefited which almost uniformly accompanies a county's change from surplus food to stamps. On the basis of incomplete figures reflecting an early stage of the change, the drop in participation in the South was at least 40 per cent; a source of food was cut off for at least 75,000 in 1966. Against strong political pressure in 1967 USDA attempted to maintain the secrecy of the figures on the food cut-off; instead, it purported to measure participation by the proportion of those certified as eligible who actually bought stamps. Even so, the record of older programs shows a tendency for participation in the food stamp program to drop as it goes on. The program in Fayette County, Pennsylvania, started with 23,670 people buying stamps in June 1961 and had 13,843 people participating in June 1966 (both months of national peak participation). USDA reports an over-50 per cent drop for Detroit from 1962 to 1965.

The effects of this failure to provide food to hungry people should now be plain to see. Mississippi is only the most highly publicized case. When families there had no work and no public assistance and the county changed from surplus food to stamps, how did they endure?

Mrs. W . . . I live with my seven children. I haven't worked since three months ago before my baby was born. I don't get welfare. I do get $5 to $10 about once a month from the baby's father. Two of my children chopped a little cotton last year, two days a week for $2 to $3 a day. . . . Two of them are in school but don't have enough money to pay for their lunches. I used to get commodities until the program ended. . . . Now we're eating some leftover commodities. I don't know where I will get any money to buy food when we run out of commodities. . . . Some days I don't have anything to eat at all. I have used my last can of commodity meat.

Mrs. B . . . I live with my five children. I haven't worked since January 21st, when I lost my Work Experience program job. . . . They haven't given me a job as they promised. . . . Since I lost the job I've been eating only what people give me plus some commodities which were left over when the program ended. . . . For breakfast we have dry rice and bread; I feed my children beans or bread for lunch, and don't eat myself. . . . For supper we eat whatever is left from lunch, if anything. I was asked for $12 to buy food stamps. I don't have $12. . . .

When they can, families borrow; many borrow regularly from the plantation owner, the white family for whom the mother does domestic work, the grocer, the neighbors, relatives who have moved North. This may be impossible for some, such as the aged and those who cannot work and have no relatives. When, as in the Delta area of Mississippi, crops grow up to the edge of the house, there can be no garden or any place for chickens to roam and forage. In some places farm land that has been removed from production for USDA subsidies lies idle next to families who have no income and no garden, while the local food program attempts to contribute to the reduction of surpluses. (Ironically, if the family were receiving public assistance, food which they produced at home for their own use would not reduce the amount of their payment because a family's growing food is considered by HEW a contribution toward self-support.) The effects show in the people: severe skin infections and ulcerations, bacterial and parasitic disease, bone diseases, heart weakness, and anemia with its accompanying poor muscle tone, general weakness and lassitude—the facts of a life of malnutrition.[7] A prevalent complaint among middle-aged women who have done field work or domestic work from an early age (and may have had repeated pregnancies) is frequent "falling out" (i.e., spells of fainting and dizziness). These women, and many men with a similar work history, reach the age (often late forties or early fifties) when they can no longer do physically taxing work; yet they are not covered by Social Security, are too young for Old Age Assistance, would be found not sufficiently "disabled" for Aid to the Permanently and Totally Disabled, would be denied Aid to Families with Dependent Children (if they had

[7] See "Hungry Children," a report issued by the Southern Regional Council (July 1967).

had children) because of the presence of the father or some arbitrariness; and general assistance, if any, is erratic and paltry. The number of such persons may be judged by the fact that pilot food stamp programs made special provision for free issuance to persons who had no income,[8] who comprised about 10 per cent of those participating.

Yet with the adoption of the Food Stamp Act USDA ruled that those who have too little income to spend anything for food pay cash for stamps. USDA has imposed this cash requirement on the program apparently out of a fanatical rejection of "something for nothing." According to one USDA official, "presumably, a couple of odd jobs could supply that minimum purchase requirement."[9] It was not a question of the cost of the program, since the government could issue at least the free bonus coupons to any family without income and disregard the rest of the allotment.

There is strong reason to believe that Congress intended that families without income receive their entire allotments without charge. The Food Stamp Act says simply that the family should pay an amount "determined to be equivalent to their normal expenditures for food." But suppose the family has no "normal expenditures for food"? In the Congressional debate Senator Humphrey answered:

The price they pay is approximately what they would normally spend for food out of whatever income they have from whatever source. When the families have little or no income they make only token payments or receive their coupons free.[10]

The agriculture bureaucrats of the USDA have their own client groups: the representatives of the white South who

[8] 26 Fed. Reg. 4138 (1961).

[9] *Wall Street Journal,* April 29, 1967.

[10] 110 Cong. Rec. 15442 (1964). Statements to the same effect were made by the sponsor of the legislation, 110 Cong. Rec. 7128 (1964), and other supporters, 110 Cong. 7150 (1964), probably relying on a similar assurance given by Secretary Freeman in the committee hearings.

dominate the agriculture committees in the House and Senate, and the powerful organizations of the prosperous commercial white farmers. The alliance of USDA and the white farmer has brought about the practical elimination of production surpluses. But farm prices have not been rising, and so the more the poor are forced to consume commercially sold food, the better for farmers.

The permanent scars left by hunger and malnutrition cannot be removed by reform of the USDA food programs, or even of the public assistance system. So long as the need for food programs continues, their chief significance will be the inadequacy of public assistance and of private employment. The rationalization of the public assistance system—by the removal of all eligibility standards except need (a goal which has been legitimated by the Secretary of HEW's Advisory Committee on Public Welfare)[11] and by complete federal funding—would diminish the vital urgency which has arisen for reform of the food programs. Only adequate medical care from childhood on, but particularly in childhood, and comprehensive public services can eliminate the physical and psychological damage revealed among poor people by the failure of the food programs. The issuance of free food stamps falls far short of what is necessary to secure the right to life.

1967

[11] See n. 1 above.

The Negro Family and the Moynihan Report

LAURA CARPER

> MRS. BOYLE: We'll go. Come, Mary, an' we'll never come back here agen. Let your father furrage for himself now; I've done all I could an' it was all no use—he'll be hopeless till the end of his days. I've got a little room in me sisther's where we'll stop till your trouble is over, an' then we'll work together for the sake of the baby.
>
> MARY: My poor little child that'll have no father!
>
> MRS. BOYLE: It'll have what's far betther—it'll have two mothers.
>
> (*Juno and the Paycock,* Act III, Sean O'Casey)

The culmination of intensive efforts to codify the life of the hapless is a document published by the Department of Labor entitled *The Negro Family: The Case for National Action* and commonly referred to as "The Moynihan Report," after the sociologist Daniel Moynihan. With the publication of this document a sociological theory which borders on an ideology has become a political weapon we are all obliged to examine. In order to understand the theoretical framework within which this document was written, we must take a cursory look at sociological thought in the recent period.

In 1960, Dreger and Miller published in the *Psychological Bulletin* a critical evaluation of the "Comparative Psycholog-

ical Studies of Negroes and Whites in the United States," which
was an examination of the relevant contributions in the field
between 1943 and 1958. They concluded that "in the areas of
psychological functioning most closely related to the sociological, social class differences show up more clearly as a basis for
differentiation between the two groups. Leadership, family life,
child rearing practices, fertility and mate selection all seem to
conform to social structure rather than to racial lines per se."

Dreger and Miller's conclusions reflected the intensive efforts
of liberal sociological and psychological thought of the period.
It was the culmination of a thoroughgoing examination of the
corrosive effects of our peculiar social organization and value
system on the Negro as compared to the white. They were unable to find a uniquely Negro personality or Negro psychology
in any class. Their conclusion became a landmark in the field
with which every investigator has been forced to contend.

In April 1964, however, *The Journal of Social Issues* published a collection of studies with an introduction by Thomas
Pettigrew and Daniel C. Thompson and a lead article by
Thomas Pettigrew which sought to delineate what Dreger and
Miller were unable to locate—a Negro personality and a
Negro psychology. Frankly admitting that in this effort social
psychology was whistling in the dark since the Negro was
notorious for his refusal to reveal his inner self to the social
investigator and since it was virtually impossible to establish
control groups of whites, Pettigrew nevertheless argued that
past findings have "underestimated the corrosive effects on
young children of impecunious ghetto living." This may indeed
be true, but the theoretical basis of the issue is that due to
the vicissitudes of his history and the brutality of white society,
the Negro has developed a recognizable psychology and a
recognizable personality which emerged under slavery, and that
this psychology is self-sustaining and transmitted from generation to generation. The studies, together with the introduction,
almost seem to argue for the existence of a racial unconscious.

The thinking here represents a powerful tendency in modern sociological thought; and it is this thinking, shorn of its somewhat hesitant and carefully hedged tone, which characterizes the ideological commitment of *The Report on the Negro Family* and the direction its authors feel national action should take.

The thesis of the Report is that the Negro poor "confront the nation with a new kind of problem. Measures that have worked in the past, or would work for most groups in the present will not work here. A national effort is required that will give unity and purpose to the many activities of the Federal government in this area, directed to a new kind of national goal: the establishment of a stable Negro family structure." The presumption is that the Negro poor are no longer merely the victims of white institutional corruption but also, to an undetermined extent, of their corrosive family life; that despite the enactment of the voting rights bill, the creation of the "Manpower Retraining Program, The Job Corps, and Community Action—et al.," *50 per cent* of the Negro population is incapable of profiting because of a psychological distemper.

The argument is supported with an array of statistics but without any effort to come to terms with the fact that variations in life style and social adjustment *within* the ghetto and between the Northern and Southern Negro poor are far more varied than between all of them and society at large. Fifty per cent of the Negro population is identified as reflecting the "social pathology" these statistics itemize, and the Negro family is recognized as its "source."

On page thirteen of the report there is a graph charting the non-white male unemployment rate and the number of AFDC (Aid to Families with Dependent Children) cases opened each year. This graph is the strongest argument the report offers to substantiate its thesis that the Negro poor have been so crippled by their situation and history that ordinary measures —which I suppose would be full employment, a radical revision of the ghetto school system, integrated education, decent housing, and a rigorously controlled police force—will no longer suffice; that what is now needed is a national effort not to alter our white social institutions but the way the Negro poor relate to each other on the primary personal level—the family.

The graph shows a direct correlation between the non-white male unemployment rate and AFDC cases opened each year between 1948 and 1961. As the unemployment rate drops, AFDC cases drop; as the unemployment rate rises, AFDC cases rise. But in 1962 a negative correlation begins to emerge; in 1963 the lines for each cross; in 1964 AFDC cases continue to rise as the unemployment rate continues to drop. Presumably, the negative correlation after 1962 shows or suggests that giving the Negro male a job will no longer insure or help insure family stability. The conclusion is that something more is needed.

I am not prepared to argue an economic determinist thesis. It is not my contention that the area of full employment is the only front on which we should fight. But I would like to attempt to explain the graph, particularly since the authors of the report direct the reader's attention to the negative correlation and argue that no government program should be instituted which aims at relieving the plight of the Negro poor until the reasons for the reversal are understood.

The first consideration in evaluating statistics is to understand their relevance. *New* AFDC cases must therefore be compared with the unemployment rate of young Negroes. A little investigation shows that the unemployment rate for non-white males as a whole is not reflected in the unemployment rate of non-white youth. Non-white youth, male and female, show a radically different set of statistics; and it is of course the young and not the mature Negro woman who would be a new AFDC case. The unemployment rate for eighteen- and nineteen-year-old non-white men rose from 23.9 per cent in

1961 to 27.4 per cent in 1963, and for eighteen- and nineteen-year-old women who would be obliged to assist in the support of their families from 28.2 per cent to 31.9 per cent. Taken as a whole, the unemployment rate of non-white men between the ages of sixteen and twenty-four during the years in question fluctuates but shows little over-all change. In 1963, the year the lines for AFDC cases and the unemployment rate converge, the rates were especially high. Where the over-all non-white male unemployment rate went down in 1963, the unemployment rate for youth went up and then went down a little in 1964. The picture for young non-white women is comparable. Their rate showed a general tendency to increase.

These figures, although they radically temper the implications of the graph, do not account for the extent of the reversal. A complete explanation must include the famous 1962 change in the social security law. There is a remarkable correlation between AFDC figures and the date of the new law, which authorized greater social and case work service to the poor. In the state of Michigan at least (I choose Michigan arbitrarily, only because I lived there and was in a position to discuss the graph with the welfare department), the department has interpreted this law as a directive to alter its standards. Prior to 1962, if an applicant was a poor housekeeper, mentally disturbed, or evidence of a male friend could be found, her application for AFDC was denied; after 1962 she was accepted if she showed need, regardless of her housekeeping practices, her mental health or her social life. Whereas between July 1960 and June 1961 33.4 per cent of the applications were denied, only 28 per cent were denied between July 1963 and June 1964. The strange graph in the Moynihan Report is the result of graphing the wrong things. The negative correlation is due to an inconsistency between youth unemployment rate and the unemployment rate of the non-white male population as a whole and to an important change in policy on the part of the welfare authorities. As a staff member

of the department informed me, "it is our policy to give everyone a chance now." The thinking behind the new policy is that
by accepting the "undeserving" poor as well as the "deserving"
poor, case-work service is made available to those who need
it most. It is inevitable that as news of this policy change
spreads among the Negro poor and as each of the states slowly
alters its policy to conform to this new view, AFDC cases will
continue to rise.

The Negro family is not the source of the "tangle of pathology" which the report attributes to the Negro community. It
is the pathological relationship between white social institutions and the Negro community which has bred the statistics
the report cites—from low scholastic averages to drug addic-
tion to arrest records to illegitimacy to unemployment rates.
This is the reason the Black Muslims have chosen to withdraw,
and this is the reason the civil rights movement has chosen to
confront us.

The statistics I have tried to examine are the supportive
evidence the report offers in defense of a social psychological
theory. In brief the argument is that American slavery stripped
the Negro of his culture and his most minimal human rights;
and that the Negro, under continued oppression, developed a
matriarchal family organization within which the male played
an inadequate role, if any. The argument continues that since
American family life is patriarchal, the matriarchal family
formation is pathological and is perpetuating a pathological
Negro culture—as the statistics show. But I cannot help wonder
with James Tobin, who published an interesting economic
study in the Fall 1965 issue of *Daedalus,* why "personal attributes which doom[ed] a man to unemployment in 1932 or
even 1954 or 1961 did not handicap him in 1944 or 1951
or 1956." Peter Townsend has pointed out that in 1930 many
Englishmen estimated that as many as a million of their fellow-
countrymen were unemployable because of their personal
problems and only a decade later found that only 100,000

could be characterized in this way. There was a manpower shortage in 1940. What appears to be a social malformation in one period becomes the problem of isolated individuals in another.

The Negro poor are distinguished from the middle class primarily by the fact that they are poor. The father is haphazardly employed and at a very low wage. He is frequently absent from the family scene. He has either deserted or been thrown out by the mother. If he is present and works, he may squander his income. The children are raised by an extended family of adult women. This picture does not focus 50 per cent of the Negro families. But it does include a significant section of the Negro poor. Is it peculiar to them?

"Matriarchy" is a cultural formation common to many oppressed people throughout the history of western civilization—regardless of their own past history and regardless of the values they themselves held. A brilliant and moving characterization of how and why such a family constellation developed among the Irish poor can be found in Sean O'Casey's play *Juno and the Paycock,* from which I took the quotation which precedes this piece. The Irish matriarchal family formation is noteworthy because it existed in conflict with an Irish patriarchal ideal.

Both Patricia Sexton and Oscar Lewis have shown that the poor Puerto Rican family is beginning to move toward the same "pathology" as the Negro: illegitimacy and families with a woman at the helm.

The same can be said of Jewish family life in the *shtetl.* Although illegitimacy was not a problem (partly because divorce merely involved a witnessed statement placed in the hand of the wife; the father was frequently absent, either as a peddler on the road, as an immigrant in America, or as a permanent resident of the house of study who came home only to eat). Newly married couples usually moved into the home of the bride's parents. Among the Hassidic Jews (Hassidism was a movement initiated by the poor), it was common for the father to leave his wife and children without a kopek in the house and depart for the Rebbe's court where he would dance and drink and spend all his money. As among the American poor, relations between husband and wife were cold and the roles of each clearly defined. The wife worked and assumed the main burden of supporting the family, and children became adults before they had ever had an opportunity to be children. The man either struggled desperately to make a living with little success or withdrew entirely into a private male society based on discourse or ecstacy and left the family to shift for itself. What the Jewish man succeeded in doing that the Negro man has failed to do is place a positive value on family desertion and personal withdrawal.

Since the Negro man does not rationalize his role as being a desirable religious achievement, it seems to me he would be easier to integrate into the surrounding culture than the Jew. After all, once integration became a variable possibility, even the *shtetl* Jew cast off what no longer served him. And the depth and extent to which oppression and poverty reduced the Jew can be measured by the disintegrative effects of the widespread Messianic movements, two of which emphasized orgiastic sexual practices as a means of insuring the coming of the Messiah.

I have chosen to detail the matriarchal organization of the Jewish family life not because it corresponds to the Negro family but because sociologists look upon Jewish family life as remarkably cohesive. Is the caricature I have drawn of the *shtetl* family accurate? Of course not. I have applied Mr. Moynihan's method of describing the Negro to a description of the Jew. I lumped a few hundred years of history together and failed to distinguish among people. Pathology is in the eye of the beholder. If one eliminates the positive social function of a cultural constellation, if one ignores the meaning personal relations have to the people involved, if one, in short, uses science to depersonalize, what emerges is always pathology. For health involves spontaneous human feelings of affection and tenderness which the Moynihan Report, like my deliberate caricature of Jewish family life, cannot encompass.

Let me also add that I am not trying to draw any direct analogies between the Irish poor, the Jewish poor, or even the Puerto Rican poor, and the Negro poor. I am seeking to show that "matriarchy" within the larger social context of what the report calls "patriarchy" is common to the way of life of poor people. And further, that people living under oppression always develop social formations which appear to the surrounding oppressive culture to be excessive or pathological. The form these so-called excesses take varies from culture to culture and person to person within the culture—but no matter how extreme the nature of the adjustment, once the social pressure which created it is removed, a new adjustment develops. A people is not destroyed by its history. What destroys a people is physical annihilation or assimilation, not its family life.

The question the report raises is the direction a government program would take to insure family stability. What is the quality of the solutions Mr. Moynihan has in mind? The report includes a detailed description of the therapeutic effects of military service. Mr. Moynihan argues that the armed forces are educational and that they "provide the largest single source of employment in the nation." He admits that "for those comparatively few who are killed or wounded in combat, or otherwise, the personal sacrifice is inestimable. But on balance, service in the Armed Forces over the past quarter-century has worked greatly to the advantage of those involved. . . . Service in the United States Armed Forces is the *only* [author's italics] experience open to the Negro-American in which he is truly treated as an equal: not as a Negro equal to any white, but as one man equal to any man in a world where the category 'Negro' and 'white' do not exist." Mr. Moynihan further states that for the Negro "the armed forces are a dramatic and desperately needed change: a world away from women, a world run by strong men of unquestioned authority, where discipline, if harsh, is nonetheless orderly and predictable and where rewards, if limited, are granted on the basis of performance." This view of the desirability of army life is patently absurd. Underlying the Report's understanding of the problems of the Negro family is its author's concept of masculinity. According to the Report "the essence of the male animal, from the bantam rooster to the four-star general, is to strut."

I cannot here counterpose my taste in men or my concept of the good life against Mr. Moynihan's—but it seems clear to me that it is for the Negro male himself to determine his sexual and social style—whether strutting or not.

The challenge to the Negro community is political. It remains to be seen whether we can make room for the poor to acquire social and economic power. This is our social problem—and not the existence of a matriarchal family organization. What is more, Frank Riessman has found that involving emotionally disturbed people among the Negro poor in the civil rights movement can resolve their personal problems. What is destructive to the Negro man and woman is social impotence here and now, and what rehabilitates them is social power and the struggle for it. It is not new for a ruling elite to characterize its poor as incontinent and shiftless. It is the characteristic way in which those on top describe those on the bottom, even when sincerely trying to uplift them. My Negro landlady encountered a helpful woman who tried to tell her that Negro culture was rooted in the life style of slavery and fixed by history. In telling me about the conversation my landlady said, "That woman thinks that if she handed me a bail of cotton, I'd know how to make a dress out of it!" The Negro is not grappling with the social system under which he lived over a hundred years ago, or even with the social system under which he lived ten years ago. He is grappling with the social system under which he lives today.

1966

Grape Pickers in California

MICHAEL VINCENT MILLER

Delano is entirely typical of the innumerable rural towns that dot the vast stretches of farmland in California's agricultural valleys. Lying off Highway 99, the main artery through the San Joaquin Valley, it is a thoroughly unimpressive-looking place, with some 13,500 inhabitants. Its business district spans three or four streets about half a dozen blocks long. There is a shady middle-class residential area on the east side with pleasant old homes. On the west and south sides an assortment of structures, from cheap tract homes to shacks, contains that portion of the Mexican and Filipino farm worker families fortunate enough to avoid the labor camps on the growers' property. Just outside town begin the miles of vineyards upon which the community's economy stands or totters. In normal times, the tempo of life in Delano is slow, though it fluctuates with the seasonal cycle of the grape crop.

Formidable obstacles have prevented the farm worker in areas like Delano from improving his pathetically low wages, from obtaining even the most rudimentary bargaining rights, from breaking free of a stigmatized and rootless way of life. With respect to the social structure it creates, this sector of American agriculture resembles a feudal system in which the laborer who tends the crop plays the role of a nomadic serf. Most field workers come from non-Caucasian minorities and thus have little chance of gaining entry into the farming community's white middle class or, for that matter, of being hired for industrial jobs in the cities. In order to get anything remotely approximating steady work, they usually have to move from crop to crop, often traveling a circuit through several states (there exists, however, an important exception to this in Delano, which will become clear later). Frequently their only homes are in the field camps, where they can't be reached easily by labor organizers who are supremely *persona non grata* on grower property. Thirty years ago, Congress excluded farm labor from the legislation that enabled industrial workers to engage in collective bargaining; subsequent bills extending this to agricultural workers have been strangled.

Numerous organizing drives and strikes have started up on California farms, but these have rarely made any real headway. Memberships were built up and sometimes slight wage increases achieved; but no meaningful contracts with growers followed.

With the cards thus stacked against them, workers in the Delano grape fields, led by the AFL-CIO's Agricultural Workers Organizing Committee and the locally based National Farm Workers Association, went out on strike in the fall of 1965. After months of intensely bitter struggle involving the entire Delano community, the strikers have won some unprecedented concessions from the two largest growers in the area. In the spring of 1966, NFWA and Schenley Industries, Inc., signed a contract that guarantees Schenley's field labor a minimum wage of $1.75 per hour and substitutes an NFWA hiring hall for the customary practice of employing directly or through labor contractors. And on August 30, NFWA and AWOC, newly merged under the AFL-CIO, beat the Teamsters' Union in an election to determine who would represent the Di Giorgio Corporation's Delano and Borrego Springs field crews at the bargaining table. No matter who had won, a representation election held on the farms of a major agricultural producer was in itself a historic event.

These achievements have considerably brightened the outlook for unionizing farm labor in America. The Delano effort, which still has a long way to go, is only a surface scratch in agriculture's traditional resistance to unions, but it is one that can't be smoothed over. The events in Delano have aroused widespread public sympathy for the farm workers and rekindled the labor movement's desire to bring them into the fold. And in recent months, there have been farm strikes in Texas and marches in Wisconsin, stirrings in Oregon and Arizona, Florida and Colorado.

II

Why did the grape strikers succeed in pushing their demands farther than farm workers have been able to do in the past? Perhaps the chief reason has to do with the ingenious manner in which NFWA, led by Cesar Chavez, drew on the heritage of moral response created by the civil rights movement, in order to dramatize the farm worker's plea for better wages and working conditions. Most previous farm strikes have remained isolated local phenomena, easily snuffed out by growers. Under Chavez's guidance, however, the grape strike became more like a movement for social justice, a cause for national liberal and radical sentiment to rally around.

The strike began at the outset of the 1965 harvest season, when AWOC's local membership, consisting predominantly of Filipino field workers, refused to pick grapes unless their $1.10 or $1.20 per hour wages were raised to $1.40. On September 8,

Filipino workers staged a sit-in at the grower-owned camps. Larry Itliong, AWOC regional director, asked NFWA's large, well-organized Mexican-American constituency to cooperate. NFWA held a meeting on September 16 and voted to join the strike.

Conditions were more favorable than usual for calling a farm strike. Constant agitation by AWOC and other groups, such as the Berkeley-based Citizens for Farm Labor, had finally killed the bracero program. Under a new public law, braceros could be brought in only when special manpower shortages warranted it and with a guaranteed minimum wage of $1.40 an hour. This had cut off one of the farmers' main sources for keeping wages depressed and breaking strikes. Although the Delano grape growers do not generally use braceros to harvest the crop, the new stricter law had created an atmosphere more conducive to demands for higher farm-labor wages.

Furthermore, it is much easier to organize workers in the grape territory than in most agricultural areas. If they are to flourish, grapevines require careful attention, involving several different operations, during ten or eleven months of the year. Even though migrant workers pour into Delano during the harvest, when jobs and wages are at a peak, there is also a semi-skilled residential population that works all year long. This relatively permanent labor force can form a solid core. Some of the resident workers live in town where the organizer can get to them, and they can pass on the message during work to those who live in the camps.

Despite these circumstances, it seems certain that the strikers would not have had much success in a traditional labor-management economic tug-of-war with growers like Schenley and Di Giorgio. Farm workers, even locally organized ones, could not gain sufficient leverage against the growers' wealth, their alliances with local and state authorities, the ease with which they could bring in scab labor. In its seven years AWOC had called strike after strike without winning any contracts. If the labor movement had ever thrown its full weight behind AWOC, these strikes might have been more effective; but although the AFL-CIO continued to provide AWOC with enough funds to stay alive, unionizing farm labor had not been one of its overwhelming enthusiasms.

NFWA was uniquely equipped to come up with a new approach to these problems. NFWA director Cesar Chavez, who had been a migrant laborer in his youth, had left the fields to spend ten years with the Community Service Organization, a group that deals mainly with the problems of California's urban Mexican-American population. CSO had close connections, financially and philosophically, with Saul Alinsky, and Chavez gained experience in grass-roots organization techniques. In 1962, he resigned from CSO and came to Delano, where he started NFWA as an independent union. In three years' time, NFWA had become a militant organization of Mexican-American farm workers, operating along highly democratic, communal lines and supporting a number of self-help projects. Since the strike began, NFWA has been able to supply the strikers with an incredible amount of welfare and morale support, including a credit union, a weekly newspaper, a three-meal-a-day strike kitchen, an indigenous theater group, and a medical clinic staffed by volunteer doctors, nurses, and dentists.

Thus with NFWA's entrance, the strike almost at once became a grass-roots movement. Yet this in itself would still not have prevailed against the grape growers. However, in the absence of a militant and, at that time, interested national labor movement, Chavez and his co-workers were able to tap another source of outside support: There has come into being with civil rights and poverty politics a kind of nerve network running along the edge of American society that can be triggered into action by an appropriate struggle against social injustice. NFWA alerted SNCC and CORE, the student movement, the churches newly awakened to social problems by the

Negro, and the Migrant Ministry, a group of clergymen sponsored by the National Council of Churches, who through working with farm laborers in the fields for many years had come to
combine their concern for the Holy Word with an interest in
radical social action.

These forces responded instantly—a steady procession of
civil rights workers, college students, ministers and priests,
and progressive union people began to file through Delano.
Some stayed on as full-time NFWA staff workers; the rest went
back to their cities and campuses to spread the word, organize
fund-raising drives, stir up support in trade union locals. They
helped farm workers man roving picket lines that tried to pull
out scabs by shouting to them from the county roads running
through the grape fields. And they formed the corps that
NFWA used to implement national boycotts of Schenley and
Di Giorgio products. The strike took on a tone of moral
urgency, such as one associates with a freedom drive in Mississippi or Alabama. NFWA carried its cause into state politics
with a three-week march from Delano to Sacramento which
ended on Easter Sunday at the State Capitol building amid a
throng of 10,000 enthusiastic supporters.

The weapon that NFWA mobilized against the growers was
not merely economic power but also moral power. It is difficult
to say just what brought Schenley to the bargaining table and
Di Giorgio to the polls. In large measure, their vulnerability
may have been due to the fact that they are national corporations; the same tactics probably would not have broken the
numerous independent growers, though they will eventually
have to fall in line now that the two local giants have capi-
tulated. Without doubt the Schenley and Di Giorgio boycotts
were effective, not because they did the two companies grievous
economic damage but because their public images were hurt.
One can imagine the feedback in Delano when the Schenley
New York office found the New Left and the churches organizing against it.

III

If Chavez's coalition of moral activists was building strong support outside Delano, it was having quite the opposite impact on the town. Delano's middle-class citizenry reacted as though Jesse James and his gang had ridden in to shoot up the place. When guards hired by the growers beat up farm workers on the picket lines, the local police arrested the farm workers. Students and ministers were frequently jailed on vague charges. The *Delano Record* took a fervent stand against NFWA. In one issue, the caption to a photograph of Chavez addressing a rally in San Francisco asked readers to notice that the U.S. flag was being flown below NFWA's own flag, as though this somehow indicated what the strikers' *real* intentions were. A group of local merchants, businessmen, housewives, and pensioners formed an organization called Citizens for Facts, whose avowed aim is to distribute impartial information about the strike but whose practice has more often been to attack NFWA and its outside help in the vocabulary of witch-hunting paranoia.

What accounts for this violent antagonism toward the strike? For one thing, the townspeople by and large have always echoed the growers' anti-union sentiments. From a strictly utilitarian angle, it is questionable whether this attitude makes sense—an argument as reasonable as any other is that the wider buying power and more stable, responsible work force created by union wage increases and hiring practices would be good for the town's economy.

But threatened pocketbooks probably did not count for as much in the town's reaction as threatened class and social values. While there is little overt white supremacy in Delano, the Mexican and Filipino laborers are treated with a genteel paternalism that keeps most of them firmly in place as second-class citizens. In the eyes of the town burghers, the image NFWA presented didn't mean simply unionism; it spelled "revolution," disorder, the Mexican farm workers' flag above the American flag.

What most profoundly shook the town were the student radicals and clergymen who took part in the struggle. Perhaps the threat that students posed was ultimately the lesser. The town could release its rage by calling them Communists and beatniks. But seeing out-of-town ministers of their own faiths engaging in "revolutionary activities" on picket lines hit the citizens where it hurts. Middle-class Delano looks to the churches for social solidarity and perhaps even salvation, but certainly not for political action. As a result bitter disputes about the clergy's role in society have broken out between Delano churches, which are strongly opposed to the strike, other San Joaquin Valley churches which have taken various positions, and parishes and archdioceses outside the region which have been some of NFWA's best support. These quarrels have considerably shaken the California denominations.

There was one other event which fed resentment in the town. About the time the strike began, the Office of Economic Opportunity awarded NFWA a grant of more than $250,000 to train indigenous farm workers in rural leadership. Growers and Delano townspeople figured this money would be used to fund the strike. Chavez asked the OEO to hold the money in abeyance; he may never see it now. But bad feeling remained, no doubt placing the federal government in the "outside agitator" category.

IV

The grape strike entered a new phase early last summer, when big labor came to Delano in full battle dress, not only to fight the growers but to engage in civil war. Battle lines were drawn between the AFL-CIO and the Teamsters, and the issues raised in that confrontation will have a far-reaching effect on future farm labor organizing in America.

From an early point in the strike, NFWA and AWOC forces had worked up considerable rank-and-file and regional leadership support among union locals throughout California. The Los Angeles, San Francisco, and Alameda County Central Labor Councils started making regular contributions to the strikers. Under the direction of Ann Draper of the Amalgamated Clothing Workers, the San Francisco Labor Council sent monthly motorcades, bearing food and clothing. The ILWU members on the San Francisco docks refused to load Delano grapes for shipping. Though Teamster support was uneven in the Valley, it was fairly strong at first in Northern and Southern California; the first big picket line in Los Angeles against Di Giorgio products was manned by several hundred Teamsters.

Some AFL-CIO high-level circles began to realize at an early date that what was happening in Delano was not the usual agricultural strike. Paul Schrade, UAW Western regional director, became a strong NFWA supporter and a key liaison between Chavez and top AFL-CIO echelons. In mid-December Walter Reuther who, like Bobby Kennedy in the Democratic party, is always sensitive to a potential political base to the left of the chief, appeared in Delano to address the strikers and join Chavez and Itliong in a march through town. Reuther followed up with $5,000 a month to be split between AWOC and NFWA. William Kircher, head of AFL-CIO organizing, and IUD's executive director Jack Conway worked to build a bridge between AFL-CIO policy and the NFWA approach. Kircher and Conway wanted Itliong's group to join the march to Sacramento, but California AWOC head Al Green refused to work with elements outside established labor, and he dissuaded the Filipinos from marching.

Toward the end of spring 1966, a change in Teamster policy quickly eliminated any further possibility that Chavez's organization might remain outside the national labor movement. Teamster organizers, attempting to unhorse both NFWA and

AWOC, appeared on the Di Giorgio grounds and started their
own organizing drive, although they drew back after a few
days upon being denounced, remarkably enough, by NFWA's
church support. But Di Giorgio, who had either encouraged
the Teamsters in the first place or who now saw a chance to
get rid of Chavez and Itliong, unilaterally arranged an election
for June 24, in which only presently employed workers would
be eligible to vote. Moreover, there were signs that Di Giorgio
foremen were passing out Teamster membership cards and ordering employees to vote for the Teamsters. In protest, NFWA
and AWOC called for a boycott of the polls and refused to
permit their names on the ballot. Needless to say, the Teamsters
won.

Subsequently, various labor, religious, and Mexican-American organizations—including California's powerful Mexican-
American Political Association—pushed Governor Brown
(who up to this point had kept himself entirely aloof from the
events at Delano) into doing something about the bizarre, one-
sided election. Brown sent in Ronald W. Haughton, a labor
relations expert from Wayne State University, to investigate;
and on Haughton's recommendations, the August 30 election
was established.

With the new election a few weeks away, the Teamsters
opened a full-scale campaign at the Di Giorgio farm. Squadrons
of top Teamster organizers arrived in Delano, looking urban
and expensive in contrast to NFWA's grass-roots style. They
brought along San Francisco public relations experts, set up
shop in one of Delano's two relatively swank motels, drove
out to the fields in new cars and minibuses loaded with fancy
sound equipment, and passed out free key chains and soda
pop to the workers. On occasion, they sought support in what
would seem forbidden territory to a labor union: William
Grami, coordinator for the Teamster Drive, gave an address
before the Citizens for Facts, in which he attacked NFWA
in terms not unlike those of his audience. By this time it was

common knowledge that the Teamsters were on friendly terms with Di Giorgio—the company published an open letter to its employees urging them to elect the Teamsters on August 30.

What brought the Teamsters into the fray? One explanation is that the huge union has a vulnerable flank to protect. If, for example, a militant farm workers' union like NFWA were to gain sufficient statewide influence in agriculture, it could call harvest strikes that might suspend work for some 150,000 Teamster food-processing workers in California canneries and packing sheds, as well as for large numbers of truck drivers. To turn over the coin—with farm workers in its fold, the Teamsters would have substantial control over agricultural labor operations at almost every point from the fields to the marketplace.

Apparently the latter possibility did not bother Di Giorgio. The Teamsters in Delano were promoting their "business union-ism" formula, which emphasizes preserving harmonious labor-management relations by using the most tranquil routes to collective bargaining. They sold the company, if not the workers.

In response to the Teamster threat, it was decided that NFWA and AWOC would become a single AFL-CIO organi-zation. There were some immediate practical reasons for this move: Staying separate would mean a split in the Mexican and Filipino Di Giorgio vote. And the merger would enable Chavez to draw freely on AFL-CIO resources and prestige. At an AFL-CIO Executive Council meeting in Chicago a week before the election, the merger received official blessings and a new name, United Farm Workers Organizing Committee. Chavez was appointed director.

v

The arrival of big labor in Delano raises questions about the sort of unions farm workers can now hope to get. How much difference is there ultimately between what the AFL-CIO and what the Teamsters' Union has to offer? And now that the AFL-CIO has absorbed Chavez and the NFWA, what impact will the centralized labor giant and the tiny democratic and activist farm workers' organization have on one another?

The two questions are closely related. The AFL-CIO victory has by no means chased the Teamsters from the farmlands. Grower by grower, crop by crop, wherever Chavez and the AFL-CIO goes, Teamster organizers will follow, and vice versa. In future struggles for votes and contracts, perhaps the chief advantage that the AFL-CIO has over the Teamsters is the grass-roots and moral-cause appeal of Chavez's group and its loose coalition of outside support.

During the Di Giorgio clash the AFL-CIO pitted its newest organizing concept, called "social unionism," against Teamster business unionism. Social unionism, as formulated by Walter Reuther and the IUD's Jack Conway, takes its cue in part from the new political mood generated by Alinsky, Martin Luther King Jr., and other community action leaders. It centers around the notion that organizing for bargaining power can be extended from the job site out into the community at large, so that not only wages and working conditions are at stake but education, housing, poverty, and unemployment as well. Thus far, social unionism is mostly ideology, although a few pilot projects have been set in motion: In Chicago UAW organizers have hooked up with the tenants' unions started by King to work out a new basis for dealing with slumlords. And Paul Schrade and other labor officials in Los Angeles have helped create the Watts Labor Action Council, a neighborhood union staffed by AFL-CIO rank-and-file who live in the area, to recruit Negroes for jobs, set up training and recreation programs, and press for better general living conditions.

It is significant that the AFL-CIO officials who became most involved in the Delano events were social unionism's leading advocates. Explaining the new concept to the press, Conway singled out NFWA as the model for what he has in mind.

Another suggestion of a shift toward the experimental within AFL-CIO ranks was brought out when the Di Giorgio election drive was at its peak. The grape strike set the stage for the first real meeting between big labor and the student movement, two groups who have not felt much trust and warmth for one another in recent years. When Chavez joined the AFL-CIO, no doubt some students who had been with the NFWA movement from its beginning felt that they had been sold out. And no doubt some AFL-CIO veteran organizers who came in to help with the campaign felt uneasy working alongside the youthful, idealistic radicals. But on the whole, relations between the student volunteers and the labor officials were remarkable for their harmony, achieved under the duress and excitement of at least a temporary common cause. William Kircher was quoted in the *Fresno Bee* just before the election to the effect that AFL-CIO organizers were strung out from Oregon to the Mexican border trying to locate eligible voters who had moved on to other crops. According to NFWA, however, these particular "organizers" were almost entirely students, along with a few activist ministers and NFWA strikers that Chavez had sent out. Apparently Kircher had conferred official AFL-CIO status upon the whole lot for the benefit of the press. While Chavez's entry into the AFL-CIO will hardly radicalize that organization, neither does it appear that the AFL-CIO will try to press Chavez into its more conventional leadership molds.

VI

The farm workers' future also depends heavily on whether the strike will have political consequences that might significantly affect farm labor legislation.

Despite their conservative social values, many California agricultural communities like Delano are by no means political throwbacks to rugged frontier individualism—*that* strange yearning seems to well up most strongly in California's suburbs.

Delano's voters, for example, are Democrats by a margin of nearly two to one. Up till now, the state Democratic party has managed to keep the growers' friendship by not actively worrying—to put it mildly—about the plight of farm workers. Pat Brown, when he was Governor of California, made promises about pushing farm labor legislation, which nobody, including himself, has taken seriously.

But now the grape strike has put California Democrats on the spot. On the one hand, the furious Delano growers and townspeople, as well as farmers elsewhere in the state, anxiously watching the stirrings around them, have been demanding that their elected guardians of law and order quell Chavez and his friends. But since the strike, farm workers cannot be ignored politically for very much longer—they are becoming increasingly well-organized, ready for action, and have gained liberal and labor support.

Perhaps there is more hope in the long run for action from Washington. Senator Harrison Williams of New Jersey, who, with Bobby Kennedy and George Murphy, held a Senate hearing in Delano, has initiated new legislation to extend bargaining rights to farm workers, and Congressman Phil Burton from San Francisco has done the same in the House. Even as they continue fighting grass-roots skirmishes, the fledgling farm labor unions must look to the lawmakers to help them win the war. Only at the federal and state levels can moral conscience pressuring for social change become translated into the kind of political power which can offset those economic and class interests that want to preserve the status quo. Marvelously inspiring as the Delano struggle has been, both for the farm workers themselves and the students, ministers, and trade unionists who helped them, anyone who reflects upon the recent events in California must conclude that, for the American dispossessed, political and economic action have to go together.

1966

Mississippi: Children
and Politics

PAT WATTERS

The controversy and clamor that have surrounded the Child Development Group of Mississippi (CDGM) show clearly some basic facts about America in the time of the Johnson Administration: what's happening to the poverty program, convolutions of national (and the new Southern) politics, "black power," effectiveness and dilemmas of the nation's liberals, and the way it is with the poor themselves.

CDGM was established as a Head Start program in the early days of the poverty program in the summer of 1965. According to the lore (and it is well to point out that there is a great body of it), civil rights activists were at the time casting about for a follow-up to the tumultuous 1964 Freedom Summer. These included the tough, grass-roots oriented Delta Ministry of the National Council of Churches; remnants of the Council of Federated Organizations (COFO), that largely SNCC-dominated civil rights alliance which had run the Freedom Summer; the Freedom Democratic party people; others, including free-lance community organizers. They were persuaded by the Office of Economic Opportunity (OEO) to undertake the job of setting up Head Start schools across the state. Establishing this least controversial of poverty programs was a formidable job in Mississippi; the people and agencies (in terms of the demonology, the power structures and normal channels) who ordinarily would have been given the task wouldn't touch it.

Whether deliberately or not, CDGM played a role which became crucial in later controversy. It served as an agent of fear to force the power structures and normal channels to involve themselves in the poverty program; otherwise all that money and those jobs would be in the hands of the nefarious civil rights "agitators." There followed frantic (and from all reports fairly typical) organization of Community Action Programs (CAP) across the state, peopled by respectable whites (in a state not too long past the days when respectability meant membership in the Citizens' Council) and middle-class Negroes. The pressure from OEO was for quick action, not quality of board membership.

The first CDGM grant was for $1.4 million; it financed 84 Head Start centers for 6,000 children from May to August, 1965. By July, Sen. John Stennis had completed his investigation of the program and had one made by the Senate Appropriations Committee staff, and concluded that federal money was being used to subsidize civil rights groups and that there was evidence of irregular handling of funds. These are the essential charges that were to be repeated in each crisis of CDGM. Most of the story is summed up in the fact that the OEO moved from a position of denying them to making them. Part of the lore is the August 21, 1965, *New Republic* article by Andrew Kopkind which claims that Rep. John Bell Williams, the Goldwater Democrat, persuaded Sen. Stennis to use his influence against CDGM for the obvious *Realpolitik* reasons. This meant more than the opposition of Sen. James Eastland, which would have been expected as automatic; Sen. Stennis is adjudged a more rational Southern racist, and, more importantly, was on the very committee from which the poverty program had to get its money.

It took until February, 1966, that first time, for CDGM to

get refunded. "Glory, glory, hallelujah, we want our Head Start School," a "romper lobby" of 48 five-year-olds from Mississippi sang to Congress at one of a number of demonstrations for refunding. The most important demonstration, however, was the fact that 50 of the 84 centers remained open, the staffs working for no pay, during the months of delay. It was in this action by the "poor," the "uneducated," who had found not only the rarity of regular-paying work in CDGM, but a sense of achievement and vision about the children, that the real meaning of CDGM (with implications beyond the yet Neanderthal stratagems of Mississippi politics) began to emerge.

The nation had in the previous summer learned to be properly choked up by the valiant little freedom schools in Mississippi. Publicity was lavished on them and their largely white college-student staffs. But there were no full-page pictures in the *Saturday Evening Post* and *Look* of the Negro staffs in the CDGM schools nor of their larger accomplishments.

In this first refunding crisis, the program's first director, Dr. Tom Levin, a New York lay psychoanalyst, was quietly eased out, and the headquarters was moved from the Delta Ministry's Mount Beulah Conference Center near Edwards, Mississippi (with its movement tone and people), to a proper office building in downtown Jackson. Dr. Levin's main contribution was the unique spirit of the schools, no small matter of significance in the CDGM saga. What invariably impresses visitors is the confident bearing and bright-faced demeanor of the Head Start children; this miracle seems to have been wrought by no more than the application of undiluted "progressive education," a commentary on mediocre norms of most Southern education. Dr. Levin seems also to have been of that variety of Northern missionary familiar through the history of the South whose revulsion from the grosser evils of the Southern way of life allowed no rapprochement with its smaller charms and its perhaps smaller opportunities for encouraging local reform. The tone of the first funded period of CDGM seems to have been largely that of the previous year's Freedom Summer when local propriety was affronted by beards and bohemianism never to be forgiven (while murder by local whites went unexpiated).

This early CDGM tone was understandable, but created perhaps a needless handicap. There were some local whites and many of the Negro middle class who might have been CDGM allies who were among those put off, and there resulted probably the weakest part of the CDGM program. This is the inability to get the kind of local support required for health examinations and the like, including in some cases even food supplies needed in Head Start centers. The problem in such a state as Mississippi, however, is that those who normally manage such resources do it so as to demean the recipient. As one local observer put it, the doctor doesn't establish a relationship with the child and his parent which would mean future treatment and better health. Instead, the person who got the doctor establishes a relationship of power over the parent and child; if a doctor is needed again, they know to whom they must go to get one—provided they are desperate enough.

Under the second funding, after Sargent Shriver, director of the OEO, had defended the program generally—while acknowledging some irregularities—CDGM received $5.6 million in February, 1966, to administer 121 centers in 28 counties for a six-month period. John Mudd, a white graduate student who came to Mississippi during the Freedom Summer to direct a summer seminar project at Tougaloo College, emerged as the new director. Miss Marian Wright, who is Negro, of the NAACP Legal Defense and Educational Fund, Inc., is said to have suggested him for the job. She is on the board of directors of CDGM. The two of them, in the despairing way of the post-1964 regulars who stayed on in the South, have been eloquent in describing Mississippi's terrible problems of race and poverty and persistent in seeking solutions. It would not be proper to call them the brains of CDGM, but their influence has been considerable. Both are well-educated, sophisticated, and movement-seasoned young people of that extraordinary kind who have persistently held to the old goals of the civil rights movement and the old dream of a fundamental change in American society—against virtually nothing but disappointment and, of late, a desertion and giving-up on both the goals and the dream by the vast majority of those, both white and Negro, who felt the same in the early sixties.

II

The new grant meant that CDGM was pumping nearly a million dollars a month into the poorest part of the economy of the nation's poorest state; a lot of jobs, a lot of power was involved. In the way of statistics, a CDGM handout proclaimed that 98.9 per cent of the 2,272 employees during the period were local residents, and the vast majority of them poor people. In this, as in education, CDGM was a startlingly successful operation; it seemed to be doing what the poverty program called for in the most straightforward manner.

Like the education theory, the organizational framework had the virtue of rational design. The staff and the advisory boards were set up on three levels: local, regional, and state; the middle layer to serve as go-between for the top and bottom. Poor people, less than well educated, including teachers, filled the jobs; there was real mobility from bottom to top. There were people who began as teachers on the local level, moved through the middle level, and served in administrative posts at headquarters. Here, in part, was the source of the spirit of CDGM which, far better than most big organizational structures, maintained a connection between action-taking power and the reality with which the action was supposed to deal. As far along as the period of the third funding, with superstrict regulations from OEO breathing a poison of caution into the superstructure, Mrs. Pearl Draine, associate director of the program for children, could reassert the old spirit by becoming fed-up with weeks of wheel-spinning to get the schools ready to open under the new regulations; she sent out the order to open 'em Monday, ready or not.

There were supposed to be 9,000 children in the centers under the second grant; the count was closer to 12,000 because none was refused. Beyond this, another 49 centers in counties not covered by CDGM were being operated by volunteers and on whatever money they could raise, serving some 4,000 children. Those in Sunflower County (home of Senator Eastland) were in this category, competing successfully for children and local Negro support with well-heeled "regular" Head Starts under the county's Community Action Program (CAP). A visit I made in early 1967 to Sunflower City, a hamlet with a majority Negro population, suggested some of the strengths underlying CDGM. The center, built of corrugated metal, was on a row of small, neat Negro homes fronting the usual rutted dirt road. "Don't Teach Children; Teach a Child," said a sign on the wall.

Inside, and spilling out into the yard, about 30 children were enjoying a play period—pushing each other in home-made wagons, laughing and horsing around (in that way of gentleness notable in Southern Negro children), taking turns sliding down a home-made sliding board—a "usual scene" in the schools. Sixty children were on the rolls; half were out because of "flu." Mrs. Eddy J. Townsend, a large-framed, retired teacher with a no-nonsense face, told how she walked a mile, to work from 9:00 A.M. to 2:00 P.M., and a mile home—for nothing. A little boy was holding on to her, quietly protesting because three others on a tricycle wouldn't let him ride. She said to him, "You go ride," and to the three, "Y'all share," and the accommodation was made. She said she had taught 23 years in public schools, and had decided to work with the Sunflower City Center, "as long as the children come."

Otis Brown, the young Negro who is director of the school, told how it was sort of a continuation of one that was started as a freedom school in nearby Indianola, and was "burned out" by whites. The building and a second-hand bus used to haul children represented a $500 investment of money raised by a "newsletter" (typed with carbons) sent to Northern patrons. Local Negroes had built the building six months before on land owned by a Negro woman next door, Mrs. Lula Mae Brooks, who was fired from her job as a maid because of her 1964 involvement in the movement, and, vowing she would rather die than be a maid again, has been a local leader since. Mr. Brown hoped to be elected mayor of Sunflower City in an election-ordered re-run by a federal court so that Negro candidates might be placed on the ballot. The election was considered a test of whether movement leaders (including Mrs. Fannie Lou Hamer of Ruleville) with their CDGM and FDP orientation could muster a strong local Negro vote against the usual obstacles —everything from economic and physical intimidation to apathy. This they were unable to do.

Looking about him at the children and the well-kept "center," Mr. Brown struggled for the words that would describe what the effort there represented to the people. He said it wasn't really a question of taking sides between CDGM and the whites in power. The main thing was to get to share in the Head Start program, but not in the old way of charity, with the whites giving orders. There ought to be an opportunity to talk things out. *"It's got to not be race,"* he said.

The opposition from Mississippi's two U. S. Senators and the whites of the state resumed with the second grant to CDGM. There were the usual charges and a flurry of concern, in a state notable for unconcern about education, over a textbook prepared by CDGM in ungrammatical language—that is, the language spoken in the homes of most of the Head Starters. On August 22, 1966, the Jackson *Daily News* (long a leading voice of Mississippi racism), announced a three-way investigation underway by not only the General Accounting Office and the Senate Appropriations Committee, but the Office of Economic Opportunity as well. In this article, CDGM was linked with the "militant black power wing of the civil rights movement," a charge that was later to figure in leaks to such journalistic reflections of the Johnsonian spirit in Washington as the Evans-Novak column. Mr. Shriver has denied ever making such a charge, but the leaks were generally attributed to OEO and they cited the "black power" complaint as the real reason for the impending end of CDGM funding. Another new charge was that nepotism figured in some CDGM hiring. The irony of this coming from Mr. Shriver's office did not go unnoted. One explanation was offered for the "nepotism" in one hamlet: all the Negroes there were related to one another.

The CDGM staff and board, meanwhile, encouraged by the genuine success of the schools and the program's involvement of poor people, had in July drawn up a request for $41 million to operate a statewide program. This was sent back as fiscally out of the question, and a new request for $21 million was submitted in what the CDGM headquarters people declare was complete good faith. Mr. Mudd described one of the more subtle terrors of the trade he has found himself in: the second proposal, a document of some 115 pages of text and numerous appendices of facts and figures, setting out with some eloquence the rationale and philosophy of CDGM, was prepared in an incredibly short time by people going nights without sleep. It was praised by educators as a remarkable social document—but from OEO in Washington it soon became evident that no one had read it in its entirety. Specialists read it piecemeal. The proposal was based on actual registration of 30,000 children in 44 counties, with local communities not already in the program setting up committees on their own to form schools. The reduced proposal was submitted to a public hearing and finally approved by more than

2,000 in attendance with a resolution saying that the full $41 million was needed, and that $29 million was a bare minimum. A copy of the resolution, beginning, "We, the poor people of Mississippi, assembled at this CDGM public hearing, August 13, 1966, declare our full support of the CDGM Head Start program," was sent to the President. His reaction is not recorded.

On September 30, the Jackson *Daily News* broke an exclusive story gleefully saying that "the controversial" CDGM would not be refunded, and that it would be replaced by a 12-man board of white and Negro leaders set up under the "personal supervision" of Mr. Shriver. Senator Stennis was quoted as saying he had been working toward just such an end. This bit of journalistic enterprise inadvertently gave CDGM a month's early warning of impending disaster, embarrassed the OEO with the disclosure that it had been setting up a new Head Start agency before ever notifying the old one that it was to be ended, and moved powerful liberal forces in the nation to the defense of CDGM.

III

At this point, the CDGM lore begins to lack definitiveness. It is not clear, for example, whether the plot to scrap CDGM and replace it with Mississippi Action for Progress (MAP) originated in Washington or Mississippi. Some on the CDGM side suspect that the group of white moderates and liberals and mainly middle-class Negroes, who have sought to build a loyalist Democratic party in Mississippi, sold the idea to Washington. Hodding Carter III, a prime mover in MAP, denies this vehemently. He said that the first call came in August from an OEO source in the Atlanta regional office, saying that CDGM could not be refunded, and who in Mississippi might set up a more acceptable group to run Head Start? Others tell the same story, but suggest the groundwork was being laid as early as May.

Whichever and whenever, MAP was set up to replace CDGM. Its board was headed by wealthy industrialist Owen Cooper, a chemical plant owner of Yazoo City. The most influential Negro member was Aaron Henry, stalwart of the civil rights movement, the Clarksdale druggist who kept a precarious balance between the NAACP and the COFO radicals through 1964. Mr. Henry, something of a folk hero, seems to have been doing merely what comes naturally for a tough-minded politician and state NAACP president. Offered such an opportunity for power and patronage, he took it. Some say it was the gravest mistake he has ever made. The bitterness of the CDGM-MAP split, with much of the Negro CDGM wrath falling on Mr. Henry, reflects continuing animosity that started with the 1964 Freedom Summer and a split between the NAACP and SNCC, and continued between NAACP and the Freedom Democratic Party (FDP). It is to some extent a class split, with the "middle-class Negro approach" embodied in the NAACP and MAP. Also involved perhaps is the subterranean feuding between the NAACP and the Legal Defense Fund, a national phenomenon. On the national level, Roy Wilkins was caught in a terrible squeeze— under pressure to support his Mississippi people in MAP (including state NAACP director Charles Evers) and threatened with loss of funds from Northern liberal sources unless he got behind CDGM. He ended up asserting support of both, saying they were not mutually exclusive. There are those, however, on the CDGM side who see the NAACP as a prime mover in the plot.

There are many stories of Mississippi politics which make the state seem like one spread-out, gossipy small town. One about Aaron Henry and Owen Cooper is that they met at a Human Relations Council banquet at which Mr. Cooper had appeared, perhaps reluctantly, to introduce the liberal former

Congressman Brooks Hays. Mr. Cooper said during dinner to Mr. Henry that he felt he had done his Christian duty in most civic affairs, but not by the Negro poor (he is much given to saying this), and that if a chance came where Mr. Henry thought he might help out, he would like to hear from him. The story is that Mr. Henry immediately thought of his new friend, Mr. Cooper, when the MAP proposition was offered. However Mr. Cooper got into it (and some see him there to further a long-range desire for the governor's chair), his presence is attributed by many to the absence of one of the key members of the moderate political coalition, Claude Ramsey, state director of the AFL-CIO. Mr. Ramsey, a shrewd survivor in a state whose white people hate labor almost as much as desegregation, demurred from this view, though making no bones of his distaste for Mr. Cooper and his labor relations. He said merely that MAP didn't look good to him from the start, and that when they asked for a labor representative, he had enough sense to know it should be a Negro one. He demurred, too, from the theory that the anti-union flavor of MAP helped induce Walter Reuther and his Citizens Crusade Against Poverty (CCAP) to throw formidable weight behind efforts to save CDGM. Ramsey's awareness, however, of CCAP's predilections (CCAP supported CDGM in the first fund fight) might have had a bearing on his reluctance to be involved with MAP.

MAP was chartered by Gov. Paul Johnson on September 13, and received a $3 million grant on October 11. Funds to CDGM were ended on October 3. From that date until December 17, when Sargent Shriver capitulated to the liberal pressures, and until January 30 when after what seemed churlish delay, he finally signed a new $5 million funding, a big-time battle was joined on the national level over little old CDGM.

In CDGM's corner, in addition to Mr. Reuther and CCAP, were the Board of National Missions of the Presbyterian

Church (by virtue of their sponsorship of CDGM through Mary Holmes Junior College, a stratagem which originally prevented veto of the program by Governor Johnson); functionaries of the Congregational Church and the National Council of Churches; the Field Foundation (which provided limited funds to let CDGM limp along); the New World Foundation; and a battery of high-powered attorneys, including Joseph Rauh, the ADA and Civil Rights Leadership Conference leader, and the prestigious law firm of Sullivan and Cromwell. CCAP coordinated the attack; one of its major achievements was keeping it alive in the newspapers, with not much help from the *New York Times*. The battle was marked by that deadly coldness and ruthlessness we have come somehow not to take as frightening in our national (not to mention international) affairs. OEO seems to have fought dirtiest (it accused, found guilty, and sentenced CDGM without bothering to notify its staff, let alone allow it to defend itself, a disregard for due process seriously being considered for court or legislative remedy in pro-CDGM circles; it asked fiscal purity far beyond its usual norms, according to much competent testimony). But the coalition against OEO—including all those churchmen—fought the fire with its own white-hot flame. Not the smallest of its tactics was to set old friends (including even his former legal counsel) upon Mr. Shriver, this culminating in the mobilization of Vice President Humphrey, an ace card, which, if not the deciding factor, was certainly one that hurried along Mr. Shriver's defeat.

Also important was the work of a blue-ribbon panel of liberals headed by Dr. Robert Spike, professor of theology at the University of Chicago (later mysteriously slain, to add a somber note) and A. Philip Randolph. The panel investigated CDGM and found the charges against it false. CCAP also coordinated letters of protest from professional groups, with plans to keep these coming in increasing numbers. To much of this, as to a full-page ad in the *New York Times,* Mr. Shriver's response can be most charitably described as overly defensive.

In the lore it is varyingly stated that this titanic battle was joined somewhere along the way, if not from the beginning, by the President himself, through the good offices of Harry McPherson, special counsel to President Johnson, and Douglas Wynn, a Greenville, Mississippi, attorney considered a special friend to the President. Here again, the lore is hazy. If all the accounts are to be followed and believed, the highest power in the land at first acquiesced in the MAP plot, but then turned about and allowed (if not directed) the Vice President to step in and save CDGM—which in effect betrayed those like Aaron Henry who had put considerable political and personal prestige into following the first signals, not to mention the unhappy Mr. Shriver.

IV

A student of Johnson's off-balancing ways, however, might make sense of the sequence of events. Stennis and Eastland were given the pleasure of seeing CDGM almost destroyed. The Mississippi moderates were given an extraordinary, if not unique, boon at the expense of the regular Democratic party right-wingers, a real hunk of patronage. In the political annals, this may eventually turn out to be the most important thing that happened, and to substantiate a claim in a highly regarded piece of lore published in *Christianity and Crisis*, by Larold K. Schulz (who is Executive Coordinator of the Anti-Poverty Task Force of the National Council of Churches). His contention was that the real aim of the President in the affair was to help out the moderates. This analysis is given credence in some Washington circles, but is viewed with more skepticism in Mississippi—where the question is asked, why should he when the real power is still in the hands of the rightist regulars? One answer is that anyone setting out to kill CDGM and replace it with a moderately controlled program would be helping the regular party rightists, because they would prefer to cope with conventional deal-making politicians than with the kind of uncompromising force CDGM seemed capable of producing—people capable of giving up all, rather than make a deal. Certainly the avoidance of such politics is a part of the art of government in the areas of concentration of poor and Negro voters, as poverty leaders in Syracuse discovered, and as Dr. King learned in Chicago. Moreover, a man like Mr. Carter complains eloquently (while disclaiming that MAP has an iota of political content) that the Administration has done nothing for the moderates but double-cross them, or why else would they have turned to a Bobby Kennedy cocktail party for funds? The truth seems to be that the moderates (even as Aaron Henry of old) keep a precarious perch with a foot in each of these volatile party camps.

Certainly, when the Vice President came in on the funding negotiations, on the side of the angels, there was the sense that various people had been betrayed, and yet some impressive authorities hint that the Vice President acted not with Presidential disfavor. So— in the end, everybody got a little and lost a little, and that is the way it is in a consensus, isn't it, no matter how it collapses.

Not the least of the debilitating effects of the battle royal over CDGM hit the Office of Economic Opportunity itself. Staffers were split in their reaction to the way the situation was handled; some of them got up a petition protesting it and were treated to a long, fatherly interview with Mr. Shriver. All three men in the unit's civil rights division quit, two of them over CDGM alone. In early 1967, a staff member in Washington said morale was at an all-time low over CDGM, over the inability to get programs of merit through political opposition in Northern cities and bad CAP boards in the South, and over the rumors that the department would have its functions and whatever was left of its spirit of innovation turned over to the mercies of the regular bureaucracies. Many old hands had left and others were working with their bags packed.

At any rate, MAP was created and proceeded with difficulty to try to set up standard-model Head Start schools in 24 counties. Similar schools are operated by CAP boards in the state. Some 40 of these were set up during the second funding negotiations, with a special task force from OEO working to convert CDGM schools to what is called delegate agencies, which means they have their own board and virtual autonomy. This seems to have been a concession to Mississippi reality by the better half of OEO when it was thought CDGM really would be killed, and suggests one hopeful fate of the remaining CDGM schools if the program finally is killed.

Also growing out of the final funding crisis was a dispute over five of Mississippi's counties which originally had CDGM schools, but were assigned to MAP. This is a sorest of sore spots, with many of the old CDGM people refusing or being refused the opportunity to cooperate with MAP. The fate of the five counties was not a pretty part of the funding fight. These counties were placed under MAP when it was set up, but on December 17, the OEO announced it would refund CDGM and place the five counties back under CDGM. During the interim, before the new grant was signed, they were to stay with MAP and that's where they still are. It was dirty pool on the part of OEO, like agreeing to a strike settlement and then, after the workers have returned to the job, changing the terms of the agreement. If they had been aware of this situation, CDGM and its allies would have fought for the five counties during negotiations and probably would have refused the refunding—as they seemed ready to do if conditions had been to get rid of director John Mudd, or the Rev. James McCree of Canton, a Negro and chairman of the board. There was some sentiment in CDGM for a fight when the five counties were taken away. But there was also some feeling (including that of some Negro grass-roots leaders) to be more

pragmatic, to take what was still a victory, and not to jeop-
ardize the greater good for the sake of a few. Such, too, was
the advice of important elements among liberal CDGM supporters who were still unwilling to face the fact that the treatment of the five counties had diminished that victory
considerably.

Many of the CDGM schools continued to operate during
the negotiation fight (as they had during the previous one),
and the willingness of its people to work for the children on
a no-pay "volunteer" basis was probably CDGM's chief
strength. The CDGM schools in the five counties continued
this volunteer operation for months after the grant was signed.
A private organization called Friends Of The Children Of
Mississippi, an offshoot (in terms of personnel and approach)
of CDGM, administered (with some foundation support) the
volunteer units in the five counties and in one other. As late
as mid-March, 1967, Friends Of The Children was operating
28 centers with 1,912 children—more than MAP was handling
in these areas.

A strategy was devised for bargaining with MAP—and, if
MAP refused, with OEO. As MAP had the money and Friends
Of The Children had the children, the proposal was that
Friends Of The Children be allowed to operate the schools
on CDGM principles, with MAP money. A meeting was held
on April 1, 1967, to discuss this and alternate strategies (including that of just struggling along without support) by the
people, mainly Negro women, who had done all the work and
lavished all their hope on the schools. Though the strategy
was finally given approval there was considerable opposition
to sitting down and bargaining with MAP. The mood was one
of sheer practicality, beyond pragmatism—born out of past
sad experience, out of the feeling that you can't out-fox the
fox.

These people had a profound distrust of American practical
political procedure, and CDGM's achievement of having built
in them real trust in a federally financed (power-structure

oriented) program became fully clear. "If Friends Of The Children falls through, if those people lose their schools," said one of Mississippi's toughest pragmatists, "how will they ever again believe in anything?"

Another offshoot is Mississippi Action for Community Education (MACE), which hoped to get private funding, to provide technical assistance and training to community organizations for any kind of action, from poverty program to boycotts, they might want to take. Such an organization was needed southwide; SNCC and CORE, before they went off on "black power," seemed headed in such a direction. MACE, with its roots in the CDGM experience, might be the beginning or the model of something big in the continuing transition from demonstration to implementation in the South.

But meanwhile, Mississippi's better people, its few white liberals and moderates, its Negroes, were split asunder in the aftermath of the CDGM battle's bitterness. Mr. Shriver's office, after the dust settled, was citing a news article that pleased it, and this was a rarity. It was in a series on CDGM by James C. Millstone in the St. Louis *Post-Dispatch,* and it suggested that happily enough, and all by accident and blunder, Mississippi now has two mutually complimentary programs, MAP, which "prepares whites to accept Negroes on equal terms," and CDGM, which "works to bring Negroes to the point where they can deal with whites as equals." More on the mark of truth are points made by Leslie W. Dunbar, director of the Field Foundation, in a lecture at the Ezra Stiles College at Yale—that it is "especially saddening to see Negro and white liberal Southerners . . . at war, as they are over CDGM," and that though "we weep and we worry at what we fearfully apprehend to be the progressive abdication of Negroes and youth from the general society," there was a strong effort to kill in CDGM probably the most important endeavor in which Negroes and white youth were still working together within the normal framework of society.

It is necessary to wade through the density of detail in the

CDGM saga to get the feel of what really happened. The mainstream modes of high-powered modern America are complicated and mean, and even so pure and simple a plan as the Head Start schools becomes caught up and altered. It is good even to sit for a while in one of the outer offices of the Office of Economic Opportunity in Washington, and observe without rancor (because we are all what we are, shaped by culture and accident) the secretaries and tired-looking men busy with all the paper work of big-organization ritual, and listen as a little flurry of excitement runs through them at a hurry-up order to ship a film to a Mr. Martinez way off somewhere in unreality. Phone calls are made for plane schedules, a messenger is sent for, effort is made to get the right name and address on the label. It is good to sit there and try to picture Mr. Martinez and whatever his poverty program effort and reality of hungry children might be, as a secretary makes her harmless, unintentionally offensive little joke in old-movie mock Mexican-English, and to remember the little girl in Mississippi at Strike City.

At Strike City, a lot of history comes together. There, the desperately poor people of the cotton plantations who attempted in 1965 to strike against the law of labor supply and demand lived in tents until Frank Smith, one of the old SNCCs who ran a voter registration effort with style in Holly Springs, came and single-handedly built fine concrete block and wood housing units and a community center. The little girl and her family lived in one of the units, and she and her mother came out to greet visitors, and took them inside to see the nice interior with the modern kitchen and the walls all blackened with kerosene oil from a faulty stove and against one wall in the living room, a bookcase, filled with books. "They are the children's," said the mother who came from the plantations and had no opportunity for education. The little girl went and took down a book and brought it to the adult visitor and, like any little five-year-old who has grown up with books, she turned the pages and pointed to the pictures and told what they were: fish and monkey and cow and clown.

To know the norm of such a family in the South is to know the achievement of such a scene, and the hope. Earlier when she first came up and looked the visitors in the eye and told her name without shyness and stuck out her black little hand to the white ones, one of the visitors had asked, "Do you go to school?" and she had answered: "To the CDGM."

That has been the chief accomplishment, the most complete one. The headquarters staff, the young white and Negro intellectuals, like to say that this is only the smallest part of it, that the bigger part is involving the poor people in a high-powered organization and letting them learn its jungle trails and trials by combat so that they can survive and flourish in the new America, change their lives and societies, and even shake the vapid foundations of those big bureaucrat-culture offices up in Washington. On this level, the Head Start, the children were an issue around which the poor people might organize. For they would see the fine effect on their little pre-schoolers and they would inevitably ask, "But what happens when they get in those regular schools?" And no one would have to answer; they would know that something had to be done about the regular schools. And one way to begin would be to register and vote and join the PTA. And soon such a community would be in action, even as the poverty program envisioned. Marian Wright said children were an obvious issue; they were precious, and whites wouldn't be too worried, wouldn't harass them. (There has been some sporadic white violence, but far less to CDGM than to the old civil rights efforts, and even less than to MAP which stirs the violent racists because of its white employees and strained efforts to enroll a few white children.) Miss Wright was asked if there were other such obvious issues. "Welfare," she answered. "Eating and kids. They're basic."

The light and the space make things plainer to see in Mississippi, or maybe it is the plain talk of the poor Negroes whose earnestness and honest values fed the civil rights movement and was the real strength of CDGM. Here are leaders, their leaders, two of them talking on the main achievements of CDGM. Amzie Moore of Cleveland, Mississippi: "The kids in CDGM are not put in a bind. They are told what to do, and what not to do. But they are left to develop as they are. They're not bashful. They talk, sing. Their little spirits have been lifted. They have become individuals. But once they get in the regular school system, I don't know if a teacher with 60 kids in her class will know this, will know how to handle them." Mrs. Unita Blackwell of Isaquena County: "The people had given up on PTA, schools, etc., teachers, etc. They wouldn't have anything to do with it. Teachers said they were ignorant. They were discouraged. You had to work on them to get them to come to CDGM parents' meetings. But when they came to CDGM, they said it feels good to know they had something to give, to help run things."

That was what was going on, and to an extent continued under the last funding, though John Mudd at its outset spoke of his pessimism about being able to achieve the "real goals." The organization was hamstrung with probably the strictest regulations and surveillance in the poverty program; its staff and grass-roots followers worked in the belief that this would be the last funding. The hope was that the people in CDGM would be able to continue its spirit and its aims in the other poverty programs, in privately financed programs or in community organizations after it is gone. But the polluted waters of the mainstream were seeping in early in that last funding period. A major policy dispute developed between the staff and the board; ostensibly it was over who should fill one of the administrative jobs, but below the surface was distrust and suspicion centered on patronage and the power involved in all those jobs to give to people.

The liberals who put together their remarkable coalition

to save CDGM congratulated themselves justifiably on having won the first major victory for justice in the South since Selma. But it was a strange victory. Few in the nation knew that it had been won, let alone what was at stake. Out of the CDGM experience, CCAP began building a national complaint center program to try to provide technical aid to similarly beleaguered groups. But generally, there was little attempt to make the obvious connection between CDGM and the rest of the poverty program, to force the issue for the whole program and not simply CDGM in Mississippi.

The issue was clearly, as John Mudd and Marvin Hoffman stated it in *The Nation,* October 24, 1966, the flaws built into "community action" programs of OEO whereby the whole community, rich and poor, theoretically work together to solve problems of poverty.

The poor are again deprived of control of factors, which most directly affect their own lives, and, as a result, lose the opportunity to acquire the competence which would allow them to sit as equals, able to represent effectively the claims of their group. In fact, a traditional authoritarian pattern, which at best approaches humanitarian paternalism, is reinforced. The few immediate beneficiaries of the programs among the poor will receive a short-term boost to their incomes through their dole as "aides," but even these gains are contingent on the acceptance of whatever strings of dependency may be implicit. The danger of spawning such shortsighted poverty programs lies in the unwitting creation of a "low-level equilibrium trap" in which the human basis for continued growth is throttled rather than liberated.

The victory of the liberals then was to preserve one deviant program, the exception that proved the rule of the general failure of the poverty program. Why wasn't the battle fought over the issue of basic policy, or why was the issue of basic policy not pressed after the victory? The answers include everything from awareness that OEO itself was about to be dismantled to discouragement over the Vietnam War, to acknowledgment of the "mood of the nation" which was no longer thought to be liberal. Another large question might well be whether most of those who fought for CDGM in Mississippi would similarly support it in any other state of the union.

v

The riddle of Mississippi remains unanswered, but it seems clear that the kind of creative and purposeful direction in the lives of the poor that CDGM set in motion is not going to be set in motion under the forces which, like the big offices in Washington, are so far from any comprehension of the reality of poverty that they cannot act meaningfully. Some put it more harshly; how can the people and institutions which in direct and indirect ways are responsible for the existence of poverty be expected to change it? Yet another way of looking at it is to say that the middle class of white and Negro Americans are no more in control of the forces that shape their lives (as witness the Vietnam War) than are the poor. Indeed, as we keep learning, so many of the poor are passed over by the controlling forces of conventional welfare that they do have the kind of potential for free action and independence of thought that sprang up so quickly in Mississippi and other parts of the South in the Negro movement and such efforts as CDGM.

One of the awarenesses in CDGM was that to lose out to MAP and the CAP committees or to the mainstream spirit of power-seeking and accommodation did not necessarily mean that poverty in the form of physical and fiscal deprivation would continue, but that alleviation of poverty would be used by the conventional forces to control those who need help. The implications for the years ahead of diminishing jobs and increasing welfarism are clear. The middle-class of the nation stands ready for whatever new halter is being prepared; the old Marxist hope that the poor might be a revolutionary force breathes anew in an ironic way in the notion that they might form a political force to fight for freedom and individualism, for control of institutions instead of vice-versa. But the struggle for survival (as with the black-belt farmers trying desperately to assert their right to live on the land—a kind of right the middle class so far seems to be not even aware of) consumes the energy and efforts of the poor.

The charge that "black power" permeated CDGM was demonstrably untrue if it meant to say the organization was under the sway of the exhibitionist sloganeers of what is left of SNCC and CORE. But if any understanding was to be had of the meaning of CDGM it had to include the knowledge that the kind of stirring among poor Negroes that it achieved had to be done by the poor Negroes themselves. The same would seem to hold true for poor whites. The Mudd-Hoffman article makes the point that such a separatist phase is necessary while the poor learn how to cope with high-powered organizational modes and methods. Only after the poor learn to cope can they deal effectively with the sophisticated forces they find on a conventional CAP board. But where outside of bad old Mississippi would most liberals concede this—and make a fight for a CDGM?

Dr. Dunbar in his Yale speech cites as a major political miscalculation the belief that a loyalist Democratic party can be built in Mississippi (or any other Deep South state) without the poor Negroes—as the forces behind MAP seemed to be trying to do. ". . . They can't go without the poor; without them they don't have the votes even to be interesting—and the Negro poor have, at least yet for awhile, a new vision in Mississippi."

This seemed to be the deepest political meaning in the CDGM battle. The Negro vote is large enough at 32.9 per cent of its potential in Mississippi to be worth a major struggle on the national level, from most accounts involving even the President. The percentage of registered Negroes is higher in most other Southern states, but, not having experienced a Mississippi summer like that of 1964, and for other reasons, none of the other Southern states have as mature a Negro movement. What has happened in Mississippi will in probably quieter ways be a continuing struggle across the South in the immediate future. The nation needs to realize better what the stakes are, and how liberals in their Democratic-party politics need to do more than save CDGM for one more funding, if there is to be real progress against racism and poverty, and for freedom for all Americans.

1967

Harlem Schools:
Parents and Teachers

JEREMY LARNER

1. De-Integration

On the first day of the spring semester in 1964, the New York public school system was struck by a boycott through which city-wide organizations managed virtually to empty every ghetto school. The object was integration; the results were eight schools paired on the "Princeton Plan," a raft of lofty proposals, and constant turmoil ever since.

Today the eight paired schools (in themselves a comedown from the sixty the Board of Ed first promised) are falling apart, decimated by attacks from reactionary parents' groups, losing their white students, and ignored by sloganeers. The fancy studies on "Educational Parks" make good reading, but the Parks themselves are twenty years from actuality, and untested at that. The most celebrated and expensive non-solution to the integration problem comes from State Commissioner James Allen, who got the Board of Ed to redesign its grade patterns from 6–3–3 to 4–4–4. The idea was to get the kids traveling to centralized schools after the fourth grade, rather than the sixth, and then on to four-year high schools a year earlier. What Allen failed to foresee was that 200 new Intermediate Schools would be required to replace the 140 Junior High

Schools, each of them servicing a smaller geographic area and therefore even more segregated. Sure enough, the new Intermediate Schools are segregated, and most prominent among them is I.S. 201, which was designed as a $5 million showpiece but opened this fall to a furor of community hostility.

Some of the parents in Harlem have been fighting for integration since the Board of Ed first paid it lip service in 1954. They had children entering segregated first-grade classes who are now graduating (usually with non-academic diplomas) from segregated high schools. In 1958, when the present site of 201 was slated for a new Junior High, the parents warned that the mid-Harlem location guaranteed segregation, and in 1959 Supt. Theobald promised not to build there. But when the site was revived for 201, the same protesters met with evasion. The Board of Ed blandly assured them that a borderline site wasn't necessary—the school would be so good that white parents would send in their children.

The Board then began making plans for a model school, and the plans were relatively good, involving reduced class size, heterogeneous grouping, a vast array of educational equipment, and a specially-chosen staff. Yet when it came to consulting with parents, the Board merely put up a front. Asst. Supt. Daniel Schreiber of District 4 would meet with the parents and the local school board and try to say whatever might pacify them. The parents claim that he often failed to transmit their complaints to the Board, since they might have reflected on his administration of the district. The local board itself— which was supposed to have been given new powers in the past year—eventually resigned over the 201 affair, its members charging that they had been used to "create the picture that the Board of Education does consult with the community, when, in fact, it does not." On one occasion Mr. Schreiber appeared at a local board meeting to accept suggestions for naming the new school, when the Board of Ed staff paper had announced the final choice the day before.

Nevertheless, Mrs. Helen Testamark—President of the Parents Council, which consists of the Presidents of the 23 Parents Associations in District 4—succeeded in meeting with Superintendent Bernard Donovan as early as March, 1966, in order to press complaints against certain rumored choices for the principalship. Although the parents appear to have successfully vetoed some of the early candidates, Mrs. Testamark does not feel there was any real communication between herself and Donovan. "He hasn't ignored us," she says, "he's toyed with us. It's like saying you don't count."

Finally in June the parents and community groups pinned down Donovan on integration and were told the school would be integrated 50 per cent Negro and 50 per cent Puerto Rican. Immediately the parent and community leaders, backed by the local board, staged a well-attended sit-in in the District Office. Donovan's response to this was to send out pink leaflets to various other districts, asking for volunteers to send their children to the big new school in the middle of Harlem. Meanwhile the projected summer session was canceled, and the local groups announced that the school would be boycotted if it opened segregated in September.

By this time, as a teacher at 201 put it, "The parents had been lied to for years. They thought they were lied to because they were Negroes—but they got equal treatment. This is the way the Board of Ed always treats parents and teachers." Not sharing this perspective, the Negroes went about creating a solid black front. The Parents Council was swallowed up by a Negotiating Team chosen in a "closed room" but nonetheless representing the community groups active in the neighborhood and eventually including three parents out of ten negotiators. As the negotiators talked to Donovan, however, as many as twenty "observers" sat around the room, some of whom came from "black power" groups. The observers may have served not only to keep the rhetoric pure but also to keep out concerned groups from the larger community. Most notably,

neither the staff of 201 nor the United Federation of Teachers
was asked to participate. One parent told me that they simply
assumed the teachers would "do their jobs"—an assumption
based on a distrust of "outside" professionals and their standards.

For the first week of school the boycott was in force, the
negotiators were meeting with Donovan, and the Board of Ed
was avoiding a head-on confrontation by keeping 201 closed
and sending its pupils (80 per cent Negro, 20 per cent Puerto
Rican) back to the feeder schools they came from. And by
Monday of the following week, lo and behold, Donovan and
the Negotiating Team came to an agreement.

11. *Images and Personalities*

Most of the parents and community leaders do not regard
themselves as black nationalists. David Spencer, for instance,
who works for MEND, a local community action project, has
one child in 201 and another in an integrated Junior High
in Astoria. But Spencer, like most of the other leaders, has
been negatively impressed by the slowness of integration in
jobs and housing as well as in education.

You say "integration"—that word has stopped a lot of things for
us. The bills that had that tag got chopped up, but it seems the
others slipped through. A man say integration, I say that's *your*
worry, because you promised it. He say it's a two-way thing, I say
I don't know, I want to see it.

In talking about 201, Spencer expresses an attitude that
comes naturally to a man who works at helping the poor to help
themselves.

I don't want segregation, but if I have it, I want it on my own terms.
I don't want anyone else coming in to tell me what's best for me.
I feel *I* know what's best for me.

The negotiators wanted two things: a special council controlled by parents and community to run the school in joint

control with the Board of Ed; and a black principal. The key to their first demand is *accountability;* for they had found that although 85 per cent of Harlem children are at least two years behind in reading levels, it was impossible for parents or parents associations or local boards to hold a teacher or a principal responsible. The average Harlem principal—as I reported two years ago* and as the principals themselves were to confirm by their response to Donovan's agreement—is a frightened mediocrity who runs his school like a fortress. The council Donovan agreed to would have had funds for outside evaluation and curriculum development; but more than that, it would have had the power to recommend and screen personnel. The agreement stipulated that a teacher would not be hired if either the Board or the council had a "sound, serious objection." The wording was vague and teachers might wonder what qualifications the council had for judging them. But no one could doubt that, for whatever reason, only a minority of Harlem teachers are teaching effectively. Concerned parents knew that their children weren't being taught, but the standard explanations place the blame solely on the children and their homes, and the bureaucracy is too vast and principled to permit a fruitful complaint.

The demand for a black principal also reflected the leaders' desire to make the school their own, to make it respect in its very structure the intrinsic human worth of themselves and their children. They wanted a black principal for an example to the children—what some of them call "a motivational image." They were mindful, too, that only four of New York's 870 principals are Negro, and not all of them have permanent appointments.

Yet to say that the demands were emotionally powerful and humanly justified is not to say that Donovan should have given in to them or that their ultimate fulfillment would have made 201 a better school. Not many good teachers are attracted to a school where parents can hire or fire, for reasons I will dis-

* "The New York School Crisis," *Dissent,* Spring 1964.

cuss later. As for the black principal, Donovan should have scoured the earth long before then to get the best one available. But he had already committed himself to a dedicated white principal, and to betray him at that point was to betray the parents, for a racial issue was raised which shattered the immediate prospects of parental participation and gave ammunition to racists of the Right and Left.

In the heat of battle, various community representatives impugned the ability of Stanley Lisser, who has had experience at two other Harlem schools. They claimed to have seven pages of complaints from parents, but refused to submit them to the then-existent Civilian Review Board. It turned out that the complaints were compiled by a black nationalist teacher who first clashed with Lisser when the teacher insisted on the right to administer corporal punishment to his pupils. This reporter was unable to document one serious complaint against Lisser, whom he found to be a thoughtful, worried man devoted to the welfare of his pupils and staff. Despite his abovementioned troubles as principal of P.S. 175, Lisser instituted a special reading program, which, though it had no chance to achieve sensational results in the short time it ran, still produced better reading scores than those at P.S. 119, where principal Elliot Shapiro enjoyed exceptionally good relations with the Harlem community.

Miss Beryle Banfield, one of Lisser's Assistant Principals, worked under Shapiro at P.S. 119, where she led a group of teachers and volunteers who produced a lengthy teachers' guide to Africa. Under Lisser at P.S. 175, Miss Banfield directed a similar group in the production of a history of Harlem, and it is worth noting that the latter is a sounder, more detailed document. If they chance to read it, members of the Negotiating Team may be surprised at Lisser's preface, where he writes:

A people stripped of pride in their heritage and without accurate knowledge of their history are a people without a guiding light or a bedrock. Whether by accident or pernicious design, the true history of the Afro-American, both in Africa and the United States, has been omitted and ignored in our textbooks and our curriculum. Not only is there a lack of knowledge, but there is a vast amount of distorted history which must be rewritten.

III. *The Crisis*

Lisser and Banfield had picked their staff together, choosing entirely from volunteers, and ending up with 55 unusually committed teachers, nearly half of them Negro.

When we picked teachers [says Miss Banfield], we wanted people who were aware that the parents needed a voice in decision-making. The parents were not kept properly informed—or they would not have produced a parent-teacher confrontation. These teachers want the same thing as the parents; we're on their side. The only shade of difference that might arise is in regard to professional matters. [But what a shade that little shade turned out to be!]

When the boycott became imminent in the summer of 1966, the teachers met as a UFT chapter (all but one are members), and decided to honor the parents' picket-line. Lisser, in an act that set him apart from almost every other Harlem principal, promised to defend them against reprisals. "You don't have to come in," he is said to have told them. "You've got to understand how the parents feel."

While Donovan talked to the negotiators, the teachers babysat for their new pupils, who milled restlessly in the gyms, yards, and lunchrooms of schools that no longer had room to teach them. On the following Monday, both Donovan and the negotiators wanted the teachers to take the kids into P.S. 103, an old school that was empty because it was condemned. The teachers inspected the school and found that the Board had provided a minimum of books and a quick dusting. They voted 44–10 not to go in. "Our relationship with the kids had been jeopardized already by a week of sheep-herding," one teacher told me. "We knew that if we took them into 103, we'd have lost them for good." Here was the first "shade of difference" that caused the teachers to defy both Board and community. "We wanted a chance to prove that we could teach these kids," Miss Banfield said later. "We wanted 201 to be opened for these kids with this staff."

The teachers assembled that Monday at 201, where they were later informed that Lisser (under pressure from Donovan) had offered his resignation and that the school was to open with Miss Banfield serving as principal until an appropriate black male could be agreed upon. Whereupon Miss Banfield immediately announced—to the cheers of her colleagues—that she would not be chosen on the basis of color rather than competence. At least, those were the phrases the newspapers zeroed in on, hailing the statement as a victory over "reverse racism." Correspondingly, the Negotiating Team felt that "Beryle Banfield broke our backs." But both Miss Banfield's words and her motives were more complex than heretofore reported. She refused partly because she felt the offer was "fraudulent": she would be principal "in name only," without the license and therefore, she felt, with no more power than other temporary Negro principals she'd seen flounder, unable to command support, materials, or full decision-making authority. She refused also because she was part of a staff that had come to serve under Lisser, a staff she knew would not have been as good without him.

That the community could so badly misunderstand Beryle Banfield is one of the most painful ironies of a situation marked by an utter lack of communication between community groups and teachers. Beryle Banfield is hardly the prototype of the Tom teacher. When her first day as Asst. Principal happened to fall on Feb. 3, 1964, the day of the city-wide boycott, Miss Banfield stayed out of school and reported instead to teach at a "Freedom School"—thereby putting her new job right on the line. Herself a product of a completely segregated Harlem education (including P.S. 119), Miss Banfield is thoroughly committed to giving Harlem children—with whom she has an impressively open way of talking—"a sense of identity," which for her involves both the African heritage and the counteracting of what she refers to as "white values." Miss Banfield is currently writing a biography of Marcus Garvey, who she thinks has been badly misrepresented. No parent could have been more concerned than she that 201 be unblemished by "teachers who are threatened."

The next day the teachers picketed the Board of Ed and got Donovan—who had been roundly criticized in the press—to refuse Lisser's resignation. At the same time the Superintendents' Association issued to the media a set of holy principles decreeing no parents in the schools forever. Later that afternoon at UFT headquarters, the teachers met for the first time some members of the Negotiating Team. Dorothy Jones of the Protestant Council admitted "we should have come to you," but said she was going to "stand my ground." Livingston Wingate of HARYOU gave a friendly lecture on the concept of Harlem as a colony which needs self-government. But any potential cooperation was stymied by Roy Innis of CORE, who denounced the white teachers for their "white values" and the black teachers for being "white-oriented." Once more the stage was set for the racist image-peddlers on either side to polarize the two groups who not only have ultimate goals in common but who are powerless without each other.

A parent delegate later referred to Wingate and Innis as "the headline-makers." "The newspaper people don't look down at the poor parent in the corner," he said, "because these fellows over-shout 'em." Another parent leader told me simply, "I knew Roy Innis when he was interested in Civil Rights."

IV. *Plans and Slogans*

The next day 201 opened for business with Lisser as principal and the Negotiating Team utterly betrayed. They had gone home thinking they had won an agreement and learned otherwise from press and TV, where they saw their defeat proclaimed "a victory over racism." They reacted with bitterness. "What we see happening in the schools is a result of racism," says Mrs. Babette Edwards of the East Harlem Protestant Parish, "but when we object, *we* are branded racist—by the same people who have always called us apathetic!"

The result was an unsuccessful attempt at a boycott, under the self-defeating slogan: KEEP 201 CLOSED/FOR EITHER DESEGREGATION/OR TOTAL COMMUNITY CONTROL. But only forty pickets appeared, including a disproportionate number of nationalists, some of whom tried to prevent entrance with their bodies and were then thrown off by police. Meanwhile attendance inside the building approached 90 per cent—an unusually high figure for a Harlem schoolday—and a dozen parents interviewed by *The Amsterdam News* were all against the boycott.

For the next few nights, hectic meetings were held in Harlem, while, on the outside, Donovan was criticized for "handing over the school." Trying to come up with something acceptable, many of the protest leaders supported a new plan devised by Dr. Kenneth Clark, wherein the Board would "contract out" 201 to an "operations board" composed of community, parents, and Columbia Teachers College. This plan, too, ran into heavy opposition, mostly from the UFT, which had decided that teachers ought to be represented on any board. Moreover, said Al Shanker, President of the UFT, "we don't know where you get such confidence in Columbia—has it made such a good record in training our present teachers?" Shanker also had objections to "contracting out" schools—a problem I will take up later.

Others shared these objections. "The education colleges have not produced a single thing of value for teaching in the ghetto," says Herb Kohl, a Teachers College graduate and the best ghetto teacher I've seen—but the Union took the rap in the community. "It's because of you," said Clark to Shanker, "our children are being destroyed."

Meanwhile union leaders, along with some national civil rights leaders, were formulating an alternative plan that the Board might present to the protesters. This plan called for an "advisory board" that could not be accused of "taking over" the school, and which would consist of parent, teacher, and community representatives. Once more, poor communications prevented community groups from realizing how effective such a board might be; for the proposal called for the Board of Ed to supply funds with which the advisory board might hire its own staff and conduct its affairs independently. The advisory board would have become the first organized group to have complete access to achievement scores; it would have had the power to employ outside agencies of its own choice to evaluate the school; and it could have hired universities or other groups to develop new curricula and to run training programs. In short, the proposed board, while advisory, would have had considerable real power.

But once again the image of power proved more important than the actuality. The Board of Ed leaked the plan to the press, thereby pre-empting A. Philip Randolph and other civil rights figures who were ready to present it to the community. Moreover, the Board prefaced the plan with a long statement of all the wonderful things they had done for ghetto schools. The Board's image was that of a generous donor, buttressed as usual by fulsome editorials derived from the handouts of its ever-busy publicity staff. The community had no choice but to reject the plan, despite a fairly positive statement from Clark. "Under the circumstances, I would've rejected it, too," said Shanker.

The outcome was that the community forces have hardened their line. "The Board of Ed says the community is uneducable," says Mrs. Edwards. "It doesn't blame itself in the slightest. Unless parents have a majority voice, I don't think any board is worthwhile."

The Board of Ed, under fire now from Mayor Lindsay, was reduced to a promise to appoint a "Task Force" of prominent citizens to investigate the whole problem of ghetto schools and to make recommendations for sweeping changes. The Task Force was supposed to have been appointed within 30 days, but as of early December no names had been announced. Mrs. Edwards and several other community leaders have turned down appointments because they don't want to serve as "buffers between the Board and the community."

v . *The Union as Devil*

"I think the Union is the Devil in this whole thing," says a wealthy white foundation director, safely echoing a fashionable Harlem opinion. He's forgotten, perhaps, that the UFT leadership came out in support of the parents' original demands to screen out teachers to whom they had "sound and serious" objections—adding only that the accused must have his "day in court." Al Shanker is well aware of the kinds of bad teachers who operate in Harlem and believes that parents have a right to do something about them. He also believes that positive steps should be taken to attract better teachers. At any rate, the stand he took brought him a deluge of complaints from the more conservative segment of his membership, who blamed Shanker for Lisser's firing. Within the UFT Shanker was skating on thin ice in his attempt to lead the teachers in a progressive direction, just as he had when he proposed that the UFT's delegate assembly endorse the Civilian Review Board. It is indicative of the strong conservative minority within the ranks of teachers that this measure passed by a margin of only 486 to 375, with two chapters taking ads in the *World Journal Tribune* to attack Shanker's leadership.

Shanker had to make it absolutely clear that the Union

would not stand for any violation of a teacher's professional status, nor any hiring or firing done on the basis of color or any other non-professional criterion. This accounts for the Union's public rejoicing in a "victory" at the time when the community felt most defeated.

Radical critics of the Union (and within the Union) tend to overlook the fact that the UFT has existed only since 1962, when it had a hard struggle simply to establish collective bargaining. Since then it has made remarkable progress in upgrading the teaching profession in New York City, despite a bad press, internal dissension, and lack of support from stuffed-shirt educators, politicians, and high-class parents' organizations. It is true that so far most of the Union's bargaining points have concerned salaries and working-conditions, with benefits to ghetto children coming only indirectly—insofar as better-paid and less put-upon teachers will tend to teach better. But in the past two years under Shanker, the Union has begun to make proposals for fundamental changes in ghetto schools and in the system that serves them.

Over two years ago, the Union voted down the Board's suggestion for forced rotation of teachers, an ill-conceived effort to send better teachers into the ghettos. The Union's resistance created antagonism in the ghetto and among the more militant teachers, who did not appreciate the professional considerations involved. Shortly thereafter, however, the UFT prevailed upon the Board of Ed to designate certain elementary schools as "More Effective Schools," where extra funds would be spent to carry out a union-developed program for the first four grades, which involved heterogeneous grouping, smaller classes, and volunteer staffs including all kinds of specialists. An MES inter-school teachers' committee now coordinates such programs in 21 schools, where reading levels have indeed been improved, although the Board is beginning to complain about the high costs.

Deriding most of the "solutions" proposed so far as "empty slogans," Shanker has come up with a series of practical ideas which would enable ghetto teachers to move beyond "survival techniques," such as setting out copy-work, buying off trouble-makers, showing movies, and playing in the park. First of all, he wants an "Internship Program" within each school, "so that teachers who know how to teach can provide on-the-job train-ing for teachers who don't." Secondly, he agrees with those educators who have long called for the abolition of the Board of Examiners, with its eccentric licensing procedures. Shanker would like the Board of Ed to rely on the U.S. Exam for Teachers, which is given at every teaching college in the country. At present 37 per cent of the New York teaching staff consists of substitutes, which means that there is no alternative to incompetent teachers. But if thousands of would-be teachers all over the U.S. suddenly become eligible to teach in New York City, the present incumbents would feel the pressure of competition.

(To which one might add, why not throw it open all the way? Why not let anyone into your internship program who has a B.A.? Why not let in VISTA workers, unemployed artists, qualified volunteers? What the parents are saying, in effect, is that the traditional teachers college formulas don't count in the teaching of ghetto children. Once an internship program is established, actual teaching success can be made the only criterion of licensing.)

Shanker also has some ideas for reforming supervision. "There is no supervision in the public schools of New York at the present time. The supervisors have all decided that it's easier to write up schedules and order supplies than to provide teaching leadership." He wants the Board of Ed to hire admin-istrators from outside to take care of finances and supplies, and to let each staff of teachers *elect* its principal from its own ranks. The principal would then bear the responsibility of head teacher. Judging by distribution of UFT chapter chairmen,

Shanker estimates that this procedure would result in the immediate creation of 30 Negro principals.

A delicate point in Shanker's proposals calls for special facilities for severely disturbed children, two or three of whom can put a ghetto class in a total state of disruption. Shanker contends that the equivalent children in middle-class schools are removed by their own parents, who can afford to send them to private classes. It's a tricky matter, however, to pick out the psychologically disoriented in a ghetto school where so many children are justifiably angry, defiant, and withdrawn. Bad teachers tend to *create* a certain number of "disturbed" children, and I have seen some boys and girls who were judged impossible by guidance teachers suddenly begin to read and write on an extremely high level, simply because they finally found a teacher whom they trusted.

Shanker will soon propose to the UFT that it accept the help of non-professional school aides, even to the point of letting them assist with the teaching. Nor has he given up on integration: he notes that at P.S. 307 in Brooklyn, 120 parents, mostly white, are bussing their children into a ghetto area to take advantage of a free all-day kindergarten, and that more parents are clamoring to do the same. Since middle-class children are evidently not too precious to be bussed to something they can't get otherwise, Shanker suggests that the city could create new ghetto facilities for inexpensive summer camps, music schools and pre-school centers.

Early in 1967, the UFT will present a new plan for community involvement in ghetto schools. Unlike the Board of Ed's plan, it will begin with the admission that pupils have been retarded in several basic skills. It will suggest that the Board single out one area—District 4, which includes 201—for immediate improvement, to be followed by two the following year and three the year after. It calls for the foundation in each area of an "Educational Development Council," which would include people from the Board of Ed as well as elected represent-

atives from the UFT and the community. Each Council would
be funded to develop definite plans for improvement, which
in turn would be subject to ratification by the Board, the local
teachers, and a congress of parents.

Until there is some plan—or planned experiment—it will
be impossible to tell which teacher, book, or method makes a
difference. Nor can teaching performance be measured and
held accountable until parents and teachers are jointly involved
in setting goals and methods.

VI. *The Future*

Since the boycott of 1964 and its disillusioning aftermath,
the fight against inferior ghetto education has shifted to a series
of local actions directed against specific schools and principals.
At the present moment there is trouble brewing at schools on
the Lower East Side and in Brownsville, at P.S. 175 and P.S.
125 in Harlem, and at P.S. 36, "the school on the rocks" being
built on Morningside Heights, where Columbia's involvement
has already been an unhappy one.

In almost every case, the activists are going it alone and not
seeking allies outside their communities. Although most of
them are not black nationalists, they have assimilated nationalist rhetoric to describe themselves and their predicament. As
an example, let me submit an excerpt from the newsletter of
the East Harlem Protestant Parish, which is directed by the
white Rev. Robert Nichols:

> Harlem has accepted the definition of itself as a colony. . . . If
> it cannot participate in White American Society, it is no longer
> going to be exploited by overseers who commute into the neighbor-
> hood by day, wreak havoc with the lives of the black people, and
> withdraw by night with big paychecks. . . . A way must be found to
> make the public school part of the very fabric of the ghetto com-
> munity.

No knowledgeable person could deny that there is some truth
in the colonial metaphor. But acceptance of the metaphor will

only tend to make it more true. Suppose, for example, that "White American Society" also accepts the metaphor and directs Supt. Donovan to cut loose the ghetto schools, so that they can be "part of the fabric of the ghetto community." Would the result be better education?

That many teachers, social workers, and other professionals do not behave with professional adequacy in the ghetto situation is an observable and deplorable fact which must be altered. But must we then conclude, along with the new romanticists of poverty (many of whom are affluent whites), that *there is no such thing* as professional knowledge, ability, or training? Clearly there are areas—for example, medicine—where letting poor people take care of themselves is no solution; it's a form of sabotage. Just as medical care for the poor must be more sensitively coordinated into the public fabric of their lives, so must teaching. If there are "outsiders" already involved in the fabric of the community, the trick is not to chase all of them away, but to use them, to make the most of them.

The fact is that most of those who employ the colonial metaphor don't mean to be taken literally. At bottom, most of their demands are for a different *kind* of help—a kind that includes participation—rather than an end to help altogether. The danger of such rhetoric is that it is believed both by those who hear it and those who speak it—in which case the waters are muddied, backlash cuts off funds, and children are filled with bitterness instead of knowledge.

The current vogue in super-solutions is decentralization. Each day an academic anarchist proposes a new theory, and budding manipulators scamper for funds to universities, foundations, and government. A move is currently afoot to start a private Junior High in Harlem, financed by the Ford Foundation, blessed by Robert Kennedy, and run by a "community corporation." In the midst of the 201 crisis, Nelson Rockefeller proposed that schoolboards be elected—a proposal that was greeted with joy by reactionary parents in Queens. Still others are proposing that the public school system be abolished, that each child receive a stipend to go to the private school of his choice, that schools be run entirely by neighborhood boards, or that schools be farmed out to private institutions.

All of these notions raise basic questions about the nature and purpose of public school systems. One hardly knows where to start—you'd think there were no good reasons for public education in the first place! Supposedly the members of a democratic society share some values—values neither black nor white—which we would like to impart to all our children. Perhaps most of us wouldn't like it if a private school in Queens collected a government subsidy to teach its kids, say, that suburbs are sacred sanctuaries, or that welfare is unconstitutional. So we would have to supervise our decentralized schools somehow, probably license them, set standards for teacher training, for achievement levels, for sanitation—and perhaps end up with a bureaucracy larger and more corrupt than the one we have now. And can anyone testify that the teachers colleges, or the educational institutes, or private industry, or even poverty groups, are intrinsically more efficient and less susceptible to corruption than the New York Board of Ed?

Many of the Harlem parents think they are demanding no more than suburban parents already have, when they ask for the right to choose teachers and set curricula. But the truth is that most suburban school boards choose only the supervisor, who then controls the curriculum and guarantees the job of everyone he hires. The basic decision is the choice of supervisor—and it is true that Harlem parents have no such choice, and that they must be given some sort of participatory equivalent. But the general rule in American education is that the more parents leave schools to professionals, the better they are. The richer the community, the more sophisticated educationally, the more it stays out of curriculum and personnel. For no teacher who has much respect for his teaching ability will be attracted to or remain in a system where his curriculum is dictated to him and the displeasure of a pupil can get him fired.

If the Harlem community got what some of its leaders say they want, they'd get no more than what crummy rural schools have. New York schools are already better than those schools. What we have to get is something more like what rich suburban schools have. And to get that we need more money, we need to attract and train better teachers, we need progress in integrating our whole society, and, most immediately, we need formalized cooperation between school and community.

If one assumes that big-city politics are here to stay, what will produce progressive results is an increased adroitness at conciliating and coordinating the various interest groups, a majority of which have a positive stake in educational improvement. Now, as never before, these groups are talking about what will work and what won't. But if the cycle of failure and frustration continues, it will only reinforce the temptation to a sterile superiority and a righteous defeat.

1966

Appalachia:
The Dismal Land

HARRY CAUDILL

In the fall of 1963 Homer Bigart came to Eastern Kentucky and wrote an article for *The New York Times* that described the ragged, undernourished people with whom he talked, and the flimsy shacks in which they lived. He told of children so hungry they ate dry mud gouged out between chimney stones. Stung into action, an image-conscious President issued an executive order creating PARC, the President's Appalachian Regional Commission. In due time the commission made its report to President Johnson and to Congress, and in 1964 its recommendations became law. Americans may comfortably assume the problems of Appalachia have been fairly faced and are well on the road to being solved. Nothing could be further from the truth.

A great deal of superficial writing has given the nation a one-sided and misleading picture of the Appalachian South. The television camera has emphasized time and again that the Appalachian mountaineers are poor, that their land is tilted on its edge and badly eroded, and that the chief industry of the region—coal mining—is in the doldrums. They have told us that the people are undereducated, suspicious, and poorly motivated.

All this is true, after a fashion. Appalachia is a rugged land.

Its once great timber stands have been reduced to pathetic remnants. Most highlanders still entertain a tenacious suspicion of government and of strangers, and out of this ancient suspicion flow many of the ills that beset the region today.

Mountaineers have traditionally looked at government as a dangerous tyrant, albeit a tyrant of the people's own creation. They have feared that if government is made strong enough to be effective it will be strong enough to enslave them. As a result the Appalachian states and people have deliberately kept their governments weak—and weak, underfinanced governments have kept the people ignorant and, in their ignorance, poor.

II

Let us look at eastern Kentucky. Here we have a territory the size of Switzerland. Like Switzerland, it is mountainous. Both regions embrace about 15,000 square miles. Each is scenically beautiful. Each contains extensive brine beds. But here the comparison ends. Switzerland is almost certainly the richest region in the world. Some 5.5 million Swiss live in their little corner on the housetop of Europe. Their banks are immense. The Swiss taxpayers support twenty-two great institutions of higher learning, including seven world-famous universities and five great medical colleges. The little republic is so desirable a place to live in that it has to enforce the world's strictest emigration laws.

The Swiss earth, by contrast, is remarkably poor; 24 per cent of the surface is barren and incapable of growing anything; about one-fourth will grow timber, though the varieties are exceedingly limited. Very little of the country is warm enough for really good crops. Yet, the Swiss have become a remarkably rich, strong, and self-reliant people, despite their poor land.

We, in eastern Kentucky, proceeding in the usual Appalachian fashion, have done precisely the opposite, though the Kentucky mountains are superbly rich in minerals. Originally, the coal fields contained some 35 billion tons of coal; approximately 32 billion tons remain under the hills. There are important deposits of high-grade petroleum, beds of natural gas, and immense strata of limestone and silica-rich sandstone.

The surface of this eastern Kentucky mountain earth is also abundantly endowed. It is rich in timber types and has more strains of oak than there are timber trees of all varieties in Europe. It is blessed with 45 inches of rainfall annually and has no barren land. There is probably not an acre of land in eastern Kentucky that, in its natural state, cannot grow something of utility and beauty.

But the Swiss miracle has not been repeated in Kentucky. The Swiss had confidence in their government and used it as a beneficial tool. They created an equitable tax system and collected the adequate revenues which are the lifeblood of civilization. They built schools, libraries, universities, and hospitals, and these institutions enriched the people in a creative, upward-moving spiral.

Our Kentuckians followed another road. We did not levy such taxes. We did not build the schools, libraries, universities, and hospitals. We neglected the one great resource that overshadows and outweighs all others in importance—the people. Consequently, we are a people in flight. Hundreds of thousands of mountaineers have moved away. While Switzerland fences people out, Appalachia sustains the greatest out-migration since the Irish exodus of the nineteenth century. In fact, central Appalachia is threatened with virtually complete depopulation within another decade or two unless we find a way to stop the present ruinous process.

By comparison with Switzerland's 5.5 million, there are only 800,000 people left in eastern Kentucky. Its counties operate 40 per cent of the nation's remaining one-room schools. One quarter of the white adults are functional illiterates. Its rainfall, shed on denuded hillsides and unchecked by dams, rushes away in ever more frequent floods. Thus water—one of the region's great assets—has become its scourge.

We and our forebears had an opportunity to build a vigorous society, but we have opted for a low-key society instead, a society that places little emphasis on human development— on skills, competence, and inquisitiveness—and the result has been the enlargement of incompetence and dependency. A quarter of the dwindling population is on public assistance. Like most of the Appalachian South, the region has been turned into a pale-face reservation.

Sadly, the experience of Kentucky's eastern counties is in no sense unique. Its failure may have been greater in some respects than those of its kindred regions—southwestern Virginia, West Virginia, eastern Tennessee, western Maryland, and southern Pennsylvania; but in the main its tragic tale has been repeated: a backwoods people has moved into a primordial forest. They began decimating their timber to obtain "new grounds" which they wore out without replenishing them with cover crops. Failing to educate their descendants, the generations perpetuated a lack of understanding of the land and its capacities. When the region was rediscovered after the Civil War the people practically gave away its great riches, effectually disinheriting their children and their children's children. Some of the mineral tracts sold for as little as 10¢ an acre. The vast natural wealth passed into the hands of land companies organized by speculators with offices in Philadelphia, Pittsburgh, New York, and Baltimore.

For more than 50 years mountaineers have sat supinely and quietly by and allowed their land, kinsmen, and institutions to be exploited by people who have neither affection nor respect for Appalachia—whose only concern is to plunder it.

III

The hidden face of Appalachia must be brought into view and seen in proper focus. It is wondrously prosperous, for the coal depression has long since passed into history. It is studded with the names of great corporations—United States Steel, Bethlehem Steel, Inland Steel, Republic Steel, International Harvester, Jones & Laughlin, Ford Motor Company, and scores of others. And there are less famous corporations, the obscure firms that own immense tracts of minerals and lease them to operating companies for royalties payable on coal, oil, gas, and limestone. There is, for example, Virginia Coal & Iron with its 206,000 acres, almost certainly the most profitable investor-owned corporation in the United States. A few years ago the president of that company told a reporter for *Dunn's Review and Modern Industry* that he managed to "carry practically all of Virginia Coal & Iron's income down to net." Of its receipts 76 per cent are tax-free at the federal level. In that year the company realized a net profit after taxes of 61 per cent of gross. It paid a dividend of 45 per cent of gross, nine times as high as that paid by General Motors.

The Kentucky River Coal Corporation owns 200,000 acres in eastern Kentucky, and during that same year its dividend was a trifle under half of its huge income.

The Big Sandy Corporation, with 75,000 acres in the fabulously rich Big Sandy region, is dominated by the Delano family and has its headquarters at Campo Bello. It has supported its investors in fine style for more than half a century.

These companies and a score of others like them have shaped the destiny of Appalachia for seventy-five years. They have set the policies followed in its courthouses and state houses, and governors and legislators have cowered before them, enacting laws that exempted them almost entirely from any effective taxation.

Consequently, Appalachia's counties are hollow shells, resting lightly on an enormously rich natural-resource foundation. In these once—and sometimes still—lovely valleys, whose scenic beauty should be worth fortunes to their inhabitants, the poor little counties huddle—shabby, starved for funds, in debt, deep in perpetual fiscal crisis. The shoddy schools and other public facilities frighten away potential investors. From their dreary ineffectiveness the more able, intelligent, and ambitious flee.

Appalachia is saddled with a colonial system. The colonial system was strapped onto Appalachia during the same historic interval when it was imposed on much of the world.

The colonialist sway in the rest of the world has ended. Only in our Appalachia does it proceed unchecked. In Tennessee, in my own Kentucky, in West Virginia, western Virginia, western Maryland, and Pennsylvania the colonial bastions erected in the 1870's, and 1880's and 1890's, and early in this century still stand. Once those same companies and their associates and minions dominated Africa, South America, and Asia. Now their benighted policies rejected so firmly elsewhere, continue in effect and force only in the Appalachian South. And there too, at last, they are being challenged!

IV

If a New Appalachia is to arise out of the present tangle the people must be educated to comprehend the truth about their land. In classrooms, in courthouses, in community action centers, in every place where people meet, the possibility of Appalachian reform must be taught. The first battle ground in the struggle may well be the college classroom, but eventually it will be waged in PTA meetings and in state and local meetings of educational associations.

Teachers and their charges pay a terrible price for our regional backwardness. They would profit immensely from meaningful reform. A severance tax of 10 cents per ton of coal, barrel of oil, and comparable measure of gas would provide $30 million annually for education—for higher salaries, better buildings, enriched curricula. We must educate people

(a) to be discontented with the present arrangement;
(b) to appreciate the immense wealth of their land;
(c) to resent its exploitation by absentee owners;
(d) to understand the availability of funds to finance the institutions the people need;
(e) to grasp the vast power they can exercise—but have long neglected to exercise—over their basic wealth;
(f) to inspire a political movement to accomplish the far-reaching changes I have advocated.

We in the Congress for Appalachian Development have proposed that the people of the Southern mountains, whose forebears pioneered the institutions of freedom at Mecklenburg, South Carolina, and proclaimed America's first Declaration of Independence, should now assert a new Declaration of Independence and of Self-sufficiency; that as Americans we are a free-born people and intend to order our communities and affairs as such.

We seek to accomplish here no more and no less than has been accomplished in rich resource regions elsewhere in the world. We think the great wealth that was pilfered from our ancestors should be returned to the people of the mountains. We ask that those people who now hold legal title should be given a better and fairer deal than was afforded our forebears. The predecessors of the present-day companies came to the mountains when our ancestors were unschooled and inexperienced, and, taking advantage of their credulity, persuaded them to sign "broad form" deeds whereby coal companies in state after state claim the right to wreck and plunder the land, often without compensation to the people who live on and hold title to the "surface estate."

Whereas ignorant people were cozened into virtually giving away their substance, we would compensate these owners fairly according to modern values, vesting many of the great tracts of minerals in public ownership. We would put the title into public corporations, chartered under state enabling laws and governed by representatives of the people. These public corporations would have the right of eminent domain and would be empowered to sell bonds to finance the developmental efforts of their districts. These Economic Development Districts, these public corporations, would go to Wall Street or other money markets and raise their investment funds by offering a sound deal to the investing public. With these funds and by due process of law they would buy much of the vast mineral holdings now controlled by the economic royalists in distant cities.

With these acquisitions the people, acting through their Economic Development Districts, would undertake a comprehensive development program. They would build lakes and dams and coal-burning steam plants. They would turn the abundant resources of fuel and water into electricity and sell it in the world's largest and fastest-growing power market. They would send it by the fast-forming power grid to the electricity-hungry cities—including those now suffocating in grime and grit from antiquated generators on their outskirts. After debt retirement, Appalachia would use the profits from the sale of its power to finance the institutions and services the region desperately needs.

It is certain that Appalachian fossil fuels will power much of the nation in the future, as they have done for so long and so consistently in the past. *The coal and water will be turned into electricity, and the electricity will be sold at a profit*. Whether these profits will go out as dividends to distant stockholders or stay behind to finance the institutions our people need so desperately and have been promised for so long, remains to be seen.

This proposal is neither radical nor new. It has been thoroughly tested in the state of Washington over the last thirty years. A single county—Chelan—with a population of 40,000 has sold more than $500 million worth of bonds for its development. It build the Rocky Reach dam at a cost of $273.1 million. The Chelan County Public Utility District paid $1.5 million in taxes and donated another million to the county and county seat. The cheap power and good schools are attracting industry, and the county is booming.

The people who designed and now operate that Public Utility District have assured me that if Appalachia's counties were similarly organized they could raise many billions of dollars by the same means and finance local, grass-roots TVAs under the auspices of the states.

The scheme the federal authorities have devised for our highlands is not a development program at all. It is a depopulation program. Some 80 per cent of the money Congress has authorized will go into roads, and these roads will lead to a few strategically located "growth centers," many of them completely outside the hills. The highways will act as efficient conveyors to move the people out of the hinterlands into a few places like Lexington, Kentucky, and Kingsport, Tennessee. There, the theory runs, they will find jobs and happiness.

I have a deeply-rooted suspicion that this undertaking reflects a scheme fostered by the great absentee holding corporations to empty the countryside in order to facilitate their extractive industries. Nothing could suit them better than to empty the long valleys of the Appalachian hinterland, to leave the little houses without inhabitants to witness or protest the destruction of the land. Then our latter-day colonialists could drill and dig and gouge and cut and blast to their heart's content. Then, without interference from troublesome local people, they could get out the minerals by the cheapest, the most technologically efficient method. Their profits would swell accordingly and their dividend rates would soar to new levels. Then, in God's good time, the stripmined landscape and its hideous streams would be sold to the federal government for rehabilitation at the cost of the taxpayers.

Was this kind of a future for Appalachia sold to an unwitting Regional Commission in 1963–64, and to an equally unquestioning Congress? How much better it would be to seize the dream President Johnson and Senators Ribicoff and Kennedy have expressed in recent months when they spoke of new cities springing up across America! They and others have proposed that the United States solve the problems of its people out in the countryside in new cities and towns, rather than in sprawling, crumbling ghettos in gargantuan supercities. They hold that new cities must be built because existing cities cannot be expanded to hold all who are destined to crowd into them. And where can we find a more likely spot for new population centers than in our own southern and central Appalachia?

The government of the United States is thinking of spending $100 billion to bring a river down from Alaska to southern California. A trifling part of this money would build scores of dams and lakes across the Appalachian South. This spangle of man-made lakes would provide flood control, industrial water, recreational water, and cheap electricity—all important underpinnings in the creation of a viable economy.

Government and private planners are at work devising the essential understanding for the fostering of new communities. The government is going to encourage them. Industry is going to move into them. Millions of people are going to inhabit them. It has been calculated that $3 trillion worth of new housing will go up in the United States by the beginning of the twenty-first century. Unless we act on the side of progress and positive good we will continue an immense American sub-territory in the hands of ruthless exploiters who live far beyond its borders and care little or nothing about its destiny.

1967

How to Succeed in Antipoverty Without Really TRYing

HERBERT KOHL

How do you get into the antipoverty business? In Brooklyn the Bedford-Stuyvesant YMCA, proposing TRY (Training Resources for Youth), may have come up with an ingenious solution. It merely takes a powerful board of directors and an initial investment of $50,000.

The first step is simple—hire a "professional" staff of social scientists, legislative specialists, and systems experts. They are easy to find, at the universities, or working for the military. Then review federal legislation to see what the government is offering and design a program accordingly. Survey the most current social-science and educational journals and develop a justification for the program "in the light of the most recent research in the field." Give this material to a systems expert and let him cast it into "modern" form (complete with flow diagrams, input, output, and feedback). Then get endorsements from leading members of the community, package and publish the project proposal, set up a token pilot project—and wait for the dividends from Washington.

The intentions behind such a proposal may well be moral. Yet one can't but wonder where that $50,000 and those ingenious experts would be if not for recent federal legislation. The YMCA, after all, has not been notoriously active in fighting poverty during its last twenty-five years in Bedford-Stuyvesant. In fact there has been discussion of closing the Y if the project is not funded.

The TRY proposal is an impressive document. It sets out plans for a semi-residential vocational training program for 500 to 1,000 jobless youths from the age of seventeen to twenty who live in the Bedford-Stuyvesant section of Brooklyn. The entire program is neatly summarized by several flow diagrams that follow these boys (the input) from entry into the program through educational, psychological, and vocational training (the phase states of the system) into jobs (the output) and through to follow-up services (the feedback). An elaborate research design incorporates continual scientific evaluation and re-evaluation. The planners envision a computer bank programmed with the characteristics of both the staff and the boys that will constantly be used to develop research projects and to indicate the effectiveness of the ongoing program. This research aspect of the program is perhaps the most novel aspect of the design and possibly the one that most excites the social scientists who have conceived TRY. Its actual usefulness in helping the boys has yet to be established.

It is also encouraging that TRY acknowledges the magnitude of the problem of unemployed youth in Bedford-Stuyvesant and hopes to help up to a thousand boys. Unfortunately TRY's portrait of seventeen- to twenty-year-old jobless youths is more a caricature than a serious attempt to describe human beings.

According to TRY's proposal, most deprived youths are neither introspective nor verbal. They do not know the origins of many of their attitudes and opinions. Hate, for example—or bitterness, hopelessness and despair? The boys are said to be "lacking [in] the ability to make connections between actions and consequences." Connections between stealing and flight, for example, or job-seeking and rejection?

"A lack of practice in introspection leads [them] . . . to superficial or incorrect explanations." Of segregation in the North, or of the strategy of prejudice and counter-prejudice? We read that the jobless youths from Bedford-Stuyvesant "must become more aware of the quality and content of their thoughts and feelings," and that the TRY project must "help them learn how to analyze their own thought processes and their feelings." And how is TRY to achieve these goals? By teaching "Life Skills" and "Life Responsibilities" that will "provide for an intensive study of community resources." In the original version of the proposal, an example of such Life Skills was presented in the unit entitled "The Policeman and Me." The plan called for the jobless black youths to talk with policemen (some may have already), visit the station house (a neighborhood landmark), and learn the difficulties of policing a ghetto. Then these youths were to meet a policeman in "real life" and, "listening to the Police Officer after having had opportunity to learn more about policing in the city should result in more appreciative attitudes towards the police and their work. Undoubtedly there will be some students who will still hold unfavorable opinions about police services in the city. The interplay of these students with the others in the DISCUSSION which follows the police officer's talk should REVEAL FEELINGS [capitalized in the proposal] with which counselors will work . . ." Good God!

The counselors are to work within "the areas of Life Responsibility" emphasized in this curriculum: "Developing and maintaining the self psychologically and physically; preparing for a career; managing home and family responsibilities; using leisure time productively; and participating effectively in the community." An admirable program for the educable mentally retarded perhaps, but also admirably designed to further alienate the already alienated. Black youths, "disadvantaged" youths, jobless or not, are not mentally retarded, nor do they need to be taught how to develop and maintain themselves, their lives, families, homes and jobs. What they need is simply the opportunity to live lives in which human beings can humanly maintain themselves. The ghetto is inhuman, not the people who live there.

Lest this seem too harsh on the TRY proposals, it must be added that their notion of "culturally deprived" youth is no different from that current in most antipoverty programs and is derived directly from the social science literature on the disadvantaged. The book most frequently referred to in the literature is Frank Riessman's *The Culturally Deprived Child* which characterizes deprived children as anti-intellectual, physical and visual, content-centered, externally-oriented, problem-centered, inductive, spatial, slow, careful and persevering—implying that non-deprived children are intellectual, aural, form-centered, introspective, abstract-centered, deductive, temporal, quick, clever, facile, and flexible—a portrait no less absurd than that of the deprived child.

Yet TRY's notion of Life-Skills education does have fascinating possibilities. The Life-Skills educator is conceived of as combining the roles of teacher, counselor, and therapist in a newer, more flexible way which certainly may be called for because of the acknowledged failure of traditional teaching, counseling, and therapy with "disadvantaged" youth. TRY may have a solution, but one has to be wary of the proliferation of "professional" roles. It isn't necessarily the role of the teacher, counselor, or therapist that has failed with the poor and the alienated. More likely it has been the individual teacher, counselor, and therapist—and what they have taught, counseled, and thought they were curing. The new flexibility of a Life-Skills educator may be desirable, but if he is to tell the same old condescending lies (as in the Policeman story), he will fail in the same old way.

The TRY project offers, in addition to Life Skills, a list of carefully selected vocational programs. The Philco Corporation, the Interstate United Corporation, and tentatively the Brass Rail restaurants have been contracted to develop training programs, and a machine-servicing corporation is also being sought. TRY has offered these corporations alluring incentives: profit (from federal funds), and the opportunity to develop a training program that can be resold to the U.S. for retraining projects in underdeveloped nations. It seems that the antipoverty program is being used by corporations to develop training methods which may easily become part of foreign aid and development packages. Thus the federal government supports research on its own "underdeveloped" population so that American business will be ready to meet an increasing demand for service and training units in Africa and Latin America. It is rumored that the TRY package has been approached by the Canadian government, even before it had been funded or tested in the U.S.

The vocational programs TRY has carefully selected involve non-unionized industries. TRY has chosen Auto and Diesel Service, Food Service, Vending Machine Service, Home Appliance Service, Business Machines Service, Heating and Air-Conditioning, and Refrigeration as the areas of training. The vocations, too, are dressed out in flow diagrams. Yet when one looks closely at the diagram, one finds that what is meant, say, by food service is, in order from entry to exit: Kitchen Man and Counter Service Worker to Short-Order Cook and Second Cook, to Steward, First Cook, Advanced Short-Order Cook, and finally to Chef and Assistant Manager. Vending Machine Service, when translated reads: Candy routeman, cigar routeman, gum routeman, etc.

So 500 to 1,000 jobless youths will be allowed to choose between working in restaurants or garages, or the filling of vending machines. But why such an elaborate program to teach these trades—aren't there vocational high schools in the city, and doesn't one learn such trades on the job anyway? Why not just give the dropouts the jobs in the first place?

But do they want such jobs? Isn't the fact that these were the only jobs available in the first place one of the causes for their dropping out of school and not looking for work? Can one feed these young people lies in modern, attractive forms and buy out their bitterness? These youths are experts at picking out the lie and silently quitting in despair. That is perhaps the true meaning of Riessman's term "non-introspective."

Here then is the dilemma of the YMCA proposal—can one accept the status quo and still do something about poverty and prejudice in America? One can seem to be doing something and yet avoid the issue through entering the antipoverty business, via neatly packaged justifications and elegant experimental designs. But if committment is to go any deeper, if social and human motives are to take precedence over narrow economic interests, then one must be committed to change and agitation, to sacrificing transient respectability, in order to win the respect of those one is trying to help. The very existence of such appalling irrational poverty and helplessness in American society is a more serious indictment of the helping than the helped. It is the YMCA that needs Life-Skills Education.

1966

Bogalusa: The Economics of Tragedy

VERA RONY

The press has done justice to the woeful catalogue of demonstrations, shootings, and court injunctions suffered by this papermill town in the past year. There has been little exploration, however, of the causes of Bogalusa's agony: automation, economic frustration, and civic myopia. For Bogalusa is no redneck hamlet, dominated by musty tradition and the paternalism of an entrenched and locally controlled industry. Until recently the town has prospered under the influence of a progressive national corporation and strong Northern-based unions. Yet it was here that the economic urgency of the civil rights movement has most clearly come into focus: Negroes and whites fighting for the same jobs in a work force drastically reduced by technological change.

Bogalusa's anguish was not inspired by the economic demands of its Negroes. It began in December, 1964, when six prominent white residents became concerned because the town's public facilities were still segregated five months after passage of the Civil Rights Act. They invited former Arkansas Congressman Brooks Hays, a racial moderate, now associate director of the Community Relations Service, to speak on the experience of Southern communities in complying with the new law.

280

When the invitation became public, a cross was burned in front of the home of Reverend Bruce Shepherd, a signer of the invitation, in whose church the meeting was to be held. Several thousand handbills with the following text were distributed door to door:

[the purpose of this meeting] is to convince you that you should help integration by sitting in church with the black man, hiring more of them in your business, serving and eating with them in your cafes, and allowing your children to sit by filthy, runny-nosed, ragged, ugly little niggers in your public schools. We will know the names of all who are invited to the Brooks Hays meeting and we will know who did and did not attend this meeting. . . . Those who do attend [will be] dealt with accordingly by the Knights of the Ku Klux Klan.

A few days later, the vestrymen of St. Matthews Episcopal Church voted seven to one against opening the parish hall for the Hays meeting; their insurance did not cover bombing. And on January 5, the invitation to Hays was withdrawn. "We searched our souls day and night," said Shepherd, a former combat bombardier in Korea. "Cars filled with Klansmen kept going by our houses. We didn't want to give in to the Klan. But we had no one with us. We didn't have labor, business, city officials, or the law. We were just six guys bucking the whole town."

Why was it that Bogalusa, like Sodom, could not produce ten good men in a crisis? A partial answer is to be found in the brief but contradictory history of the town itself. In 1906, the Great Southern Lumber Company decided that Bogue Lusa —Choctaw for "smoky water"—would make an ideal location for the world's largest sawmill, to be surrounded by a town "laid out with . . . care and provision for the future." This care and provision included company houses, utilities, hospital, YM- and YWCA. But within fourteen years the monster mill, consuming fifty acres a day, had almost depleted the surrounding forests. Great Southern responded by instituting the first large-scale reforestation program in the history of the Southern lumber industry. By 1938, however, the local timber resources proved inadequate, and the company sold out to the Gaylord Container Corporation, a paper-products firm that in 1955 merged with the much larger Crown Zellerbach Corporation.

Crown knew little about the South when it came to Bogalusa. Its headquarters are in San Francisco and its 26,000 employees are scattered for the most part across the Pacific States. Since 1955, its sales have risen 58 per cent, to $622 million, making it the second largest paper-products manufacturer in the country. But in this highly competitive industry, this means only 4 per cent of the market. It also means continual plant modernization to keep pace with the industry's rapid technological change; by 1957, Crown had already built a new bag plant in Bogalusa.

Bringing the same progressive spirit to bear on its relations with the community, Crown began divesting itself of such utilities, houses, and stores still under traditional company control. But in 1960, the demands of competition collided with those of communal harmony. As Board Chairman Reed O. Hunt later explained: ". . . to make the mill fully competitive in the industry it had to be extensively modernized. . . . It was also clear that the mill was greatly overstaffed and that the work force would have to be reduced. . . . We made every effort to explain the situation to the union but tension inevitably developed."

This tension erupted in August, 1961, into a strike that lasted seven months. The company insists that, while it was a costly strike for all concerned, there was no residue of bitterness. But Paul Phillips, international president of the United Papermakers and Paperworkers, which maintains white and Negro locals in Bogalusa, hotly disagrees: "All that consultation stuff is malarkey. The company made those decisions unilaterally—that's why we struck. Our people felt the rug had been pulled out from under them."

Between 1961 and 1965, Crown spent more than $35 million on plant modernization and laid off 500 Bogalusans, black and white. There was no program, city-, company-, or union-sponsored, to attract new industry or to retrain displaced workers. They were merely placed in Crown's pool of unassigned labor, known as the Extra Board, where from time to time they could find temporary work. Since the Extra Board was segregated in 1961, displaced Negroes had access only to the most menial jobs. Nevertheless, unemployed whites were shocked to find themselves confronting Negroes in the same predicament—and in the context of a civil rights movement determined to destroy the social equilibrium upon which they depended.

In this tense social climate Crown Zellerbach confronted Executive Order 10925, signed by President Kennedy in March, 1961, requiring all firms under government contract to provide equal-employment opportunities for their workers. Crown waited more than a year before it moved, and moved, by its own admission, only its mouth. "We were aware that this was the first initiative in Bogalusa to alter the accepted pattern of race relations in the community and that we were taking it after a prolonged labor dispute," Chairman Hunt recalled for the stockholders. ". . . We felt it was essential to move ahead on the basis of a patient and thorough explanation. . . ."

In doing so, Crown ignored the experience of other Southern firms which have desegregated without incident: namely, that once a policy of integration is announced, a clear-cut procedure pursued with reasonable speed is far less inflammatory than a "patient and thorough explanation"—particularly if it lasts a year and a half! This lengthy study period was not, however, entirely Crown's responsibility. The other major parties were the white paper unions; their sentiments were immovable. When the company invited Victor Bussie, president of the Louisiana AFL-CIO Council, to assist in these discussions, these Unionists told him to go home. Bussie, one of the South's most effective labor leaders, was somewhat non-plussed by the United Papermakers and Paperworkers and the International Brotherhood of Pulp, Sulphite and Papermill Workers, who share jurisdiction over the 2,900 workers at Crown and another 13,000 in the state: "The state council has managed to keep the allegiance of most locals throughout the integration crisis, but not the paper unions; 45 per cent of them have disaffiliated. Most of these locals are in small towns, and the bulk of their membership consists of farmers who quit the land recently or one generation back. It's the most funda-mental kind of Southern conservatism, the hardest kind to reason with."

There was another, though silent, partner to this company-union talkathon which lasted from the spring of 1962 until December, 1963—the General Services Administration, which had awarded several lucrative federal contracts to Crown. During this period, the agency completed twenty-four reviews of the company's fair-employment practices and found them in compliance with government policy. GSA obviously based its approval on the company's *plans* for integration, since the plant remained totally segregated. But finally, in early 1964, Washington began to prod Crown into action.

Separate plant entrances for Negroes and whites were abolished, along with separate drinking fountains (which now have long spouts and paper cups). The toilets, always a hazard, were integrated but with partitions between the white and Negro sections. Only after violence erupted last year did the company try to desegregate its restaurant. But no sooner did the Negroes arrive than the whites left, and the private con-cessionaire was forced to close. The integration of time clocks was delayed until 1965, and, although the signs have been re-moved from the pay windows, Negroes are still to queue up at their old windows.

However, Crown's most significant act was to integrate its Extra Board in May, 1964, enabling Negroes as well as whites to be assigned to jobs on the basis of seniority. But the company frankly concedes that the impact of this innovation was limited: "Due to the manpower situation in the mill, the labor turnover since the policy was put into effect has not been great. Consequently, few Negroes have been able to obtain permanent jobs in progression lines formerly set aside for whites. Few whites have moved into jobs formerly held by Negroes."

To the white workers the integration of the Extra Board, after three years of reduced employment caused by automation, was the nightmare of Negro competition come true. The Klan lost no time exploiting the fear of job loss to Negroes; its ranks increased during 1964 to an estimated 800 members in a population of 22,000, reportedly the highest concentration in the South. And to job anxiety was added the agitation for civil rights legislation, the national outcry at the murders of Chaney, Schwerner, and Goodman, and finally, the passage of the Civil Rights Act, Title VII, which guaranteed the widening of the fair-employment breach so cautiously opened by Crown Zellerbach.

About noon on July 3, 1964, the day after the Civil Rights Act became law, two Negro girls, about twelve years old, sat down at the lunch counter of Woolworth's and requested service. Within an hour, a hundred white men had assembled in front of the store; they remained there until dark, although the children had long since fled.

In the rare, fortunate Southern community, a danger signal like this is promptly answered by a firm call for law and order from the powers that be. Here, the mantle rested on Crown Zellerbach, whose $19 million annual payroll provides 70 per cent of Bogalusa's income and which employs two of the town's four commissioners and several of its councilmen. But the company chose to remain silent. So did Mayor Jesse F. Cutrer, the protégé of Vertrees Young, a prominent local moderate and retired Crown vice-president. The resounding stillness extended

into December before it was broken by the ill-fated invitation
to Brooks Hays. When the Klan responded by intimidating the
entire community, it ignited the racial confrontation that still
continues.

At the time, the vigilante victory in forcing the withdrawal
of the invitation was complete—inside Bogalusa. But the Hays
episode was widely reported by the press, and Crown's switch-
board in San Francisco was soon deluged with calls from news
media, irate citizens, and government officials. The company
no longer hesitated to make its influence felt; a few days later
Mayor Cutrer notified the Bogalusa Civic and Voters League,
which represents the Negro community, that his police would
provide full protection for the testing of public accommoda-
tions, starting on January 28, 1965.

The first day of testing went smoothly, and Mayor Cutrer,
clearly relieved, declared the tests successful—and concluded.
But the Voters League, fired up by indignation, publicity, and
hope, scheduled a rally to launch a systematic assault on all of
Bogalusa's segregated facilities.

"That was February 1st, and the [Negro] Union Hall was
packed. People in the aisles, in back, everywhere," Jacqueline
Hicks, a leading militant, recalls. "Bill Yates and Steve Miller
of CORE were telling us how much we could do in Bogalusa
if only we stuck together and kept fighting. . . . We never had
a meeting like that in this town before."

Meanwhile equal excitement was stirring on Columbia Road,
the town's main street, where white men were assembling and
talking about the two white "outsiders" from CORE bringing
trouble to Bogalusa.

Yates and Miller had arrived at the Robert Hicks home on
East Ninth Street, where they were to spend the night. At 11:15
P.M., Chief of Police Claxton Knight came to inform them that
he could no longer guarantee their safety in Bogalusa; he ad-
vised them to leave at once. It was a paralyzing moment for the
Hickses: their two youngest children were at home, and it had

not been easy to finance the pleasant, sprawling ranch house. "But we didn't even have to remember Chaney, Schwerner, and Goodman. We just knew that if Yates and Miller left our house at that moment, we would never see them alive again," Bob Hicks recalls. Informed that the two CORE workers would stay, Chief Knight took his leave with a parting warning: "We have better things to do than protect people who aren't wanted here."

While CORE, alerted by Yates and Miller, reached out frantically for help from Washington, word of the impending siege at the Hickses' flashed through Jewtown, Poplas, Moden Quarters, and other widely separated Negro sections. Within minutes, carloads of armed Negroes poured into East Ninth Street. Now the rumors began to travel the other way; the Klan never came near East Ninth Street. The Movement had finally arrived in Bogalusa.

These events still did not elicit a law-and-order statement from Crown or the unions. Not until April 2 did the local Crown manager speak out against violence and intimidation, a reticence the company explained by insisting that civil rights are a community responsibility.

The international unions made no statement at all; nor did their locals take advantage of the mediation efforts of the AFL-CIO's Bussie, who returned to Bogalusa in April to help establish communications between the town officials and the Voters League, now under new leadership.

This changing of the guard is a frequent occurrence in the civil rights struggle. The old preacher-teacher-insurance-agent leadership of the Voters League lacked the nerve for the aggressive enterprises of Bogalusa's aroused Negroes. By April, A. Z. Young had assumed the presidency and Bob Hicks the vice-presidency of the organization. Both men had developed their skills in the service of Local 624, the Negro wing of the Pulp, Sulphite Union: Young was the local's president for a decade;

Hicks was a trustee for years. Their union experience equipped them to voice those fundamental economic grievances that do not surface in every civil rights battle but could hardly be suppressed in Bogalusa, where the median income for Negro families is $2,200 a year.

The Voters League launched a vigorous campaign for more and better jobs—whose thrust was naturally directed at Crown. The League pounded away at the statistics: 9,000, or one out of three, Bogalusans are Negroes; yet of Crown's 2,900 employees, Negroes account for a mere 390, or one out of seven, and they are grouped in the poorest paid and least skilled jobs. At Crown as elsewhere, the demand for more jobs is inseparable from that for better jobs, since Negroes cannot hope to become a significant part of the work force without access to skilled jobs.

The Voters League's first proposal was jobs for women, who presently lack any alternative to working as maids for $18 a week. Crown, which employed 200 white women, did not have a single Negro woman on the payroll. But the League's fundamental demand was access to better-paid skilled jobs. "I came to Crown in 1950," said Otha Peters, the current president of Negro Local 624, "the same time as Hilton Beard, the president of our white local. I couldn't go beyond porter, so I make $2.16 an hour, while Hilton, who is a millwright, makes $3.45. Sometimes we talk about it, and Hilton says, 'You should've been born a white boy.'"

When Chairman Hunt announced the integration of the Extra Board, he acknowledged the limitations imposed on this policy by the low labor turnover, due to automation and reduced sales, which left the plant operating at half capacity. And he did not mention that only nine Negroes had moved into formerly white job lines during the first year of integration. Pedro Mondy, official of Negro Papermakers Local 189A, said it could hardly be otherwise: "Take the recovery room in the paper mill. There are twenty-two jobs; before '64, the top seven-

teen were restricted to whites, the bottom five to Negroes.
Now supposing that after the company announced the integration, the senior Negro wants to move into a white job, which he
knows how to handle 'cause he's done it in emergencies. He's
got to leave *his* job, give up his seniority, go into the Extra
Board, pass a tough test, and then wait his turn on the Extra
Board. If he does get the job, he'll be the first one laid off.
And if it's more than six weeks since he left his old job, he
can't go back—he's out of luck."

Repeated conferences during the first half of 1965 between
the company, the unions, the Voters League, and local officials
failed to produce a single new job for a Negro in Bogalusa.
The pace of demonstrations accelerated, as did the physical
attacks by white men and the jeering by white women and children. On June 2, Washington Parish Deputy Sheriff O'Neal
Moore, a Negro, was slain by night riders. On July 8, Henry
Austin of the black Deacons for Defense shot a white man
who attacked a Negro child during a demonstration. Nearly
100 people were arrested during those hectic weeks. And on
July 10, CORE obtained a federal injunction ordering the
police to provide full protection to civil rights workers (subsequent injunctions have been issued against local officials, the
Klan, and individual members of the police).

Five days after the injunction, Crown Vice-President Francis
M. Barnes flew from San Francisco to confer with the Bogalusa Voters League. It was a pilgrimage at least partially
motivated by the prodding of the GSA, which had just awarded
Crown a new $12 million contract.

Confronting Barnes were three Negro women who had applied at Crown and "been turned around so often" that they
kept asking local plant manager Roy Ferguson to repeat his
assurance that henceforth the applications of Negro women
would be accepted. Next followed an illuminating exchange
between management and Bob Hicks:

Ferguson: "All jobs are open, Mr. Hicks, at this time. They may not have been open in the past."

Hicks: "Not all jobs are open because they have some jobs for colored and some for whites as of today. My job is predominantly colored. I put in for this other [paste machine operator] my experience. I had done this job for a number of years before this automation came in. These [white] men had no experience, yet they were selected and put on that job. And then the same thing . . . you must take a test. It doesn't require a test for a man to do work that he has been doing for years. And in the department where I work, they bring white men in on these jobs that have training in other departments . . . yet we have to show them or they can't make it. . . . But the job I'm in, no white men have ever worked in it. . . . Yet and still, you turn right around and hire these [white] men that did not pass the test to come to work in the job that is especially for Negroes. Now these are the facts."

Crown Lawyer: "Would you go over that again?"

(The tests that Hicks referred to were instituted in January, 1963, after the company's announced intention of complying with Presidential Executive Order 10925.)

League Lawyer: "An employee told me that an examination for a manual labor category contained a question: 'If a man was fishing for two hours and caught three fish, if he fished the next day for five hours, how many fish would he catch?' "

Barnes: "What did he use for bait?" (Laughter)

Hicks: "Since the white man was hired before the test [was instituted] and promoted in the line of progression and wasn't subject to a test, why subject a man to a test now because he is black?"

As Robert F. Collins, one of the League's attorneys, said in summation: "The real issue is what, if anything, the company is willing to do to compensate for the past discrimination. To merely say that at this point you are going to be fair is not enough." This is the view that most appalls the company and the white unions.

No company answer was forthcoming or expected at this meeting, although Negroes credit it with two improvements later negotiated with Local 624: Negroes need no longer leave their old jobs and enter the Extra Board to apply for formerly white jobs, and they retain seniority on their old job in the event of return. But later, Delos Knight, Crown's public relations officer in Bogalusa, spoke quite frankly about the League's demands: "Papermaking is still an art. Despite all the new machines, men still have to hold the paper up to the light to see if it's okay. You can't turn the whole plant upside down and fire the people already working for you in order to right the wrongs of the past. There is no instant solution. This company cannot be expected to solve these problems by itself. The government will have to lay down industry-wide guidelines." President Phillips of the Papermakers put it in even stronger terms: "Even in all-white plants in the North, the top machine jobs take five years of training. You can't do more than start Negroes and whites in *all* job lines. . . . If you try to place every man according to seniority, you'll have to shut down the mill. The whites won't stand for it."

Thus the economic tragedy of Bogalusa, planted by automation and nurtured by the indecision, delay, and timorousness of Crown Zellerbach and the unions, has become by default the problem of the federal government. Until recently, the voices of Knight and Phillips seemed to echo more loudly in Washington than those of Bogalusa's Negroes. Despite warm expressions of interest from the President's Commission on Fair Employment Practices, the last five months of 1965 saw no increase in the number of Negroes in white job lines at Crown. On December 18, the commission finally acted. Chairman Franklin D. Roosevelt, Jr., conferred in New Orleans with top officials of Crown and the Negro and white locals of the United Papermakers. He extracted a pledge from both locals to accept full integration of functionally related job lines, according to seniority, without bars to competent Negroes.

Though the details remain to be settled, the agreement appears to be a major triumph for law enforcement and for

Bogalusa's Negroes. But this triumph may be more apparent than real. "Sure, the agreement sounds good," says Bob Hicks. "But three days after it was made, a Negro recently promoted into a white job line found twenty hooded Klansmen waiting for him in the company parking lot, about ten yards from the mill entrance. They told him he'd better quit, and he did. The company said it couldn't do a thing about it. A few days ago, a Negro high school senior in a formerly all-white school was beaten up for the third time; he wants to quit, too. But Crown still won't discuss any community problems with the Voters League. And as long as the Company keeps these attitudes, Bogalusa's troubles will continue.

1966

Notes on the Welfare State

IRVING HOWE

1. *The Abstract Model*

Ferment, conflict, innovation, violence, a measure of madness
—all these and more characterize the American scene in the
late sixties. The image of social stability, which dominated
both liberal and conservative thought only a few years ago,
has proved to be an illusion. The welfare state in which we
live is strained by tension and clash. But before examining
these, let's look at the welfare state as an idea or model in
order to gain some historical perspective. A model is not a
picture, either still or moving; it lacks, and in order to serve
its purpose it must lack, the dynamics of reality. It may articulate skeletal structures but it cannot describe either the processes of change or idiosyncratic traits.

Among current models of contemporary society the most

This article appeared originally as "Notes on Here and Now" in the
Fall 1967 issue of *Partisan Review*. © 1967 by Partisan Review.

useful, I think, is that of the welfare state. By the welfare state one signifies a capitalist economy in which the interplay of private and/or corporate owners in a largely regulated market remains dominant but in which the workings of the economy are so modified that the powers of free disposal by property owners are controlled politically.

The welfare state is constantly being reconstructed. The model we advance for it may suggest an equilibrium, but in the actuality from which the model is drawn there persist serious difficulties, conflicts, and breakdowns. If the welfare state could reach, so to say, a point of internal perfection, the point at which it would all but approach its "ideal type," it would comprise a system of regulated conflicts making for pluralist balance and stability. But this point of perfection cannot be reached, if only because the welfare state appears within a given historical context, so that it must always be complicated by the accumulation of problems provided by a capitalist economy and a specific national past; complicated, further, by concurrent international conflicts which, as we now see, can crucially affect and distort its formation; and complicated, as well, by a series of pressures, ranging from status ambition to moral idealism, which it is not, as a society, well equipped to handle.

Within certain limits having to do with basic relations of power and production, the welfare state remains open to varying sociopolitical contents, since it is itself the visible evidence of a long and continuing struggle among classes and groups for greater shares in the social product. That the welfare state exists at all is due not merely to autonomous processes within the economy, or enlightened self-interest on the part of dominant classes, or moral idealism, as over decades it has stirred segments of the population into conscience; no, the welfare state is importantly the result of social struggle on the part of the labor movement. If the working class has not fulfilled the "historic tasks" assigned to it by Marxism and if it shows, at least in the advanced industrial countries, no sign of revolutionary initiative, it has nevertheless significantly modified the nature and softened the cruelties of capitalist society.

In a curious way—the analogy need not be stressed—the welfare state has served a function similar to that of Communism in the East. I do not mean to suggest an equivalence in value, since for myself, as a socialist, there can be no question that it is immensely more desirable to live in a society that allows political freedom and thereby organized struggle and independent class action. Yet, from a certain long-range perspective, one could say that both the welfare state and the Communist societies have had the effect of raising the historical expectations of millions of people, even while offering radically different kinds of satisfaction and sharing in common failures. Both have enabled previously mute segments of society to feel that the state ought to act in their behalf and that perhaps they have a role in history as active subjects demanding that the state serve their needs. The contrast with earlier societies is striking, for in them, as Michael Walzer writes, the dominant conviction was that

. . . the state always *is* more than it *does*. Pre-welfare theorists described it as a closely knit body, dense and opaque, whose members were involved emotionally as well as materially, mysteriously as well as rationally, in the fate of the whole. The members ought to be involved, it was said, not for the sake of concrete benefits of any sort, but simply, for the sake of communion. Since loyalty was a gift for which there was to be no necessary return, it could not be predicated on anything so clear-cut as interest. It depended instead on all sorts of ideological and ceremonial mystification. . . . The state still does depend on ideology and mystery, but to a far less degree than ever before. It has been the great triumph of liberal theorists and politicians to undermine every sort of political divinity, to shatter all the forms of ritual obfuscation, and to turn the mysterious oath into a rational contract. The state itself they have made over . . . into a machine, the instrument of its citizens (rather than their mythical

common life) devoted to what Bentham called "welfare production." It is judged, as it ought to be, by the amounts of welfare it
produces and by the justice and efficiency of its distributive system.

What occurs characteristically during the growth of the welfare state is a series of "invasions," by previously neglected or
newly cohered social groups demanding for themselves a more
equitable portion of the social product and appealing to the
common ideology of welfarism as the rationale for their demands. (Again an analogy with Communism: the dominant
ideology is exploited and violated by the ruling elite, yet can be
turned against its interests.)

In its early stages, the welfare state is "invaded" mostly by
interest groups—economic, racial, ethnic—which seek both
improvements in their condition and recognition of their status.
An interest claim that is made through norms the entire society
says it accepts is harder to reject than one which sets up new
norms not yet enshrined in the society's formal value system—
and that, in passing, is one reason it is today easier to press
for desirable domestic legislation than to affect foreign policy.
In its later stages—which I believe we are just beginning to
approach in the United States—the welfare state is subjected
to a series of pressures that morally are both more grandiose
and more trivial than those of the usual interest groups; since
now it becomes possible for claims to be entered with—and
against—the welfare state by those who yearn forward to what
they hope will be a splendid future and those who yearn back-
ward to what they imagine was a golden past.

This course of "invasions" is by no means completed in the
United States and indeed is scandalously frustrated by racial and
social meanness. As long, however, as there are groups trying
to break in and powers trying to keep them out, we can be
certain that the welfare state will be marked by severe conflict,
even though the "invading" groups may differ from decade to
decade. Nor is there any certainty whatever that the welfare

state will prove receptive to all the claims likely to be made by groups largely outside its system of dispensation. It is possible that the legitimate demands of the Negroes will not be met and that this would, in turn, lead to the virtual destruction of the welfare state as we know it; but if that were to occur it would not, I believe, be the result of an inherent dynamic or ineluctable necessity within the welfare state as a socioeconomic system, but rather it would be the result of a tradition of racism so deeply ingrained in American life that it threatens to survive, and overwhelm, any form of society.

This process of "invasion" is one that a good many of the younger American radicals find troublesome and concerning which I find a good many of them confused. Except for a few who have developed a snobbish contempt for the working class, they recognize the justice of the claims made by deprived groups trying to gain a larger share of power, goods, and recognition; but they fear that once this happens there must follow among the once-insurgent groups an adaptation to detested values and a complacent lapse into material comfort. In part, the young radicals are right. At a particular moment, a once-insurgent group may settle for what seems too little— though we ought to be suspicious of contemptuous judgments made by people who have not shared in past struggles or have merely grown up to enjoy their rewards. At a particular moment, a once-insurgent group may move from the drama of popular struggle to the politics of limited pressure. Right now, for example, the trade unions seem relatively quiescent; having won major victories, they may for a time content themselves with minor adjustments; but with time they are likely to raise their horizons of possibility and again come into conflict with the existing order; and in any case, it takes a peculiarly sectarian mentality not to see the tremendous potentialities of the recent UAW demand for something approaching a guaranteed annual wage for blue-collar workers.

Simply to stop at the point where formerly rebellious groups are "absorbed" into society is to miss the point. For what the young radicals fail sufficiently to see is that when a major social group breaks into the welfare society, then—even though full justice is by no means done—the society nevertheless undergoes an important betterment. The United States after the "absorption" of the labor movement is a different and, on the whole, better society than it was before. By a certain judgment the unions have succumbed to the system, though we should remember that only rarely had they claimed to be its intransigent opponents. Yet even in their relative quiescence of the last few decades, the unions have performed an extremely valuable function: they have maintained a steady pressure, more than any other institution, in behalf of domestic social legislation which benefits not only their own members but a much wider segment of the population.

If—it is a large if—the Negroes succeed in establishing themselves within the society to the extent that the labor unions have, there will occur changes which can only be described as major and perhaps revolutionary—though there will not have occurred that "revolution" which various kinds of ideologues hope the Negroes will enact for them. Were such victories to be won by the Negroes, there would probably follow a certain relaxation among them, a settling-down to enjoy the fruits of struggle, such as occurred earlier among trade unionists. But if past experience is any guide, there would follow after a certain interval a new rise in social appetites among the once-insurgent group, so that it would continue to affect the shape of society even if no longer through exclusively insurgent methods.

Is there, however, a built-in limit to this process of "invasion"? Almost certainly, yes; and by habit one would say the point where fundamental relations of power seem threatened. But we are nowhere near that point; a large array of struggles await us before reaching it, and we cannot even be sure, certainly not as sure as we were a few decades ago, that this point can be located precisely. The history of the Left in the twentieth century is marked by a series of dogmatic assertions as to what could not be done short of revolutionary upheaval; the actuality of history has consisted of changes won through struggle and human will which have in fact achieved some of the goals that were supposed to be unattainable short of apocalypse.

11. *Some Other Models*

The model of the welfare state I have been using here is of course an extrapolation from the complexities of history, and even if we are to content ourselves with it we must acknowledge the presence in our society of elements it cannot account for and which, indeed, conflict with it. Even the traditional *laissez-faire* model of capitalism, which by common consent is now obsolete, retains some importance. There are aspects of the society—certain segments of the economy, certain sectors of the country, certain strands of our ideological folklore—in regard to which the traditional model of capitalism retains much relevance, so that in discussing the welfare state, or welfare capitalism, one must bear in mind the earlier historical form out of which it emerged. More immediately, however, there are several models which should be looked at, not merely or even so much as competitors but rather as supplements, necessary complications, to the welfare state model.

The Garrison State. The war economy is like a parallel structure, a double aorta, of the welfare state, at some points reinforcing it through an economic largesse which a reactionary Congress might not otherwise be willing to allow, and at other points crippling it through sociopolitical aggrandizement such as we can observe at this very moment. In consequence, we can never be free of the haunting possibility that if our military expenditure were radically cut there would follow a collapse or a very severe crisis in the welfare state. Nor can we be sure that gradually the military arrangement will not overwhelm and consume welfare. But these, I would stress, are matters of political decision and thereby of social struggle; they will be settled not through some mysterious economic automatism but through the encounter of opposing classes and groups.

The Mass Society. This theory proposes a model of society in which traditional class antagonisms and distinctions have become blurred and in which there occurs a steady drift toward a bureaucratic, non-terrorist and prosperous authoritarianism, with a population grown passive and atomized, "primary" social groups disintegrated, and traditional loyalties and associations become lax. Herbert Marcuse writes: "Those social groups which dialectical theory identified as forces of negation are either defeated or reconciled within the established system." In simpler language this means that the working class which Marxism assigned to revolutionary leadership seems either unwilling or incapable of fulfilling the assignment. That there is a tendency in modern society toward a slack contentment it would be foolish to deny. But I think it sentimental to slide from an abandonment of traditional Marxist expectations to a vision of historical stasis in which men are fated to be the zombies of bureaucratic organization, zombies stuffed with calories, comfort, and contentment; or to slide from the conclusion that revolutionary expectations no longer hold in the West to a Spenglerian gloom in which we must yield the idea of major social change and indulge ourselves in compensatory fantasies about the last "pure" revolution of the third world.

More fundamentally, the trouble with the "mass society" theory is that, if pushed hard enough, it posits a virtual blockage of history. Yet the one thing that history, including the history of the last several decades, teaches us is that, for good or bad, such an eventuality seems most unlikely. Even in what seems to some disenchanted intellectuals the murk of stability, change is ceaseless. Twenty years ago who would have supposed that Russia and China would be at each other's throats, or that the seeming monolith of Communism would disintegrate? That a conservative French general would succeed in ending a colonial war in Algeria after both the liberal and radical parties failed? That in the United States Catholic students would be picketing Cardinal Spellman's residence? That a silent generation would appear, to be followed by a remarkably articulate one, which in turn . . . well, who knows? What looks at a given moment like the end of days turns out to be a mere vestibule to novelty.

One interesting offshoot of the mass-society theory, popular in some academic and student circles, declares that in a society where revolution is impossible and reform ineffectual, the only remaining strategy of protest is a series of dramatic raids from the social margin, akin to the guerrilla movements of Latin America. Insofar as this strategy draws upon the American tradition of individual moral protest, it has a decided respectability if only, I think, a limited usefulness. Insofar as it is meant to satisfy an unearned nostalgia, it is utterly feckless. Raising hell is a fine American habit, and if hell is even approximately identified, a useful one. But in contemporary society there is always the danger that the desperado exhausts himself much sooner than he discomfits society, and then retires at the ripe age of 30½ muttering about the sloth of the masses. Or he may be crushed in the embrace of a society always on the lookout for interesting spectacles.

A far more serious and honorable version of this strategy is that of absolute moral conscience, for example, that of the young people who, while not religious, refuse the Vietnam war on moral grounds. Their protest is to be respected. If they are simply bearing witness, then nothing more need be said. If, however, it is claimed that they stir other, more conventional and sluggish segments of the mass society into response, then we have abandoned the ground of moral absolutes and moved to the slippery terrain of effectiveness and expediency—and then what they do must be scrutinized as a political tactic, open to the problem of consequences both expected and unexpected.

Liberal Pluralism. This theory, associated with the name of Daniel Bell, sees the society as a pluralist system in which competing pressure groups—some reflecting socioeconomic interests and others refracting the aspirations of status groups —tacitly agree to abide by the "rules of the game" and to submit their rival claims to the jurisdiction of technical experts. Superficially, this approach is congruent with the one I have here outlined, insofar as it traces the effects of political clash within a given society; fundamentally, it is divergent from the approach I have taken, insofar as it accepts the society as a given and fails to penetrate beneath political maneuver to the deeper contradictions of social interest. Still, whether we like it or not, this theory helps describe a good part of what has been happening in the United States these last few decades, especially when one confines oneself to the local texture of political life. I think, however, it is a theory inadequate on several counts:

It fails to consider sufficiently that within the society there remain long-range economic and technological trends threatening the stability, perhaps the survival, of the pluralist system: that is, it asserts a state of equilibrium too readily.

It fails to recognize sufficiently that even when the society is operating at a high degree of efficiency and what passes for a notable benevolence, it does not satisfy human needs and instead gives rise to new kinds of trouble with which it is poorly equipped to deal.

It fails to acknowledge sufficiently that the very "rules of the game" are prearranged so as to favor inequities of power and wealth.

III. *Some Complications of Reality*

The welfare state does not appear in a vacuum; it arises at a certain point in the development of capitalist society and must therefore confront the accumulated tradition and peculiarities of that society. In Britain it comes to a society where serious problems remain of a pre-modern and pre-democratic kind, difficulties having to do with aristocracy and status. In France it comes to a society where the necessary industrialization has just been completed. In Sweden it comes to a society with a minimum of historical impediments or world political entanglements and therefore functions best of all—though here, as Gunnar Myrdal describes it, the welfare state tends to break down organs of rural and village self-government. In the United States it comes at a time of severe historical and moral tensions: the former concerning our role as a world power and the latter a long-term shift in the country's pattern of values. Let us glance at the second.

For some decades now there has been noticeable in this country a slow disintegration of those binding assumptions which, operating almost invisibly, hold a society together and provide its moral discipline. These values can hardly be evoked in a phrase but we can at least point to a few: a creed of individualist self-reliance linked with a belief that the resultant of unrestrained struggle among private persons (atomized economic units) will prove to be to the common good; a conviction that the claims of conscience, seriously entertained, and the promptings of will, persistently accepted, are in fact equivalent; a belief in work as salvation and therapy; a steady devotion to privacy, rigor, control, and moral sobriety. In short, the whole American mythos which we have inherited from the nineteenth century and which in retrospect has been remarkably successful in unifying the country.

During the last few decades, however, this creed has proven inadequate to the American reality, with the evidence ranging from the crisis of urbanization to the gradual decay of religious belief. Perhaps the most striking evidence has been the way in which the WASP elite has slowly been losing its hegemony in American society. So far as I can tell, this loss of hegemony, accompanied by a decline in self-confidence, has occurred more on the social surface than at the economic base, but with time it is bound also to affect the latter.

The American creed served to unify a nation that in its earlier years had largely consisted of a loose compact of regions. Once these regions were gradually melted into a nation, the unifying ideology began to lose some of its power and the sociocultural elite articulating the ideology began to decline. Precisely the unification of the country through the cement of this ideology gave an opportunity for new interest groups and competing moral styles to press their claims.

This process could not, of course, act itself out autonomously. It was always intertwined with social struggles. And as it slowly unfolded itself at the center of society there occurred crisis reactions at the extremes: on the right, a heartfelt cry that morality is being destroyed, religion mocked, our way of life abandoned; on the left, an impatience to be done with old ways and to plunge joyously, sometimes merely programmatically, into experiment. The earnest suburban middle class which only a few years ago was shaking with indignation at the collapse of standards, and the hippies of Haight-Ashbury and East Village—these form symmetrical polarities along the spectrum of American moral life, each reacting to the gradual decay of American convictions and neither absorbed by the kind of pluralistic moderation and maneuvering encouraged by the welfare state. Both the little old lady in tennis shoes and the young hippie in sandals are demonstrating their hostility to the "role playing" of the current scene. Both provide complications of response which our increasingly rationalized and rationalistic society finds it hard to handle. For in a sense, the kind of issues raised by Barry Goldwater and the SDS are symmetrical in conern, if sharply different in moral value. Both of these metapolitical tendencies are re-acting to long-range historical and cultural developments at least as much as to immediate political issues.

What then are the political consequences of this gradual deterioration of the American value system?

The traditional elite can no longer assert itself with its former powers and self-assurance. One reason Adlai Stevenson roused such positive reactions among intellectuals was that it seemed to them that he was a figure in the old style, for which, in their conservative disenchantment, they had de-veloped a sudden fondness.

The image of America inherited from folklore, textbooks, and civic rhetoric proves unusable, and the result is an enor-mous barrier of intellectual and emotional fog which prevents people from apprehending their true needs.

At the margins of the welfare state there spring up apoc-alyptic movements and moods, seemingly political but often in their deepest impulses anti-political (they want not a change in power relations but an end of days). Reflecting the pressures of the fading past and the undiscovered future, these move-ments confound, yet sometimes also refresh, the politics of the welfare state.

IV. *Inner Problems of the Welfare State*

It is not only the distinctive American setting which affects our version of the welfare state; there are also certain char-acteristics which seem to be intrinsically dysfunctional or at least unattractive. A few of them:

Especially in America, the welfare state fails to live up to its formal claims. At best it is a semi-welfare state; at worst an anti-welfare state. It allows a significant minority, the chronic poor, to be dumped beneath the social structure, as a *lumpen* deposit of degradation and pathology.

The welfare state may gratify the interests of previously deprived minorities and thereby benefit the society as a whole; but while doing this, and perhaps because of it, the welfare state tends to dampen concern with such larger values as justice, fraternity, equality, and community. At least for a time, one consequence is that fundamental issues of power are muted; for better or worse—I think for worse—the system as such is hardly an issue in public debate.

Yet here again we ought to beware of a sin prevalent among intellectuals: the sin of impatience with history. For even in its brief existence, and with its own "historical tasks" far from fulfilled, the welfare state has witnessed the growth of an enormous body of social criticism, as well as the appearance of the militantly idealistic young, both of which insist that we pay attention to precisely the larger issues. If the welfare state lulls some groups into acquiescence, it also grants a succeeding generation the relative affluence to experiment with its life-styles and cry out against the slumbers of their elders. The crucial question, to which no answer can yet be given, is whether this concern will remain limited to a tiny segment of the population, driven wild with frustrated reachings toward transcendence.

In its own right, the welfare state does not arouse strong loyalties. It seems easier, if no more intelligent, to die for King and Country, or the Stars and Stripes, or the Proletarian Fatherland than for Unemployment Insurance and Social Security. The welfare state makes for a fragmentation of publics and, at a certain point, a decline in political participation. By one of those accursed paradoxes history keeps throwing up, the welfare state seems to undercut the vitality of the democratic process even while strengthening both its formal arrangements and its socioeconomic base.

But again a word of caution. It should not be assumed that in a country like the United States, despite the rise of group interest politics and the atomization of social life, the traditional claims of the nation no longer operate. For they do, even if in a muted and more quizzical way. Millions of people still respond to the call of patriotism and the rhetoric of democracy, even in their corniest versions. The centrifugal tendencies set into motion by the welfare state must always, therefore, be seen against a background of historical traditions and national sentiments which lie deeply imbedded in collective life.

The welfare state cannot, within the limits of the nation-state, cope with the growing number of socioeconomic problems that are soluble only on an international level or do not really fit into the received categories of class or group conflict. As Richard Titmuss says:

> It is much harder today to identify the causal agents of change—the microbes of social disorganization and the virtues of impoverishment—and to make them responsible for the costs of "disservices." Who should bear the social costs of the thalidomide babies, of urban blight, of smoke pollution, of the obsolescence of skills, of automation, of the impact on the peasants of Brazil of synthetic coffee which will dispense with the need for coffee beans?

The welfare state provides no clear or necessary outlook concerning the role of the nation in the modern world. It is almost compatible with any foreign policy, despite our too-easy assumption that domestic liberalism is likely to go together with restraint in foreign policy. The welfare state can be yoked to a foreign policy which saves Titoist Yugoslavia and destroys Vietnam, which provides food to India and shores up dictators elsewhere in Asia, which proclaims and begins the Alliance for Progress and sanctions the Dominican intervention. The consequences are severe dislocations within the welfare state, splits between groups oriented primarily toward the improvement of their own conditions and groups oriented primarily toward improving the place our society occupies within the world. Of this, more later.

Within its terms and limits the welfare state finds it very difficult to provide avenues of fulfillment for many of the people whose conditions it has helped to improve—the workers displaced by automation, the Negroes given the vote but little else, the young seeking work that makes sense. That is why there now appear new formations, such as the subculture of the alienated young, responding primarily to their felt sense of the falseness of things. If the revolt of the radical right was, in Richard Hofstadter's phrase, an outburst of status politics —the anxious need of an insecure segment to assert itself in the prestige hierarchy—then the revolt of the alienated young is, among other things, an anti-status outburst—a wish to break loose from the terms of categorization fixed by the society. That, in the course of this effort, the young sometimes settle into categories, styles, and mannerisms quite as rigid as those against which they rebel, is something else again.

v. *Politics of the Welfare State*

The politics of the welfare state extends back into the early twentieth century, through a variety of parallel and competing traditions—the labor movement, the Socialist movement, the various liberal groups, the moral pressures exerted through Christian action, the increasing role of the Jews as a liberal force. But for our present purposes we can date the beginning of welfare-state politics as a style of coalition to the early thirties and perhaps even more precisely to the election of 1932, one of the few in American history which marked a major realignment of political forces. In that election the unions began to play the powerful role they would command during the next few decades; large numbers of Negroes began their historic switch to the Democratic party; the city machines found it expedient to go along with Roosevelt's policies. And soon significant numbers of intellectuals would begin their entry into practical politics. This coalition would remain a major

force in American life during the next three or so decades.
When all or most of its component parts could be held together,
formally or informally, and it could command the practical
issues and/or moral appeals to win a good cut of the middle-
class vote, this coalition could often win elections on a national
scale and in many industrialized states. When there were group
defections, victory went to the right. In general one can say
that this coalition was most successful whenever it managed
to link strong economic interests with moral urgencies, the
politics of pressure with the traditions of American liberalism
and populism. I believe that this lesson still holds, despite
sharply changed circumstances.

What specific forms did this coalition take? It could be one
or more of the following:

> a bloc of organizations and movements cooperating for a
> legislative or electoral end;
>
> a long-range concurrence in electoral behavior, so that
> certain expectations could reasonably be inferred—e.g.,
> that even if we do not have self-conscious classes or dis-
> ciplined publics there are at least certain fundamental
> recognitions of common interest;
>
> intermittent activization of class and interest groups when
> aroused by specific issues—e.g., "right to work" laws,
> Negro rights, etc;
>
> various electoral and political arrangements within and
> across the political parties.

Now one way of looking upon recent American politics is
to conclude that in recent years the liberal-left coalition has
gradually disintegrated and, with the Vietnam war, seems
virtually to have come to an end.

There are plenty of signs. The electoral blocs seem to function with less assurance and predictability than ten or twenty
years ago. Workers reaching a measure of affluence are less

likely to follow the signals of their union leadership; they may veer off into middle-class styles or lapse into racialism. Still, when certain issues are clearly drawn along class lines, as for example during the last presidential election or the earlier struggles around "right to work" laws, the labor vote can still cohere into a major force.

Similar signs of change seem to be occurring among the Negroes, where the massive commitment to the Democratic party may—though it certainly has not yet—come to an end. And among younger people there is a growing inclination to respond to politics as if group interest were somehow vulgar or even reprehensible and what mattered most were political "styles" and moral, or pseudomoral, appeals rising above socioeconomic concerns.

Why then has this coalition devoted to defending and extending the welfare state come to a condition of crisis? A few answers suggest themselves:

As the interest groups become increasingly absorbed into the welfare state, their combativeness decreases, at least for a time. They develop a stake in the status quo and become economically and psychologically resistant to new kinds of insurgency. Thus, while a general case can and should be made for a community of interests among the unions, the Negroes, and the unorganized poor, these groups will often clash both in their immediate demands and their basic political styles.

What I would call the "rate of involvement" among the interest groups and moral-issue groups is likely to be sharply different at various moments, and the result is unavoidable friction. When the unions were surging ahead in the thirties, they received little help from the churches; it did not even occur to anyone at that time to expect much help. The Catholic Church in particular was regarded as a major center of political reaction. Today we witness the astonishing and exhilarating rise of ferment within the Catholic community, while the unions, though still fierce guardians of yesterday's gains, are not notable as centers of innovation.

Ideally there ought to be cooperation between those committed to a politics of pressure and those committed to a politics of insurgency; but in practice the latter often tend to define themselves through dissocation from the former (perhaps on the "principle" that you strike out most violently against your closest relatives) while the former feel their survival and even their honor to be threatened by the latter. As long as the wretched Vietnam war continues and social stagnation consequently characterizes our domestic life, this conflict is likely to be exacerbated.

The programmatic demands advanced by the liberal-left groups for domestic reforms during the thirties have by now either been mostly realized or require merely—but that's *some* merely!—quantitative implementation. By itself this does not yield a dramatic or inspiring perspective; it does not excite the young, it barely arouses those in whose behalf it is advanced, and it proves more and more inadequate for coping with the new problems we all experience more sharply than we can define.

There has occurred over the Vietnam war a split between groups focusing primarily on domestic issues, mostly the unions, and the groups focusing primarily on foreign policy, mostly the middle-class peace organizations and radical youth. During the twentieth century, with the possible exception of the 1916 election, foreign policy has never played a decisive role in American elections; or, to modify that a bit, disputes over foreign policy, such as the interventionist/isolationist quarrel in the thirties, did not threaten the survival of the liberal coalition. Today this is no longer true, and cannot be true—even though I am unhappily convinced that in an electoral showdown the moral protestants, among whom I wish to include myself, would prove to be a very small minority. Never in the past has it been possible to rally a successful liberal-left movement on issues of foreign policy alone or predominantly. Whether it can be done today remains very much an open question.

We are living through an exhaustion, perhaps temporary, of American liberalism. It is not, at the moment, rich in programmatic suggestions. It has lost much of its earlier élan. It has become all too easily absorbed into establishment maneuvers, so that it shares a measure of responsibility for the Vietnam disasters and ghetto outbreaks. It has not developed new leaders. In short, as its most intelligent spokesmen know, it is in a state of moral and intellectual disarray.

Yet in fairness one should add that pretty much the same difficulties beset most or all other political tendencies in the United States. One of the remarkable facts about our political life is the paucity of specific proposals to come from the far left or far right. A comparison with the thirties is instructive, for whatever else was wrong with American radicalism (almost everything) at that time, it did advance specific proposals for legislation and thereby agitation. Today that is hardly the case. "Participatory democracy" may be a sentiment as noble as it is vague, but even its most ardent defenders cannot suppose it to be a focused proposal for our national life. And by a similar token, it is interesting that Governor Reagan did not really try to dismantle the welfare state against which he had mock-raged during his campaign.

I think that for the next period we shall have to live and work within the limits of the welfare state. There is only one possibility that this perspective will be invalidated, and that is a racial conflict pitting white against black—a tragedy which even the most puerile advocates of "nose-to-nose confrontation" must recognize as utterly disastrous. Unless we are to delude ourselves with the infantile leftism of the talk about "Negro revolution" (sometimes invoked most fiercely by guerrillas with tenure), the first point on the political agenda must be a renewed struggle for the fulfillment of the claims advanced by the welfare state. And that, in turn, means a simultaneous struggle to end the Vietnam war and to bring large-scale economic help to the Negro ghettos.

VI. *A Word About the Future*

If one could view the present moment with detachment, one might say that we are witnessing the breakdown of the old political coalition which helped usher in the welfare state and perhaps the slow beginnings of a new coalition to improve and transcend the welfare state. In this new coalition the labor movement would still have—it would have to have—a central role, but no longer with the decisive weight of the past. The churches would matter a great deal more, and so would the American "new class," that scattered array of intellectuals, academicians, and technicians. Issues of foreign policy would occupy a central place in the program of such a coalition, as would those concerning "quality of life"—though, I am convinced, the immediate major domestic concern remains the realization of the welfare-state expectations for the American Negroes. In such a coalition there might come together the tradition of moral protest and the bearing of witness with the tradition of disinterested service. All of this could occur only through a radicalization of American liberalism: a politics unqualifiedly devoted to democratic norms but much more militant, independent, and combative than the left-liberal world of today.

Whenever in the past American radicalism has flourished somewhat, it has largely been in consort with an upsurge of liberalism. There have been two major periods of radical activity: first during the years immediately preceding World War I and then during the thirties. The notion that radicalism can grow fat on the entrails of liberalism is a crude error, an absurdity.

But all of this remains hope and speculation. Before such

a new coalition emerges, if ever it does, there is likely to be severe tension and conflict among its hoped-for component parts. The Vietnam war stands as a harsh barrier, political and psychological, which must be broken down in order to take care of our business at home—which is by no means to accept the quietistic and reactionary argument that until the war is ended nothing can or should be done at home.

Even the full realization of the "idea" of the welfare state would not bring us to utopia or "the good society." The traditional socialist criticisms in respect to the maldistribution of power, property, and income would still hold. But to continue the struggle for such a realization is both a political and human responsibility. And through the very struggle to realize the "idea" of the welfare state—if I may offer a "dialectical" observation—it is possible to gain the confidence, strength, and ideas through which to move beyond the welfare state. Unfortunately, American intellectuals do not seem well equipped for keeping to this dual perspective: they either lapse into a genteel and complacent conservatism or they veer off into an ultimatistic and pseudo-utopian leftism. Yet, when one comes to think of it, why should it be so difficult to preserve a balance between the struggle to force the present society to enact the reforms it claims to favor and the struggle to move beyond the limits of the given society? Tactically, to be sure, this creates frequent difficulties; but conceptually, as a guiding principle, I think it our only way.

1967

Notes on Contributors

PAUL BULLOCK, Associate Research Economist at the Institute of Industrial Relations at U.C.L.A., supervised the study "Hard-Core Unemployment and Poverty in Los Angeles," a report which was prepared under a contract with the Department of Labor many months prior to the Watts riot of 1965. He is currently at work on a book about Watts today, and is also studying the problem of police and prison records in relation to employment in urban ghettos.

LAURA CARPER has been a teacher for twenty-one years: six years teaching Hebrew and fifteen years teaching dramatics in settlement houses and community centers. She is currently taking courses that will allow her to teach in a city school system. Miss Carper has contributed anonymously, pseudonymously, and in her own name to *The New York Review of Books*.

HARRY CAUDILL has long been an active critic and participant in attempting to solve the problems of his native Appalachia. He is a practicing attorney in Whitesburg, Kentucky, has served three terms as Fletcher County Representative to the State Legislature, and has given special attention to natural resource conservation, improvement of education, and the question of strip mining in his state. He is the author of NIGHT COMES TO THE CUMBERLANDS and has been elected Chairman of the recently formed Congress for Appalachian Development.

WILLIAM B. GOULD is a practicing attorney, specializing in labor law and labor arbitration. From 1961–1962 he was Assistant General Counsel for the United Automobile Workers in Detroit, from 1963–1965 a lawyer for the National Labor Relations Board in Washington, and has also been a consultant to the Equal Employment

Opportunity Commission. Mr. Gould has contributed articles to the *Labor Law Journal, Cornell Law Quarterly, London Economist,* and other periodicals.

MICHAEL HARRINGTON is the author of THE OTHER AMERICA (1962), THE ACCIDENTAL CENTURY (1965), and TOWARDS A DEMOCRATIC LEFT, to be published in May, 1968. Active in the civil rights movement for over a decade, Mr. Harrington has been a longtime associate of the Fund for the Republic, organizational secretary of the Worker's Defense League, special consultant to the A. Philip Randolph Institute, and in 1964 was elected Chairman of the Board of Directors of the League for Industrial Democracy.

CHESTER W. HARTMAN has been a frequent contributor to various journals as an expert on planning, housing, and relocation. He is currently Assistant Professor in the Harvard Department of City Planning and Acting Assistant Director of the Harvard Center for Urban Studies. He has been Director of the Legislative Commission on Low-Income Housing for the Commonwealth of Massachusetts, and Research Fellow in Sociology in the Department of Psychiatry, Harvard Medical School.

IRVING HOWE, the editor of *Dissent* magazine, is the author of a number of books, including WILLIAM FAULKNER: A CRITICAL STUDY, POLITICS AND THE NOVEL, and THOMAS HARDY. He is the co-author of two books, THE U.A.W. AND WALTER REUTHER and THE AMERICAN COMMUNIST PARTY: A CRITICAL HISTORY. Mr. Howe is a Professor of English at the City University of New York at Hunter College.

PAUL JACOBS is a writer and social critic who has been on the staff of the Fund for the Republic's Center for the Study of Democratic Institutions for the past ten years. He is the author of, to name a few, IS CURLY JEWISH (1965), a political memoir, THE STATE OF THE UNIONS (1965), an analysis of the American trade unions, co-author of THE NEW RADICALS (1966), and has just completed LOS ANGELES IS AMERICA AND IT'S TERRIBLE, to be published this year.

HERBERT KOHL, educated at Harvard, Oxford, and Columbia, taught in the New York City public school system, Harlem, from 1962–1965. He is the author of THE AGE OF COMPLEXITY, 36 CHILDREN, and TEACHING THE "UNTEACHABLE." At this time he is Director of The Teachers and Writers Collaborative at Columbia University.

JEREMY LARNER is the author of the novels DRIVE, HE SAID and THE ANSWER and co-author of THE ADDICT IN THE STREET, a book of interviews with heroin addicts. He is a member of the English Faculty at the State University of New York, Stony Brook.

ROBERT LEKACHMAN, Chairman of the Department of Economics at Stony Brook, State University of New York, is the author of AGE OF KEYNES and A HISTORY OF ECONOMIC IDEAS. A member of the Board of Editors at the *Journal of Economic Issues,* a contributor to *Commentary, The Atlantic,* and other national periodicals, Mr. Lekachman is a Consultant to the Office of Education and a Rockefeller Fellow.

DEBORAH MEIER is well acquainted with public schools. The mother of three children who have attended school in Chicago, Philadelphia, and New York City, Mrs. Meier was active in the Philadelphia Get Set program of 1965–1966 during its first year of operation. A former member of the South Side of Chicago CORE, Mrs. Meier has taught elementary school in Chicago and is presently in the New York City school system, teaching in Harlem.

MICHAEL VINCENT MILLER is a native San Franciscan and has studied at Berkeley and taught at Stanford. He is the co-editor of the anthology REVOLUTION AT BERKELEY (1965) and a contributor to *Dissent, The Nation,* and *The Alantic Monthly.* Mr. Miller is an instructor in the Department of Humanities at M.I.T.

s. M. MILLER is Professor of Education and Sociology, New York University. He is the author of several books, including SOCIAL CLASS AND SOCIAL POLICY, APPLIED SOCIOLOGY, THE

SCHOOL DROPOUT PROBLEM—SYRACUSE, and editor of MAX WEBER—SELECTIONS. Mr. Miller is also Program Advisor in Social Development at the Ford Foundation.

PAMELA ROBY is a research sociologist at New York University and the Russell Sage Foundation.

VERA RONY first encountered the South as a student at the University of North Carolina. She has worked as an aircraft mechanic in Seattle and as education director of the Beltmaker's Union, ILGWU, in New York. From 1956 to 1964 Miss Rony was Executive Director of the Workers Defense League, and from 1962–1964 was Executive Director of the League for Industrial Democracy. Since 1965 she has travelled through the South gathering material for a book on Southern labor, from which her article is excerpted.

BEN B. SELIGMAN is a professor of Economics and Director, Labor Relations and Research Center, University of Massachusetts. His article is based on his forthcoming book PERMANENT POVERTY: AN AMERICAN SYNDROME. Professor Seligman edited the volume POVERTY AS A PUBLIC ISSUE and is the author of MOST NOTORIOUS VICTORY: MAN IN AN AGE OF AUTOMATION. He was research director of the Retail Clerks International Association for almost a decade before joining the faculty of the University of Massachusetts in 1965.

STEPHEN THERNSTROM's SOCIAL MOBILITY IN A 19TH CENTURY CITY (1964) will be reprinted in a paperback edition this year. Associate Professor of History at Brandeis University, Mr. Thernstrom also serves as an associate of the M.I.T.-Harvard Joint Center for Urban Studies. His current work in progress is a social history of modern Boston.

HOWARD THORKELSON is a graduate of the Yale Law School, a member of the New York Bar, and an attorney at the Center on Social Welfare Policy and Law at Columbia University.

PAT WATTERS has been Director of Information of the Southern Regional Council since 1963. From 1952–1963 he was a reporter, city editor, daily columnist and book editor for the Atlanta *Journal.* Mr. Watters is the co-author of CLIMBING JACOB'S LADDER, a study on Negro voting and politics in the South. He has contributed articles on the South and race relations to *The Nation, The New Republic, The Atlantic,* and other periodicals.

About the Editors

Jeremy Larner is the author of the novels *Drive, He Said* and *The Answer* and co-author of *The Addict in the Street,* a book of interviews with heroin addicts. He is a member of the English faculty of the State University of New York, Stony Brook.

Irving Howe, the editor of *Dissent* magazine, is the author of a number of books, including *William Faulkner: A Critical Study, Politics and the Novel,* and *Thomas Hardy.* He is co-author of two books, *The U.A.W. and Walter Reuther* and *The American Communist Party: A Critical History.* Mr. Howe is Professor of English at the City University of New York at Hunter College.